The Constructive Mind

The Constructive Mind is an integrative study of the psychologist Frederic Bartlett's (1886–1969) life, work, and legacy. Bartlett is most famous for the idea that remembering is constructive and the concept of schema. For him, 'constructive' meant that human beings are future-oriented and flexibly adaptive to new circumstances. This book shows how his notion of construction is also central to understanding social psychology and cultural dynamics, as well as perceiving, imagining, and thinking. Wagoner contextualizes the development of Bartlett's key ideas in relation to his predecessors and contemporaries. He also applies Bartlett's constructive analysis of cultural transmission in order to chart how his ideas were appropriated and transformed by others who followed. As such, this book is also a case study in the continuous reconstruction of ideas in science.

Brady Wagoner (Ph.D. University of Cambridge) is Professor of Psychology at Aalborg University, Denmark. His research focuses on social and cultural psychology, constructive remembering, social change, and the development of dynamic methodologies. He was the co-creator of the *Sir Frederic Bartlett Internet Archive* and is an associate editor for the journals *Culture & Psychology* and *Peace & Conflict*. He has received a number of prestigious professional awards, such as the Sigmund Koch Prize in 2009 and the Gates Cambridge Scholarship in 2005. He is currently editing *The Oxford Handbook of Culture and Memory*.

The Constructive Mind

Bartlett's Psychology in Reconstruction

Brady Wagoner

Aalborg University, Denmark

CAMBRIDGE
UNIVERSITY PRESS

CAMBRIDGE
UNIVERSITY PRESS

University Printing House, Cambridge CB2 8BS, United Kingdom
One Liberty Plaza, 20th Floor, New York, NY 10006, USA
477 Williamstown Road, Port Melbourne, VIC 3207, Australia
4843/24, 2nd Floor, Ansari Road, Daryaganj, Delhi – 110002, India
79 Anson Road, #06-04/06, Singapore 079906

Cambridge University Press is part of the University of Cambridge.

It furthers the University's mission by disseminating knowledge in the pursuit
of education, learning, and research at the highest international levels of
excellence.

www.cambridge.org
Information on this title: www.cambridge.org/9781107008885
DOI: 10.1017/9780511920219

First published 2017

A catalogue record for this publication is available from the British Library

ISBN 978-1-107-00888-5 Hardback

Contents

Figures

Foreword
Active and Developing Patterns: Remembering
into the Future

Jaan Valsiner

This book is a carefully crafted monument to one of the most profound thinkers in twentieth-century psychology. Frederic Bartlett's name in psychology is usually associated with his 1932 book *Remembering*, and in psychologists' habitual discourses about their own field of knowledge his contributions are located in the domain of the so-called 'memory research.' Of course, combining the terms 'memory' and 'research' has all the allure of basic science. 'Research' is the unquestionably glorious central term in the social discourses about science, and the value of 'memory' for our everyday lives goes undisputed for anybody who is worried about finding one's parked car in a humungous parking lot of an equally grandiose shopping center. Pressures upon our ordinary psychological capacities are not necessarily reduced in the 'Internet age.'

Yet there is a twist. While at first glance that label seems very clear – we all worry about how not to forget important events of the past – the content of this category of 'research' is extremely wide. Everything ranging from the neuroscientific study of retaining the information at neuronal levels to that of countries' maintenance of their national identities may end up labeled as 'memory research.' Yet when a certain corpus of perspectives is grouped together as 'X-research,' it is likely to be seen as a conglomerate of empirical presentations ('the literature') and dismissive of theoretical integration efforts, and often opposed also to 'practice.' Such dependence on 'research' is detrimental to any science where theoretical goals come first, and practices determine if the empirical investigations are of any real value.

The value of ideas prevails over classifications. I would claim here that Frederic Bartlett was never involved in 'memory research,' even if – for his intellectual interests – the phenomena of remembering were of utmost importance. As the reader of the present book soon understands, Bartlett's actual contributions to science are much wider and more multi-faceted than their usual presentation in history of psychology narratives has been. As the reader can discover from Brady Wagoner's careful analysis of Bartlett's intellectual history, he can be seen as one of the revered and mis-presented (as well as misunder-stood) scholars in psychology who are considered 'classics,' while their constructive ideas are left to gather intellectual dust on the pages of introductory textbooks-dominated knowledge base of the field.

What is at stake in the case of Bartlett's contributions is the study of human processes of construction of novelty. This is the core issue for all developmental perspectives in the biological, social, and human sciences (for detailed coverage, see Carré et al.[1]). In this, Bartlett's thinking resonates well with the major developmental thinkers of the twentieth century – James Mark Baldwin, Lev Vygotsky, and Hans Driesch. Yet Bartlett was unique, linking the ideas coming from social anthropology of his time with the best of psychology of his time. Uniting the intellectual input from his Cambridge interlocutors with the best of German psychological heritage – the introspective focus of the Würzburg tradition of Karl Bühler and Oswald Külpe – Bartlett was educated by the life-worlds of the (at that time labeled) 'primitive' peo-ple of the Torres Straits and other far corners of the world. Variations in cultural practices between different societies were the basis for Bartlett to work toward creating a general science of the human *psyche*. All human beings are involved in the universal process of negotiating the adoption of new ways of living while trying to adhere to their estab-lished historical traditions. The tension on the border of the tradition and innovation is what Bartlett studied. That issues of memory are important on that border goes without saying. But equally important is the future – pre-knowable only through imagination.

The place where the history of a society and its future are collectively under the process of re-negotiation is its folklore and traditions of mate-rial culture. Hence Bartlett's basic interest is on how images and stories become reconstructed from generation to generation, across persons in a society, and – ultimately – in any person's reconstruction of the socially relevant myth stories. Social conventionalization of newly re-constructed traditions is a universal process that is both necessary and inevitable. As the readers of this book find out, that is what *remembering* is about – it is *memory needed for the future*, rather than the test of accu-racy about reflecting upon the past.

The human *psyche* is inevitably personal. Human psychological con-structivity is always individual – even if that individual is embedded in a social group, community, or society as a whole. Hence, the methodology of its study is necessarily based on individual case studies – with a focus

[1] Carré, D., Valsiner, J., and Hampl, S. (Eds.) (2016). *Representing development*. London: Routledge.

of the tensions on the border of past and future. Bartlett did not have to face the naïve normativity of his colleagues who could ask "how big was your sample?" to evaluate his work. Generalization based on single cases was the accepted scientific norm in Bartlett's time – only to vanish from psychology in the second half of the twentieth century. It is only in our time that it is coming back to its appropriate relevance for psychology as science.[2] All basic knowledge in history of psychology has come from careful analysis of single cases, even if subsequent efforts have been made to replicate these on samples. These would necessarily fail because of the non-ergodic character of psychological phenomena.[3] Mathematical proof of non-ergodicity leads to one – but fundamental – epistemological conclusion: *inter-individual variability is not isomorphic with intra-individual variability* in case of the open systems. This has profound significance on how psychology as science needs to operate: inference from samples (inter-individual variability) to the organization and development of individuals over time (intra-individual variability) is in principle impossible. All the empirical work conducted on samples *and extrapolated to interpret the functioning of individuals* is consequently useless. Empirical research practices – supported by social norms of what is called 'good methodology' (i.e., large samples, random sampling, etc.) – are rendered mute because of the wrong starting axiom (that of ergodicity). Psychology, as science, needs to return to careful analysis of single cases, in new ways.

The contrast between non-developmental and developmental views on the processes of remembering is best exemplified on the simple issue – what is an 'error'? Researchers who have tried to continue Bartlett's work have demonstrated their own non-developmental axiomatic stances by projecting the notion of 'error' into the accounts persons give in the Bartlettian re-telling experiments. Omitting some detail from a re-told story is de facto indeed an 'error' until it becomes linked with a confabulation that introduces a novel extension to the old. Here the omission – forgetting – works for the future. Movement through 'erring' in relation to what was the case in the past is potentially

[2] Molenaar, P. (2004). A manifesto on psychology as idiographic science: Bringing the person back into scientific psychology, this time forever. *Measurement, 2,* 201–18; Valsiner, J. (2015). Generalization is possible only from a single case (and from a single instance). In B. Wagoner, N. Chaudhary, and P. Hviid (Eds.), *Integrating experiences: Body and mind moving between contexts* (pp. 233–44). Charlotte, NC: Information Age Publishers.
[3] Molenaar, P.C.M., Huizinga, H.M., and Nesselroade, J.R. (2002). The relationship between the structure of inter-individual and intra-individual variability. In U. Staudinger and U. Lindenberger (Eds.), *Understanding human development* (pp. 339–60). Dordrecht: Klüwer.

the starting point for innovation. The whole of the human mind works at the intersection of 'erring' and imagining.[4] The basic principle introduced by James Mark Baldwin over a century ago ('persistent imitation') – "trying, erring, and trying again … and so on!" – guarantees the uniqueness of human striving for a better future.

This book also illustrates the short-sightedness of orthodoxies in science. Not only can (dead) authors be dealt with as such, but also their ideas can be declared 'dead.' This happened to Bartlett's schema concept in the 1970s, and has happened – directly by declaration or indirectly through omission – to many other fruitful perspectives in psychology. Introspection as the core for psychological investigation is a good example – dismissed over the whole twentieth century, it necessarily re-emerges in new forms when psychology moves toward the study of higher psychological processes that indicate what *being* human is.[5] In our multitude of feelings into the world, we live, love, kill one another, pardon the violence under the banners of national heroism, and gossip about our neighbors. The mundane, the monstrous, and the sacred are deeply intertwined in our ordinary lives, where we are making our ways of being, relating the desired or dreaded imagination of the future with the selective reconstructions of the past. A return to the heritage of Frederic Bartlett is actually an act of remembering into our futures.

Last (but not least), I have deep personal satisfaction in seeing the present book published. Its author has been my student and friend whom I consider to be the most careful analyst and further developer of my own scientific *oeuvre*. His careful and constructive elaboration of ideas is visible from the first to the last page of this book. Contemporary academic scholarship would have much to learn from the present book and its author, and I hope the readers will appreciate the deep scholarship they encounter on the pages of this book. Through such work, remembering the ideas from the past is illuminating the future of a discipline that is in great need for constructive innovation.

---

[4] Sato, T., Mori, N., and Valsiner, J. (Eds.) (2016). *Making of the future: Trajectory equifinality approach in cultural psychology.* Charlotte, NC: Information Age Publishers.

[5] Valsiner, J., Marsico, G., Chaudhary, N., Sato, T., and Dazzani, V. (Eds.) (2016). *Psychology as the science of human being.* Cham: Springer.

Acknowledgments

This book is the result of over a decade of research and discussion. If I had to give it a beginning, I would place it toward the end of my first term at the University of Cambridge at which time Alex Gillespie recommended I read Bartlett's book *Remembering* to develop my own research ideas. I was fascinated and went on to do a study of conversational remembering using the method of repeated reproduction, published as 'sociocultural mediators of remembering.' The summer after my first year in Cambridge, Gillespie and I won a British Academy grant to build an online archive for Bartlett, which put me to work on gathering most of Bartlett's *oeuvre*. I am also grateful to my then Ph.D. supervisor (late) Gerard Duveen for introducing me to social representations theory, which as he showed owes much to Bartlett's theorizing and as such is covered in the present book. The Cambridge adventure itself would not have happened if it was not for the support of Jaan Valsiner, my parents and the Gates Cambridge Scholarship.

The conception and writing of this book did not begin until after I had already left Cambridge and started working at Aalborg University. At around the same time, Ivana Marková began her book *The Dialogical Mind* for Cambridge University Press; it has been helpful and supportive to share the journey with her, as well as many others who have been a part. I am particularly grateful to many of my Aalborg colleagues for their interest, ideas, and feedback on my writing. Principally, I would like to thank Jaan Valsiner, Vlad Glăveanu, Ignacio Brescó de Luna, Svend Brinkmann, Luca Tateo, David Carré, and Sarah Awad. This excellent group of researchers was brought together thanks to the Danish National Research Foundation, which awarded a grant to create *The Niels Bohr Professorship Centre for Cultural Psychology*. Outside of Aalborg, I must also thank Rainer Diriwächter, Eric Jensen, and Seamus Powers for their suggestions on the book manuscript. Finally, Paula Cavada deserves acknowledgment for tolerating all the weekends and nights I spent writing, and for her comments on the text.

Some of the research and thoughts discussed in these pages appeared in earlier publications. Although all of these have been rewritten for the present book, I am grateful to the publishers for the permission to draw from the following:

> Papers on Social Representations (2012)
> Theory & Psychology (2013)
> Doing Psychology Under New Conditions (2013)
> The Catalyzing Mind: Beyond Models of Causality (2014)
> Forum Qualitative Sozialforschung/Forum Qualitative Social Research (2015).

Introduction

Like the reactions it studies, psychology is living and oriented forward: there can be no end to its achievements.

(Bartlett, 1936, p. 52)

Man's life and search are a perpetual adventure ... all our advances towards self-knowledge are promises without end.

(Bartlett, 1951, p. 462)

Human beings are constructive. This means they are oriented forward in their actions and experience. From this perspective, what characterizes human beings is their innovating adaption to the environment. From primitive tools and classifications of the world to modern weapons of warfare and scientific theories, humans have persistently developed novel ways of acting and organizing their worlds. Every new generation must balance the need for continuity with the past and the need to innovate for the future. The tension between *conservation* of the old and *construction* of the new manifests itself in the life of every group and every individual. Both individuals and groups are dominated by their past but also creatively orient to the uncertain future; they are both curious and fearful, seeking out the strange while finding security in the familiar. Understanding the constructiveness of human beings in facing the future with the resources of the past was at the core of Frederic Bartlett's psychology. This book aims to explore how his ideas help us to understand human beings as constructive agents situated in a complex social and material world.

In writing this book, I came to realize that 'constructiveness' provides a unifying concept to approach Bartlett's *oeuvre*. Constructiveness is at the heart of his diverse contributions to both theory and methodology, yet it has been generally misunderstood. Bartlett's celebrated theory of constructive or reconstructive remembering, for example, has typically been taken to mean that memories are inaccurate and distorted. In contrast, Bartlett saw 'constructive' as a positive, future-oriented characteristic that could also lead to accuracy in memory. Rather than lamenting

1

the follies of human memory when compared with literal reproduction of information by computers, he saw it as entirely functional within the needs of human life. In a similar vein, the leading memory researcher Daniel Schacter (2012) has recently begun to speak of '*adaptive* constructive processes' to highlight the neglected functional meaning of the word.[1] At a general level, Bartlett consistently emphasized constructiveness throughout his career to show that novelty emerges through human adaptation to the ever-changing environment. He was critical of mechanistic methodologies that simply looked at how a certain stimulus caused an isolated response, or an input led to a given output. This focus on predicting human behavior led most of psychology to adopt a one-sided view of human beings that greatly underestimated their creativity and agency in meeting new challenges.

According to Bartlett, psychology needs an approach that looks at the whole, active person or group constructively using the past in order to move toward the future. We are here concerned with the mind as a unity, not separate mental faculties, and how it operates in interdependence with an environment that is at once social and material.[2] Thus, psychological processes (e.g., imagining, thinking, and remembering) cannot be adequately understood without taking account of the context in which they operate and the material on which they work. They occur *through* a certain environment and carry a particular history. Although Bartlett is most famous for how he uses this approach to study remembering as a constructive process, his contribution is much more wide ranging. His ideas are particularly instructive in that he developed a constructivist theory that works on and between different levels (e.g., individual and group), and applied it to a variety of topics (e.g., perceiving, imagining, remembering, thinking, group dynamics, political propaganda, cultural transmission). The breadth and diversity of his approach is part of the reason he has become a seminal figure for a variety of social scientific fields.[3] How Bartlett has been selectively interpreted and used by different groups of psychologists and to some extent anthropologists will be discussed in depth in this book.

Bartlett's work has been and continues to be a key source of inspiration for psychology and across the social sciences. Despite this, a rather skewed understanding of it is now in circulation, especially in psychology. This has come from the limited attention paid to his broader thinking about culture and group dynamics (which sets the frame for his famous experiments), as well as his holistic, affective, and temporal approach to psychological processes. Neglecting these aspects of his thought has consequences for interpreting any part of it. As a result, even his most widely known concepts have taken on meanings very different from their original use, without any acknowledgement that a change has occurred. For example, 'schema' is often now understood as a knowledge structure in the head that stores information, a notion Bartlett was trying to overcome (see Chapter 4). I have also already mentioned that 'reconstructive remembering' is now typically taken to mean that memory is distorted, rather than that the past is accessed, formed, and used by individuals and groups to meet the needs of the present. It is also worth noting here that Bartlett theorized construction in its dynamic relationship to the conservation or retention of the past, rather than as an invention out of nothing.

The reconstruction of Bartlett's psychology in this book likewise aims to use the past in order to make advances on problems facing the discipline today. This book is the first extended and integrative reconstruction of Bartlett's work and legacy.[4] A book that simply 'reproduced' Bartlett's ideas as they were in the original would be unhelpful – it would be much better simply to read Bartlett's own works. An act of reconstruction brings the past to bear on the present in a movement toward the future. This is not to say that we can be sloppy in our scholarship, but rather that we become engaged with the past in the pursuit of particular aims that help to select what is relevant from the past. The aims of this book are not only to explicate and contextualize Bartlett's ideas but also to adapt them to advance psychology as it is now practiced. Although this book is the most extensive reconstruction of Bartlett's ideas to-date, it is of course necessarily selective and open-ended. Its objective is to stimulate a renewed surge of interest in Bartlett and his legacy, leading to new interpretations and reconstructions that shed light on issues not covered by him or in this book.

In interpreting and reconstructing ideas from the past, we need to proceed with some caution. When major earlier figures are remembered, there is a tendency to reproduce them in our own image rather than engage with them on their own terms. What we tend to recognize as valuable are those ideas and practices we see as akin to our own and what we criticize are those that violate contemporary norms of scientific practice. From this perspective, the history of a discipline becomes a progressive march toward the present way of doing things. This attitude blocks us from using the past to critique and develop current ideas and practices in a discipline. Major thinkers of the past often had very good reasons for thinking and doing things differently than is routinely done today. If the past is a foreign country, we need to be willing to step into the native's territory, learn about their beliefs and practices on their terms, to avoid holding a rather empty and stereotyped view of them. This involves familiarizing oneself with the general background of ideas and practices within which key thinkers developed their approach. By doing such an analysis, we also see that original ideas tend to be a synthesis of already existing ideas rather than the creations of a lone genius.[5]

I am not implying we should avoid criticizing ideas from the past – just the opposite. It is only through a thorough understanding of a thinker and their context that their limitations become fully clear. What we need to be wary of is what Bartlett (1918) called 'conventional criticism,' whereby something is criticized simply for being different from some conventional idea or practice. This kind of criticism is particularly easy to do and unsurprisingly it is widespread in everyday life and often in science as well. To further develop a science, however, one must move beyond this form of criticism to one in which different positions are analyzed for their ability to generate further knowledge and cope with different phenomena. I will consider this book a success if it is effective in generating a constructive dialogue on a number of key issues for psychology and other social sciences such as: the understanding of an experiment; the relationship between individuals and social groups; the conceptualization of schema; what makes remembering constructive and social; how to think about and study thinking; and how culture and ideas are transmitted and transformed in science and society.

In our efforts to interpret the past, we cannot free ourselves from the background we bring with us, nor should we. It is precisely our own background that provides a way into another's way of thinking, but we must be willing to let the other have a voice as well (cf. Gadamer, 1989). It is worth mentioning at this point my own background as a cultural psychologist, from which I was originally drawn to Bartlett and have reconstructed his work in this book. Cultural psychology (re)emerged[6] in the 1990s and encompasses a heterogeneous group of thinkers that nonetheless share a common interest in the ways persons and social-cultural worlds mutually make each other up (Shweder, 1991). In other words, human beings both are molded by culture and create culture. Culture here is not a thing, bounded group, or variable to be manipulated, but the medium through which we live our lives (Valsiner, 2014). The central idea is that people act on the world on the basis of the meaning they give to it (Bruner, 1990). This principle is effectively captured in Bartlett's idea that all psychological processes involve 'an effort after meaning.' From this standpoint, it makes little sense to develop abstract models of psychological processes that are removed from the social and cultural existence of the people studied. As we will see, many cultural psychologists – including Jerome Bruner, Michael Cole, and James Wertsch – have taken inspiration from Bartlett on this point. I will argue that Bartlett's approach is both compatible with many of the central premises of cultural psychology and capable of offering new insights for developing this field.

The reconstruction offered here thus involves attending to Bartlett as a researcher of culture and a truly 'social' (as opposed to individual) psychology. It is only by drawing out this often-neglected side of his thought that we can fully understand his ideas. This is not a point I simply presuppose, but one I will demonstrate in considerable detail in the pages to follow. Also I have not shied away from criticizing approaches that neglect or underemphasize the social and cultural as well as the holistic, affective, and temporal dimensions of his work. On this point, critique often falls on *early* work in cognitive psychology for two main reasons. First, it was by far the most successful subdiscipline to appropriate Bartlett's work and propagate definitions of his concepts and methods for the discipline as a whole. Second, it was originally very explicit in its efforts to remove the social, cultural, and historical from its scope, so as to reduce the complexity of the phenomena under study (see e.g., Gardner, 1985, for an early summary of the field). This is a methodological strategy that Bartlett in fact devoted numerous pages to refuting. Although recent work in cognitive psychology has moved away from this strategy toward a more Bartlettian position,[7] many of the earlier interpretations of Bartlett's work nonetheless persist. The fate of notions such as an experiment, schema, and reconstruction all provide illustrative examples of the transformation of ideas away from their social, cultural, temporal, affective, and holistic understandings. I will consider each of these in detail in the chapters of this book and also highlight some lesser-known research inspired by Bartlett's work, which demonstrates that his ideas can be taken in a different vein than is typically done today.

Consequently, although this book is centered on Bartlett it encompasses a much wider terrain. Research for it very quickly became an enormous task. I found it necessary not only to read through Bartlett's entire *oeuvre*, but also to follow up on the wide range of different thinkers who influenced him and those who later appropriated his ideas. Bartlett's writings are full of insightful ideas but he does not frequently offer fully worked-out analyses of them, something he himself often admits. The task of further developing many of his suggestive concepts was often left to others coming after him; thus it made sense to follow on some of these efforts in this book. In each chapter of this book, I discuss the thinkers who both preceded and proceeded him. The predecessors help to better contextualize his approach, while those who came after him show how current understandings and evaluations of concepts and methods have reached us today (or alternatively not reached us) as well as how they have been developed.[8] Thus, this book can be read in two ways: first, as an explication of Bartlett and his legacy and second, as a case study in the diffusion and reconstruction of ideas in a science. In the pages of this book, we see the different sources that Bartlett brought together in his thinking, the development of his ideas over his career, and how these ideas have been selectively appropriated and transformed by others who have followed him.

In short, this book aims to explore the context, development, and appropriation of Bartlett's ideas. In doing so, it furthers the development of psychology toward a social and culturally inclusive study of the mind, which puts constructiveness at its center. It is my contention that one can be both accurate and constructive in this project; however, this requires being explicit about where transformations of his approach have taken place and could potentially take place. I speak of 'misunderstandings' only when a thinker attributes a position to Bartlett that he did not hold, and try to avoid it when a thinker is explicit about elaborating his approach in a given direction. As Bartlett's own studies showed, the transmission of culture involves both the processes of simplification and elaboration, aspects of the material are both omitted and added in ways that transform the whole. I should mention here my own selection in focusing on the theoretical side of Bartlett's work as opposed to his applied research.[9] In this book, I will only describe his applied research in so far as it has directly influenced his theoretical and methodological ideas (viz., his work on skill done during Second World War). I am also well aware that I have only covered a few selected examples of the recent explosion of research inspired by Bartlett's work. Future reconstructions will have to fill in some of these remaining gaps.

Preview of this Book

The first chapter of this book, 'Life and Work of a Cambridge Psychologist,' outlines Bartlett's life, ideas, and influence and situates them in historical context. Understanding Bartlett's particular intellectual trajectory requires attending to his personal biography, the Cambridge context, wider shifts in the discipline of psychology, and major historical events, such as the First and Second World Wars. As Bartlett (1932, p. 15) himself said: "The study of any well developed psychological function [e.g. a person's thinking] is only possible in light of a consideration of its history." In the chapter, we see how Bartlett's thought develops through different influences throughout his life as well as the tension between his institutional role and his own scientific production. Describing Bartlett's life and work further functions to contextualize the different phases of his career and thus the core concepts thematized in the proceeding chapters. The five chapters that follow are ordered to track the approximate chronological development of Bartlett's thinking, though each chapter does not confine itself to a particular period of his life. Instead, each chapter focuses on a specific theme and follows the pattern of (1) describing the intellectual context from which his ideas emerged, (2) explicating Bartlett's work, and (3) showing how subsequent thinkers reconstructed it. Let us consider each chapter in turn.

Chapter 2 'Experiments in Psychology' explores the meaning of an experiment. It aims to review and contextualize Bartlett's early experimental studies, done in the 1910s but only published as a systematic monograph in 1932 with the release of *Remembering: A Study in Experimental and Social Psychology*. These experiments provide concrete examples from Bartlett's research to be drawn upon in the explication of his theoretical ideas in the chapters that follow. The chapter begins by situating Bartlett's methodology within the continental research tradition of his time, which was in a state of transition from a focus on elements (à la the method of psychophysics) to a focus on wholes (later culminating in Gestalt psychology). The defining feature of Bartlett's early experiments is his holistic treatment of human responses, in which the basic unit of analysis is the active person relating to some material within the constraints of a social and material context. This manifests itself in a number of methodological principles that contrast with contemporary understandings of experimentation in psychology. The contrast is further explored by reviewing the history of 'replications and extensions' of Bartlett's experiments, demonstrating how his methodology was progressively changed and misunderstood over time. An argument will be made for reintroducing an open, qualitative, and idiographic experimental method, along the lines of the one Bartlett practiced.

Bartlett's famous 'experiments on remembering' were actually first pursued as contributions to diffusionist anthropology (see Bartlett, 1916b, 1920a). The Bartlettian universe is one in which culture (e.g., folklore, designs, ceremonies) is continuously reconstructed in communication and action. Bartlett was well aware that his experiments left aside the wider social and cultural dynamics of the diffusion and reconstruction of culture, and set out to address this gap. Chapter 3 'Cultural Diffusion and Reconstruction' explores the broader theory of social and cultural dynamics that he developed through his wide anthropological readings rather than his experimental studies. His framework is a development of diffusionist anthropology, particularly as his mentor W.H.R. Rivers understood it. In fact, Bartlett had originally intended to go into anthropology but was convinced by Rivers that psychology would be the best preparation for it. Through a number of historical contingencies, he never left psychology. Nevertheless, his early writings highlight the interrelation of cultural and psychological processes, and cover anthropological topics, such as cultural contact, folklore, and symbols. The chapter focuses mainly on Bartlett's first book on psychology, *Psychology and Primitive Culture* (Bartlett, 1923), though there is coverage of other material, including his later works dealing with cultural dynamics, such as his book *Political Propaganda* (Bartlett, 1940). It also contextualizes his theory in relation to the anthropology of his day (viz. Haddon, Rivers, and Lévy-Bruhl) and discusses Moscovici's (2008) Theory of Social Representations as a contemporary extension of Bartlett's diffusionist ideas.

In the next phase of his career, Bartlett's theory of cultural dynamics was used as an analogy to develop his famous concept of schema. Chapter 4 'Concept of Schema in Reconstruction' explores Bartlett's reconstructive theory of remembering, his most well-known contribution, through an analysis of the schema concept. No other concept in Bartlett's psychology has generated as much attention as that of schema. However, contemporary schema theories generally think of schema as a knowledge structure in the head that stores memories. In contrast, Bartlett (1932) used it to provide the basis for a radical *temporal* alternative to traditional *spatial* storage theories of memory. He took remembering out of the head and situated it at the enfolding relation between an organism and its environment. The basic model for this approach is how we adapt normalized patterns of response and the just-previous-body-position to the ever-novel present moment, much like groups adapt to new challenges on the basis of their established cultural patterns. This explains why memories tend to become generalized over time. However, higher psychological functions (i.e., those involving self-reflection, such as remembering, imagining, and thinking) involve a process of "turn[ing] around upon [one's] own schema and to construct them afresh" (Bartlett, 1932, p. 206). In doing so, we break determination by schema (i.e., the seamless flow of action in context) and with it take active control over our mind and behavior. The chapter contextualizes Bartlett's concept of schema within his general theory and other theories of his time (viz. the trace theory of memory and the work of Henry Head); examines its temporal dimensions in relation to embodied action and memory 'reconstruction'; shows how these temporal dynamics are abandoned by early cognitive psychology's 'schema' theories (which revert to the metaphor of static storage); and explores how we might fruitfully bring schema back into psychology as a temporal, embodied, dynamic, holistic, and social concept. The social nature of remembering is the main focus of the chapter that follows.

At the end of Part I of *Remembering*, Bartlett formulated his reconstructive 'theory of remembering' at the level of the individual through a discussion of 'schemata' and 'images.' However, in Part II of the book Bartlett further elaborated his theory to highlight the social and cultural framework in which remembering occurs, thus connecting it up with his earlier work on cultural diffusion (discussed in Chapter 3 of this book). David Middleton once said to me that when he first read *Remembering* the pages of the first half of the book had all been cleanly cut, while the second half (on social psychology) remained uncut and thus unread. This story is an example of a larger bias in Bartlett scholarship (at least until recently) toward the more cognitive side of his thought, at the expense of his understanding of the social and cultural situatedness of mind and memory. Chapter 5 'Social Psychology of Remembering' outlines the principles of his social psychology and their importance for understanding the psychology of remembering. It begins by contextualizing Bartlett's approach in relation to Jung's and Halbwachs's theories of collective memory. These two psychologists represent opposing views, the former biological and the latter social. This is followed by a discussion of what Bartlett understood by social psychology and how it was implemented in the study of the 'matter and manner of recall.' He illustrated these ideas with examples taken from his 1929 trip to South Africa, at which time he was able to at least partially realize his early ambition to do anthropological fieldwork. The chapter ends by considering how others (viz. Nadel, Bateson, Cole, and Wertsch) have developed his social psychology of remembering through a number of psycho-anthropological field studies from the 1930s until the first decade of the twenty-first century.

Chapter 6 'Thinking about Thinking' describes the last major phase of Bartlett's research career. This was the period just before the study of thinking became the study of cognition, at which point the focus shifted from a person's experience solving problems to an emphasis on mental errors and distortions. A research program on thinking was a natural extension to the ideas presented in *Remembering* (1932). This took form in a number of studies on what came to be called 'constructive' or 'everyday thinking' (Bartlett, 1938a, b; Carmichael, 1939a, b, 1940). Bartlett's St. John's Fellowship Dissertation (1916b), in fact, already includes a number of ideas for developing this program. However, the Second World War interrupted this development by shifting Bartlett's research toward the production of knowledge to aid in the war effort. This wartime research focused on understanding complex skill in human–machine interfaces and how they could be modified to improve information flow. Bartlett's notion of complex skill was itself an extension of his schema concept. The principles discovered about skill became the framework for Bartlett's book *Thinking: An Experimental and Social Study* (1958), while the cognitive revolution that followed shortly afterward picked up on the idea of information and machine interactions. The chapter highlights the comparative dimensions of Bartlett's approach to thinking: namely, the comparison of (1) thinking with bodily skills, (2) different varieties of thinking (e.g., in closed systems, science, everyday life, and art), and (3) the thought patterns of different social groups. It makes the argument that each kind of thinking needs to be understood on its own terms rather than through the standard of logical thinking.

This book's concluding chapter 'Conclusion: From Past to Future' summarizes and synthesizes the core findings of the previous chapters. It both outlines the key themes of Bartlett's constructivist approach and points out how his key ideas have been reconstructed by others. Like Bartlett's method for analyzing cultural transmission, it attends to what was omitted, retained, and added at different times. The approach sketched out here aims to overcome the one-sided focus on human reactivity by including people's history, material, and social environment, wider experiences, aspirations for the future and, most of all, the constructive ways in which humans live and are oriented forward. As a final note, it is important to stress here that *construction*, on both individual and collective levels, does not occur out of nothing; rather the past serves as a source for innovation in the present. In this way the continuous development of ideas requires flexibly engaging with the past, as this book has aimed to do in relation to Bartlett and his legacy.

Notes

1. Significantly, Schacter (2012) begins his article with a discussion of Bartlett's theory as a framework to understand these processes.
2. Bartlett's focus on how material culture conditions psychological processes connects up well with the materiality turn in social sciences. In contrast to some interpretations of Bartlett's work (e.g., Douglas, 1986), the social and cultural dimensions never entirely disappeared from his approach. However, they did take an increasingly subordinate role, especially toward the end of his career (see Chapter 1).
3. Bartlett has been influential in social, cognitive, cultural, discursive, and ecological psychology, and the disciplines of anthropology, sociology, the philosophy of science, and ergonomics.

4. An earlier edited book titled *Bartlett, Culture and Cognition* presents a range of different perspectives on Bartlett rather than an integrated framework for understanding him. Nonetheless, it has been an important source for this book, particularly in following up how his ideas have been appropriated by others.

5. Bartlett (1958) himself discussed his approach as a synthesis of ideas coming from others, a perspective that clearly fits his own theory of constructive thinking.

6. I say 're-emerged' because cultural psychology has been born multiple times through psychology's short history (Wagoner, Chaudhary, and Hviid, 2014). Its first incarnation was in the mid-nineteenth century in the guise of *Völkerpsychologie*, at which time social and cultural psychology were synonymous.

7. Extended, situated, and distributed cognition (see e.g., Sutton, Harris, Keil, and Barnier, 2010) are all highly compatible with a Bartlettian approach.

8. In this latter endeavor, I have been particularly inspired by the historians of psychology Kurt Danziger (1990, 1997, 2008) and Jaan Valsiner (2012; Valsiner and van der Veer, 2000).

9. Bartlett's applied research became particularly important after the Second World War, but was already present in research he did during the First World War.

1 Life and Work of a Cambridge Psychologist

> To separate psychology from the psychologist is an entirely artificial procedure.
>
> (Bartlett, 2010[1959], p. 988)

> If I am to say what sort of a psychologist I am, I think I can say only that I am a Cambridge psychologist. The trouble about this is that Cambridge psychology of the laboratory type has never committed itself to any hard and fast and settled scheme of psychological explanation. I hope it never will.
>
> (Bartlett, 1936, p. 40)

Bartlett's statement aptly expresses both the theoretical and institutional position he occupied in psychology. He spent his entire working life in Cambridge, from 1909 until his death in 1969. Over his long and distinguished career, he was able to exert a considerable influence on the development of psychology, particularly in Britain.[1] This has come primarily from the importance placed on his most famous book *Remembering*, and his 30-year directorship of the Cambridge Laboratory. Throughout his career, both his own research and the Cambridge department of psychology continued to change in response to new influences. Interestingly, his research and that of the institution diverged in crucial ways: as the institutional leader, he promoted a kind of research that was at odds with much of his own work, including his most famous books (viz., Bartlett, 1923, 1932/1995, 1958). In this, we see a tension between factors promoting the construction of new scientific ideas (often interdisciplinary in nature) and factors involved in the promotion of psychology as an independent and dominant discipline. To understand this tension, we need to attend how biographical, historical, and institutional influences were woven together through his life.[2]

In what follows we will chronologically consider the different phases of Bartlett's life and work, and the different influences and factors that shaped them. The story begins with Bartlett's upbringing in the Cotswolds, an area of west central England then known for its progressive liberal values. It was here that he first developed his interest in

12

psychology as well as a lifelong passion for cricket. The second phase covers Bartlett's early years in Cambridge as a philosopher and the events that definitively turned him away from that discipline toward anthropology and psychology. The third phase describes his activity during the First World War, conducting theoretical and applied research, as well as seeing traumatized patients at the local hospital. The fourth phase highlights both Bartlett's role as institutional leader and his continued interest in and development of a thorough social and cultural psychology. The fifth phase then describes the founding of the Applied Psychological Unit and the work done during the Second World War, which later feeds into Bartlett's research program on thinking. The concluding section of this chapter examines the development of Bartlett's ideas through a life-course analysis and outlines how he left a controversial legacy for those that followed.

From the Cotswolds to Cambridge

Frederic Bartlett was born on October 20, 1886 in the small town of Stow-on-the-Wold, located in the beautiful Cotswolds hills of west central England. He claimed to have found record of members of the Bartlett lineage living in the area as early as the fourteenth century in the local cemetery. Throughout his life, he remained proud of his birthplace and even retained something of his regional accent. The region was then known for its non-conformist ministers, progressive liberal values, and political radicalism. Bartlett's family was no exception to this. His father was an intelligent 'outspoken and deeply convinced liberal'[3] who ran a local shop for the manufacture and sale of boots and shoes; he believed in education and was highly supportive of young Frederic's ambitions. Many on his mother's side of the family worked in building and farming – his maternal grandfather owned a quarry. Bartlett had only two siblings, an elder brother and a mentally disabled younger brother.

Bartlett spent the first 14 years of his life as a 'normal country boy, largely outdoors,' helping in the harvest and playing cricket, which would remain a lifelong passion and also help him to develop his later research on skill (see later; Chapter 6). At the age of 14 he attended a private primary school in his hometown, which he recalls was 'pretty good' though not quite adequate in mathematics, something he regretted. The local secondary school had closed, which led his family to consider sending him to boarding school. This possibility had to be scrapped when Bartlett suffered from a severe attack of pleurisy, which brought him near to death. Being too weak to attend school, he was left hardly with any formal education under his belt. Instead, he was self-educated, with the support of his father and the local non-conformist minister, both of whom had considerable libraries. He spent much of his time in independent reading and walking through the surrounding countryside – the doctors had prescribed 'a life in the open air' (Bartlett, 1956, p. 81). Bartlett recalls that he was "learning something about the habits of birds and beasts, exploring ancient and overgrown roadways, walking far in all weathers, and, as strength returned, playing every game [he] could get" (p. 81). With the encouragement of his father, who purchased a typewriter for him, he also tried his hand at writing stories and novels with 'reasonably good' results. Literary writing remained an interest throughout his life and probably also influenced his later exploration of folk stories.

At the age of 17, Bartlett's father persuaded him to start a higher education by taking a correspondence course from the *University Correspondence College*, dependent on the University of London, with headquarters located in Cambridge. Given Bartlett had little exposure to formal schooling, it is not surprising that he found it 'very hard going' and failed his initial exams in three of five subjects, passing only in English and logic. It took long and hard work, combined with help from local people, for him to pass the failed exams on second and third attempts. By the end of his degree, things got progressively easier and he graduated B.A. in 1909 with First Class Honours, specializing in logic and philosophy. His interest in these topics had come about by chance when, at the start of his degree, a friend of his father suggested that he should take a course on logic. Bartlett later reflected, "it seems odd that this suggestion, made, as it appeared, very much spur of the moment, should have settled pretty much all of my future."

His strong interest in logic led him to read widely in related areas, such as psychology. He first encountered psychology through the works of the analytic psychologists G.F. Stout (1860–1944) and James Ward (1843–1925) – the former was a student of the latter at Cambridge. Bartlett (1936, p. 39) comments, "My way into science was by the philosophy of it." The first book he read in psychology was Stout's *Manual of Psychology*, which was the textbook used for nearly the first quarter of the century by most British universities. He also read Ward's famous article 'Psychology' in the *Encyclopaedia Britannica*, which he cycled once a week 18 miles to the nearest public library to read, bringing back home copious notes with him. Bartlett (1968b) directly credits Ward and Stout for his own conception of the mind as an active and complex system, but later moves away from their analytic description of the mind toward a functional approach that investigates the conditions under which different reactions take place. Ward's psychology was itself highly influenced by German philosopher Lotze's "constant reiteration of the fundamental importance of life and activity" (Bartlett, 1925d, p. 450). Additionally, there was C.S. Myers's *Text-book of Experimental Psychology*, which fascinated Bartlett to the point of trying out its exercises at home with crude instruments made of "cardboard, pins, bits of string and 'elastic glue'" (Bartlett, 1936, p. 39), which he used for "bothering and confounding [his] relatives and friends with a lot of odd questions" (Bartlett, 1956, p. 81). Over a decade and a half later, Bartlett would co-author the third edition of the *Text-book*.

Upon finishing his degree, the Principle of the Correspondence College invited him to become a tutor in Cambridge. Bartlett recalls, "I accepted without hesitation and on a misty morning in the Autumn of 1909" left Stow for Cambridge. This turned out to be a good decision as he thoroughly enjoyed his work, and had time to both play a lot of cricket and take a M.A. from London University in 1912, gaining 'special distinction' in sociology and ethics. His chief interest at that time remained in philosophy, especially logic – his first two publications were successful in this subject (see Bartlett, 1913, 1914). For the young Bartlett, psychology studied the whole range of conscious life descriptively (as Ward and Stout practiced it), whereas logic was normative with its focus on valid processes of thinking. Over 40 years later, he would publish an elaborated typology of thinking processes in his book *Thinking* (1958), which includes analyses of the psychological processes by which people solve problems in logic, science, everyday life, and art (see Chapter 6).

On the strength of his success in his previous two degrees, Bartlett decided to start another undergraduate degree in moral sciences at the University of Cambridge, which involved immersion in a range of philosophical discussions as well as some exposure to the psychology laboratory.[4] On entering the University, students become affiliated with both a department and a college. Bartlett chose to apply to St. John's College "principally because W. H. R. Rivers was there" (Bartlett, 1956, p. 81). W.H.R. Rivers (1864–1922) was a leader in psychology, anthropology, and medicine, which were all competing interests for Bartlett at that time. Through the efforts of his family, friends, and himself, he was able to enter the University in the autumn of 1912. Bartlett's admittance is really quite remarkable when one juxtaposes his middle-class rural background and absence of formal schooling with the ultra-competitiveness of the University of Cambridge. Most Cambridge students had elite upper-class pedigrees with lots of private tutoring. Yet, Bartlett would excel in this new environment and within 10 years become the director of the Cambridge Laboratory, the most prestigious center for psychology in Britain; although, as we will see in the next section, there would also be some stumbles along the way.

Cambridge University: From Philosophy to Psychology

In 1912, Cambridge University was an intellectually vibrant environment as well as a conservative institution that religiously guarded its tradition. These two tendencies of *construction* and *conservation* would become essential to Bartlett's approach to social and psychological processes. Cambridge constructiveness could be seen in the dynamic exchange of ideas occurring across different areas of knowledge. Bertrand Russell and Whitehead were working on their *Principia Mathematica* and the young Wittgenstein had just arrived. The world famous economist J.M. Keynes had started work at the university and the Bloomsbury group, an eccentric collection of writers, philosophers, artists, and intellectuals of all kinds, was in full swing.[5] This forward-looking, constructive atmosphere coexisted with a rather conservative institutional background. In one of his books, Bartlett (1923, pp. 48–9) even compared the Cambridge Colleges with social groups in primitive cultures in their adherence to tradition and conservation of their institutions! Given Bartlett's upbringing in the intellectual freedom and religious nonconformity of the Cotswolds, it is of little surprise that this latter side of Cambridge never really charmed him.

Psychology itself, as an upstart discipline, seemed to attract people, like Bartlett, who were progressively minded and had some disdain for the University's conservatism. There was even a story circulating in Cambridge psychology, and published in a number of places by C.S. Myers and Bartlett, that the university could have had the first psychological laboratory in the world if only it had not been so conservative – Leipzig is generally given the distinction of having the first laboratory, which was opened by Wilhelm Wundt in 1879.[6] The story goes that in 1877 Ward and Venn together proposed to the university Senate that a laboratory of psychophysics should be established, but that it was rejected when a "theologically minded mathematician" argued that it "would insult religion by putting the human soul in a pair of scales" (Bartlett, 1937c, p. 98). Bartlett admits to never having seen a record of the proceedings and no one has uncovered it since. Regardless of whether it is in fact true or not, the story clearly expresses a general sentiment in psychology about the constraints imposed by the University's conservatism on what the founders felt to be a progressive new discipline.

Other milestones in the establishment of psychology as an independent discipline at Cambridge were better documented. Since 1878 Ward and Stout had been offering philosophy courses in analytic psychology, but it was not until 1891 that Ward managed to secure a small room for psychophysics in the physiology laboratory. In 1897, W.H.R. Rivers arrived and began to lead psychology away from philosophy. Rivers was perhaps Britain's first experimental psychologist and certainly the leading figure in the psychology of vision at that time. At Cambridge, he ran a course on 'experimental psychology' in the psychology laboratory at that time in its third location. This course was taken by C.S. Myers, who was later made responsible for running the laboratory and in 1907 occupied the first lectureship entirely devoted to psychology. The Cambridge laboratory began to produce a considerable amount of experimental work during this time, which in 1904 led Ward, Rivers, and Myers to found the *British Journal of Psychology* as a forum for publication. Against the hostility of some conservative Senate members, Myers also succeeded in getting psychology accepted as a subject for examination in ordinary Cambridge degree in 1909 and as a degree program in itself in 1912. It is interesting to note that although Ward, Rivers, and Myers worked for decades to carve out an autonomous space for psychology, they themselves remained highly interdisciplinary in their own research, a tension that would manifest itself in Bartlett's career as well.

The emergence of psychology out of philosophy also occurred in Bartlett's life trajectory. When Bartlett arrived in Cambridge, he was still very much a philosopher. He says that he had at the time "a very predominant philosophical bias in [his] outlook upon life" (Bartlett, 1936, p. 39). He signed up for the Moral Sciences Tripos focusing on philosophy with some topics in psychology. He had considered a career in philosophy but two events put him off the idea. The first involved an encounter early in his study with two of Britain's most distinguished philosophers, G.E. Moore and Bertrand Russell, at a kind of intellectual sparring activity called 'squash.' Bartlett recalls,

There was a prolonged discussion on whether the rats said to be seen in an advanced state of delirium tremens were real or not. MacTaggart thought they were not real; Moore argued that they were not real in any ordinary sense of the word and Russell rather played one off against the other. When I was appealed to as a sort of umpire I know I was completely flummoxed and I believe I tried to agree with them all. Anyway I came away feeling very depressed.

The second incident that turned him away from philosophy occurred at the Moral Sciences Club soon after the first. Bartlett gave a paper defending Henri Bergson's *Creative Evolution* (1907/1911) to a Cambridge crowd, who being rather unsympathetic to Bergson heavily criticized his paper to the point that Bartlett left the encounter rather dejected. Although Bergson is only rarely referred to in Bartlett's published work, his influence can be seen in Bartlett's conceptualization of time, memory, habit, and organismic activity (see Chapter 4).

Fortunately, Bartlett had also begun to become better acquainted with psychology as part of his degree. In fact, one of the first Cambridge notables Bartlett ran into was Stout, at a St. John's College Garden party, whose *Manual* had initially sparked Bartlett's interest in psychology. Bartlett was also tutored at the college by Rivers, which meant he would meet up with him during the term to discuss his progress. In terms of classes, Bartlett was a member of the last group of students Ward taught. He recalls,

It was an unforgettable experience. The class was a small one, but good, and contained several people who have since done much for psychology in this and in other lands. When Ward had doubtfully assured himself that we were worth instructing, he distributed to all of us copies of the complete proofs of his new book [*Psychological Principles*[7]]. He said we would take it paragraph by paragraph, and we could raise whatever questions we pleased. With simple-minded enthusiasm we made a corporate effort and arrived at lectures armed with many enquiries. Whereupon Ward sadly but firmly pointed out to us that we could not possibly have read what he had written since nearly all these questions were answered 'later on.' By this time his spell was upon us, as it was set upon nearly everybody who came into personal contact with him. Above everything else we desired him to talk just as he liked; so we dropped our questions. At this, more sadly, and yet more firmly, he pointed out that we could not possibly have read what he had written, since hosts of unanswered questions abounded there.

(Bartlett, 1937c, pp. 99–100)

In May 1913, a new well-provisioned psychological laboratory was opened to replace the previous one, described as 'damp and rat-invested.' On the opening day, Bartlett was asked by Myers – the laboratory's founder, director, and sponsor – to carry out some experiments on visual perception for visitors to the laboratory. The experience fascinated Bartlett and inspired him to develop his own research on perception (Bartlett, 1916a, 1918), which would eventually lead him into the topics of imagination and remembering. In the autumn of that same year, Bartlett took a course in experimental psychology, run by Myers and the laboratory assistant Cyril Burt. The laboratory exercises were apparently rather tedious and in general without clear links with the teaching nor everyday life. Throughout his life, Bartlett had an ambivalent attitude to the laboratory: on the one hand finding it trivial and boring, and on the other hand feeling that strict methodology training was good for a scientist. Going through his notes from that time, Bartlett (1956) recalls,

We worked in the main with the stock-in-trade of Helmholtz and Hering, of Wundt, of Blix, Goldscheider and Von Frey, of G. E. Müller, of Kraepelin. There were a few refreshing excursions into the fields of the Würzburg school, a little of Wilhelm Stern, and a little, a very little, of the new psychology of mental tests, and of Jung's form of word associations. It was Germans, Germans all the way, and if we were going to stick to psychology then to Germany sooner or later we must all surely go. (p. 83)

This emphasis on the German tradition of experimental psychology is particularly important in understanding the experimental method Bartlett himself develops, a point that will be discussed in detail in Chapter 2. Let me simply point out here the "few refreshing excursions into the fields of the Würzburg school," which sets the stage for his own experimental methodology. Because of the impact it had on Bartlett's thinking, it is worth briefly describing here the fierce debates that the Würzburg School prompted in the first decade of the twentieth century (see also Kusch, 1999).

The debate was focused on whether 'imageless thought' was possible and through what methods of investigation could the question be approached. On one side, Wundt argued that experimental psychology must limit itself to the study of *inner perception*, in which some external stimulus could be varied and the subject's experience was *immediately* reported. Wundt believed that this experience could be decomposed into sensations, images, and feelings. On the other side, Würzburg psychologists argued that a rigorous experimental methodology of thought was possible, using *retrospective* self-observation (e.g., Bühler, 1908). In this method, subjects or 'observers' were given an experimental task, such as providing a word association, making a judgment or solving a thought puzzle. They were to silently resolve the task and then immediately afterward provide a detailed introspective report or 'experiential protocol' of how they arrived at the solution. Their aim was to access the *process* of thought. In their analysis, the Würzburgers borrowed heavily from Brentano's 'act psychology' to highlight *intentional* aspects of consciousness irreducible to Wundt's sensationist typology. Thus, they emphasized the active goal-directed character of mind. This debate was carefully followed at Cambridge, especially by Bartlett's mentors James Ward and Charles Myers, who adopted opposing views. It is thus not unsurprising that Bartlett had an active interest in the Würzburg approach, sometimes borrowing from them and at other times criticizing them. Through his career, there is a trend from the former to the latter position. The Würzburger's findings and concepts in relation to Bartlett's research will be further elaborated in Chapters 2 and 6.

Because of his previous degrees, Bartlett was allowed to complete his B.A. in moral sciences in only two years, which he did in 1914 with distinction. The then laboratory assistant Cyril Burt moved to London to work with Charles Spearman leaving the position open. Myers offered it to Bartlett, who had reservations about taking it because he imagined himself at that moment pursuing anthropology instead. Rivers convinced him to take the position, arguing that the best preparation for anthropology would be rigorous training in the methods of psychology. As a result of a number of historical contingencies, described in the next two sections, Bartlett never left psychology. Nonetheless, anthropology would continue to exert a considerable influence on him, especially in the first two decades of his career, at which time about half his publications dealt with topics in that area (e.g., folklore, symbols, cultural contact), albeit with a psychological twist (see Chapter 3). It was in fact the anthropological study of the transmission and transformation of culture (i.e., the process of conventionalization) that originally inspired him to develop his famous experiments on remembering, which will be described in the next section.

First World War: The Cambridge Laboratory

Bartlett had barely settled into his new position when the First World War broke out. Most of the Cambridge men left to aid in the war effort. Bartlett was not eligible to participate due to his previous health problems, and thus remained in Cambridge during the war. He was put in charge of running the psychology laboratory as 'relief director,' though there was not much activity with most of the staff and students away. During this period, he must have spent most of his time working on his own experiments, which he submitted for his *St. John's Fellowship* in 1916 and then again in 1917, at which point it was successful, making him a fellow there. For his application, he submitted three essays: "An experimental study of some problems of perceiving and imagining" (Bartlett, 1916b), "Feeling and criticism" (later published as "The development of criticism" – Bartlett, 1918), and his *Dissertation* on "Transformations arising from repeated representation: A contribution towards an experimental study of the process of conventionalisation" (Bartlett, 1916b). These studies would later be rewritten for his most important book *Remembering* (1932/1995) (more on that below). In this section, I first briefly describe these experiments and then discuss some other biographical influences on him during this period.

Bartlett's experimental studies involved ideas coming from two main intellectual currents: German experimental psychology (mentioned earlier) and Cambridge diffusionist anthropology, which analyzed the spread of cultural forms. The German tradition of psychology taught him experimental techniques for accessing and analyzing mental life as an active process (see Chapter 2), while Cambridge anthropology, founded by A.C. Haddon (1855–1940), provided the focus on the transmission and transformation of cultural elements (e.g., decorative designs, cultural instruments, and burial practices) as they move from one social group to another (see Herle and Rouse, 1998; Chapter 3). In relation to the latter, Rivers (1912a) had coined the word 'conventionalization' to describe the process by which cultural elements are progressively changed in the direction of existing social conventions when they enter a new group. Later in his life, Bartlett (1958) goes as far to describe this period of his thinking 'the "conventionalization" phase' (p. 144), which lasted well into the 1920s.

Bartlett's first studies grew out of some standard visual experiments Myers had asked him to perform on visitors to the new Laboratory of Experimental Psychology on its official opening in May 1913. The variety of participants' interpretations to the same diagrams and pictures given inspired Bartlett to design further experiments that looked at what the participant themselves contributed to the perceiving response. Using the method of presenting subjects with some material for a fraction of a second (via tachistoscope[8]) and asking them to describe what they had seen, he was able to demonstrate the influence of attitudes, interests, and conventions on perceiving. For example, one participant transformed a satellite looking object with a hand pointing at it into an airplane during an air raid, which was a common occurrence in Cambridge at the time of the First World War. Participants were selectively attending to and constructing the material based on previous social and personal experience.

Conventionalization was even more evident in the experiments Bartlett started in 1914 to specifically study the process. For example, in *the method of repeated reproduction* participants were asked to reproduce material after increasingly longer time periods, in some cases after several years; and in *the method of serial reproduction* one participant's reproduction was passed to another, who reproduced it and so on, like the party game 'Chinese Whispers.' His most famous results come from the use of the Native American folk story called *War of the Ghosts* as material to be remembered and reproduced. Participants systematically changed the story in their reproductions of it to look more and more like a conventional English story. For example, 'hunting seals' became 'fishing,' 'war cry' became 'noises,' proper names were forgotten or changed, puzzling elements were either rationalized or omitted. Thus, Bartlett powerfully illustrated the work of conventionalization at a psychological level in a controlled experimental study, providing a mechanism for what his mentors had observed in their field studies. These early experimental studies will be described in detail in Chapter 2.

In the rest of this section, I highlight some other contemporaneous influences on the development of his approach.

As with Myers and Rivers, Bartlett also worked during the war with soldiers being treated at the Cambridge hospital. This undoubtedly left a considerable impact on his thinking, sensitizing him to the role of personal history in setting internal conditions for behavior, as well as the value of working with single cases: "The man who knows intimately but one mental life will the sooner enter others, than the man whose observation has grasped the external form and movements of thousands of people, but has gone no further" (Bartlett, 1923, p. 23). For these reasons and the need to see a person in light of his or her history, Bartlett (1932/1995, p. 15) likens an experimental psychologist to a clinician. He recalled his clinical work in the following terms:

> There was no properly trained medical personnel available for dealing with these cases, and as a psychologist with practical interests I was invited to see what I could do to help them. I had discussed current treatments of 'shell shock' with Myers and Rivers and, like all psychologists of the period I had read everything I could get of the work of Sigmund Freud ... I cannot say whether what I was able to do was of much, or indeed of any, use to these patients: none of them was allowed to stay long in Cambridge. But I myself learned two lessons ... The first concerned the value to the psychologist of collaboration with medically trained experts, and the second that psychological insight and understanding always demands a consideration of the internal, and personal, conditions of behaviour as well as a study, and if possible a control of external circumstances.
>
> (Bartlett, 1964, quoted in Winter, 2012, p. 213)

In this quotation, Bartlett reveals the influence of Freud on his thinking. Although Bartlett would later criticize psychoanalytic approaches, they were clearly influential at this time (see Forrester, 2008). It is noteworthy that many of the terms he uses to describe his subjects' transformations of stories and images in remembering come from psychoanalysis – for example, 'rationalization,' 'condensation,' and 'substitution' (his other terms come mainly from diffusionist anthropology). However, he seems to go to great lengths to avoid using the term 'unconscious,' preferring instead 'unwitting.' Unlike his mentors, Bartlett would later develop a distaste for psychoanalysis as an approach to psychology[9] and devoted a number of papers to critiquing it – for example, its treatment of folklore (Bartlett, 1920), repression (Bartlett, 1928a), and the collective unconscious (Bartlett, 1932/1995, p. 281ff).

Toward the end of the war, Bartlett did applied work on 'detecting sounds of weak intensity' (Smith and Bartlett, 1920a, b), which was used to select personnel to monitor German submarines. This kind of applied research would help to grow the Cambridge Laboratory in the postwar years and eventually come to dominate it (see later). His colla-borator in this research was Emily Mary Smith, who would later become his wife "to the mutual satisfaction of them both," as he put it. At the time, Smith was a leading 'animal psychologist,' having pub-lished an important book titled *The Investigation of Mind in Animals* (1915), which shows her particular admiration for Pavlov's work. Thus, through personal contact Bartlett developed knowledge of this field as well; in fact, he tends to adopt a biological language in much of his writings, using words like 'organism' and 'adaptation.' Furthermore, it was not out of ignorance that behaviorism never got a foothold in Cambridge – Bartlett and Smith (1920) published an article critiquing Watson's characterization of "thinking as merely the action of a lan-guage mechanism," and Bartlett (1927a) critically reviewed Watson's (1925) book *Behaviorism*. Nevertheless, Bartlett does continue to use the terminology of 'response' and 'conditions,' though he considers these to include a much wider range of factors than would Watson, including the 'internal conditions of response' (e.g., attitudes) and the framework imposed by group membership and social setting on action and experience.

Between the Wars: Institutional Leader and Social Psychologist

When the war ended "Psychology, everyone found, had changed" (Bartlett, 1936, p. 40). Having treated soldiers with psychological injury or shock during the war, Rivers and Myers returned to Cambridge with new purpose. On the back of this experience, psychoanalysis seemed all the more important to them, though they were also critical in their engagement with it (Forrester, 2008). Rivers spent the postwar years pouring out lectures, essays, and books that integrated psychoanalytic insights into anthropology and social psychology. He remained at this time 'extremely close' to Bartlett and played a key role in the develop-ment of his thinking about social and cultural processes (Chapter 3). Similarly, Myers became heavily involved in the debate over whether 'shell-shock'[10] should be recognized as a mental illness caused by experiences in war. The involvement of many psychologists with trau-matized soldiers during and after the war brought the topic of memory to the fore. There appeared to be more to memory than association and trace decay, as had been researched in the standard experimental studies up until that time; Myers and Rivers argued for the need to introduce feeling and meaning into memory's study as well as psychoanalytic notions such as repression, suppression, and dissociation (Collins, 2001).[11] These developments undoubtedly contributed to Bartlett's turning toward the subject of memory – more on that below.

Having grown tired of the struggle to establish psychology in the face of University conservatism, Myers decided to leave Cambridge to found the *National Institution of Industrial Psychology*. But before doing so, he made sure that the position of 'Reader in experimental psychology,' which had been offered to him, was passed onto Bartlett with the same salary and conditions in 1922. That same year Rivers died without warning of a strangulated hernia.[12] These developments left Bartlett without a senior in Cambridge psychology, except Ward who was by that time long retired and would himself die three years later. Consequently, Bartlett became director of the Cambridge laboratory at the age of 36, a position he held until his retirement in 1952. Being in the most senior position in Cambridge for 30 years, at a time when psychology was still a fledgling but quickly growing discipline, Bartlett had considerable power to shape its course in Britain. Strangely, in this position he successfully promoted a narrow brand of experimental psychology that was practically minded, anti-intellectual, asocial, and applied, which were characteristics at odds with much of his own work (Costall, 1992). This discrepancy can be partly explained by the conflicting demands of institutional leader and research scientist. In the former position he worked to establish psychology as an autonomous and dominant discipline, whereas in the latter he was more motivated by his own personal research interests. The approach he developed in his most famous books highlights the 'construction' tendency, in that he weaved together ideas coming from philosophy, anthropology, sociology, and psychology into a new form, whereas in the position of laboratory director he grafted psychology onto the natural sciences and worked to secure its position there.

As laboratory director one of the first battles Bartlett took up was to move psychology from the 'moral sciences' (i.e., philosophy) to the 'natural sciences' tripos, which was only fully accomplished in 1934.[13] Part of this move involved bringing applied areas of psychology into the laboratory. Bartlett was already teaching Myers's course on 'the psychology of the soldier,' which he published as a book in 1927. From the late 1920s onward, Bartlett served on many research committees and brought in a steady stream of government funding for work on applied areas, especially on the military and industry. This applied link was not so much Bartlett's innovation but a continuation of developments that had already been set in motion by Myers. Costall (1992) points out the problem with Bartlett's institutional advocacy of applied, experimental psychology that such funding permitted:

Bartlett seems to have never questioned whether the strong practical emphasis of Cambridge psychology would in itself ensure its 'human significance.' The problem is that some real life situations are extremely artificial and restricted – not least, those occurring in industrial and military work. Yet it was exactly such situations, involving routine, repetitive motor movements or monitoring of display screens, that came to dominate the applied research at Cambridge. (p. 636)

Costall (1996) describes how Cambridge psychology of the laboratory increasingly became a kind of 'glorified button pushing' (p. 307), in which strict experimental methods became not simply a means of study but an end in itself. In this endeavor, social and cultural issues had little place. At best, the experimental psychologist was to pass on the latest methods to the researcher in the field (Bartlett, 1937a). In his entire time as director, Bartlett never hired a social psychologist to his laboratory, though he supported those pursuing social issues, as long as they were working somewhere else (Costall, 1992).

Bartlett also became editor-in-chief of the *British Journal of Psychology* in 1924, a position he kept until 1948. A large percentage of the articles were done under his supervision. In 1931 Bartlett was appointed as the university's first professor of experimental psychology, further signaling the growth of the laboratory. On top of his skill as director, committeeman, and editor, Bartlett was a gifted teacher. All these combined factors led to an extremely strong Bartlettian influence in British psychology. In fact, Bartlett actively used his institutional position to make sure that his students got the "lions share of the Professorships of Psychology in Britain; and indeed quite a number elsewhere in the Commonwealth" (Broadbent, 1970, p. 3). Crampton (1978) points out that of the 16 professors of psychology in Britain in 1957, 10 had done their postgraduate study with Bartlett or Myers.

At the same time that Bartlett was securing the institutional position of psychology through its placement in the natural sciences and application to the military and industry, he was developing a more radical social perspective closely aligned with his anthropological interests. This can be most clearly seen in his early book *Psychology and Primitive Culture* (1923), which was based on lectures Rivers had encouraged him to give at the Bedford College for Women in the University of London. The content of the book is a further development of the work on conventionalization, but rather than being experimental in focus (like his *Dissertation*), it explored how wider social processes lead to particular outcomes in intercultural contact, very much inspired by Rivers and his anthropological approach. It is this work that provides the background through which we should interpret Bartlett's famous experiments described earlier. In this book, Bartlett makes the argument that sociology might be able to ignore psychology but the reverse was certainly not true: human action and experience are deeply social to the core. To explain them outside of the particular group in which they occur leads to speculation and guess work. An elaborated account of these arguments can be found in Chapter 3. Here I simply point out that while Bartlett, the institutional leader, was beginning to define psychology in terms of the laboratory and asocial processes, he was in his published work advocating psychology as a thoroughly social science.

While still in his 'conventionalization phase,' Bartlett wanted to continue to explore anthropological problems through the lens of psychology in a book that was to be titled *A Contribution Towards an Experimental Study of the Process of Conventionalization*. A publishing agreement with Cambridge University Press was even secured. However, Bartlett (1958, pp. 144–5) recalls: "There came a time when I began to write this book, and I labored heavily through two or three chapters, but it did not go well. I tore up what I had written and for some time there followed a most unpleasant period when it seemed that I had taken a lot of steps to get nowhere at all." The plan for the book on conventionalization[14] is actually close to the structure that Bartlett would later adopt for his most influential book *Remembering*, published in 1932. The first part was to include his experimental studies on conventionalization while the second would explore conventionalization from a more social perspective. The shift in focus to the topic of remembering should be understood against the background of the postwar period, in which memory became salient through commemorative practices (e.g., poppy flower remembrances and the 2-min silence) as well as clinicians' discussions of soldiers' war trauma (see earlier). In fact, a third of Bartlett's (1927b) book on *The Psychology and the Soldier* dealt with 'mental health and disease in warfare.'

Two features of Bartlett's book title *Remembering: A study in experimental and social psychology* immediately stand out for comment. First, Bartlett uses the gerund of the verb to describe remember*ing* as a concrete activity rather than an elusive thing or substance. Second, the study of remembering was to be part of social psychology. In both respects, he was clearly breaking with the dominant tradition of research following Ebbinghaus's (1885/1913) classic *Memory: A Contribution to Experimental Psychology*, which saw memory as a mental faculty for retaining individuated pieces of information and that worked in independence of history, context, and social processes. Despite the freshness of Bartlett's (1932/1995) approach, he does seem to back down somewhat from the radical social position of *Psychology and Primitive Culture* (Costall, 1992; Douglas, 1986). Over half of *Remembering* is devoted to descriptions of his experiments, which are not fundamentally different from their presentation in his *Dissertation*. The new interpretation of his results came from contact with the neurologist Henry Head, from whom Bartlett adopted the concept of 'schema' (see Chapter 4). The middle section of the book uses the concept to develop a 'theory of remembering,' which provides an alternative to the idea that memories are stored as individuated traces in the organism; instead, each act of remembering is conceptualized as an 'imaginative reconstruction' built out of the massed affects of previous experience (i.e., schema) and what recurs in the form of images. However, formulating his theory with the previously physiological concept of schema suggested an approach focused on the individual rather than on social processes.

It was not until page 239 that the social psychology is directly discussed and it appears as somewhat more of an add-on than an integrated part of his approach – thus, making it easy to neglect. In the second half of the book, there is a chapter on 'conventionalization' that further develops some of his earlier ideas about cultural diffusion (see Chapter 3 – 'some principles of cultural change'), and is probably leftovers from his unfinished book on the subject. Bartlett's 'social' psychological theory of remembering is elaborated mainly in Chapters 14 and 15 of *Remembering* (see Chapter 5). Material for these chapters came primarily from Bartlett's visit to South Africa in 1929, where he was invited to give a talk as President of the Psychology Section of the *British Society for the Advancement of Science*. On this trip, Bartlett was able to finally realize his earlier anthropological ambitions and vividly experience first-hand the intercultural contacts which he had written about at length in *Psychology and Primitive Culture* and continued to be of interest throughout his life. During the trip he took copious field notes, which filled a journal, now kept at the Cambridge University Library. The journal served as a source for later publications. In one of them, he vividly describes a day visiting a group of natives in an isolated region:

One day, certain of the leading members of this small nation group collected together all the available oldest people of the community, and some of the youngest, and I was invited to watch them re-enact some of their ancient, fast disappearing, or perhaps already obsolete, cultural practices. It was an occasion on which the traditional and the novel were mingled, though I do not think that we were very much aware of anything incongruous at the time. The natives sat on skins, or robes, or on the bare ground in their established order of precedence; but a European made armchair was produced for my greater comfort. Native beer was handed round in ceremonial fashion, regalia and clothes, now little or never seen in public, were donned and their functions demonstrated ... We watched the ancient fire-drill, which none of the young could perform, and everybody got very excited when we saw the first glow and the spiral of smoke, and soon the fire was leaping into flame. I had never seen this before and I think some of the natives had not either ... We talked long about old ways of life, some of which still persisted, though not openly. Then, as the day wore on, my turn came. I had to try and describe something of English life and practice. I handed round photographs, which were greatly admired, but apparently extremely hard to perceive with any understanding.

(Bartlett, 1955b, p. 270)

After the publication of *Remembering* (1932/1995), Bartlett's research concerns centered around developing stronger methodologies for social psychology and anthropology. In a number of articles, he argued for the use of psychological methods to deal with anthropological problems (e.g., Bartlett, 1937a, 1943, 1946b), while also commenting on the dangers of doing so without sensitivity to the local contexts.[15] Additionally, he began a program of research on 'constructive' or 'everyday' thinking, which was a clear extension of his studies on remembering (Bartlett, 1938a, b; see Chapter 6). In this research, he removed sections from the middle or end of a story and asked his participants to complete them in the most plausible way. This task illustrated how previous experience in the form of schemata is used to 'fill in gaps' in a constructive and predictive way. Part of Bartlett's analysis involved comparing the thinking processes of different social groups. A student of his also used this method to compare Bartlett's studies in England with constructive thinking among Greenlanders (Carmichael, 1940). This data helped to counter French anthropologist Lévy-Bruhl's (1926/1985) claim that 'primitive' people were tolerant of contradiction in their thinking while Western people adhered to the rules of logic. Bartlett and Carmichael found that the everyday thinking of both English and Greenlandic people consisted of single generalizations which were 'strongly socially colored,' further affirming arguments already made in *Psychology and Primitive Culture*.

Finally, in 1935 Bartlett formed a group of psychologists, anthropologists, and sociologists who were focused on social issues. The group met twice yearly until 1938, and in 1939 published their discussions in an edited volume appropriately titled *The Study of Society*. The book begins by highlighting the contemporary necessity of understanding wider social phenomena:

There is to-day widespread recognition of the fact that the future of human civilization depends to a high degree upon Man's capacity to understand the forces and factors which control his own behaviour. Such understanding must be achieved, not only as regards individual conduct, but equally as regards the mass phenomena resulting from group contacts, which are becoming increasingly intimate and influential.

(Bartlett, Ginsberg, Lingren, and Thouless, 1939, p. vii)

This was a time of major social crisis, including an economic depression, a political movement to the far right, and feeling that another major war was on the horizon. In this context, the government initiated an 'anthropology of the home' in order to better understand the social climate and people's view of the danger of war. The government's 'mass-observation' project and Bartlett's interdisciplinary working group should be seen as a complementary pair (see Roiser, 2001). As war approached Bartlett became increasingly interested in mass culture and 'political propaganda,' publishing a book with that title in 1940. In this book he applied his diffusionist ideas to modern society, demonstrating the relationship between social organization (e.g., totalitarian and democratic societies) and the different forms of mass communication (see Chapter 3). When Second World War arrived in 1939, psychology would again be put to work to aid in the war effort and in a more substantial way than it had done before, as will be discussed in the next section.

Second World War and Its Aftermath: The Human–Machine Interface

In the First World War, psychology had devised numerous forms of selection tests to identify personnel for all kinds of mental and bodily activity required of different military roles, which Bartlett (1927b) discussed in *Psychology and the Soldier*. He had himself investigated listening to sounds of weak intensity in order to select people to monitor German submarines during the war (see earlier). Intelligence tests were also widely used at this time for the selection of army officers and were advocated in the postwar years by Charles Spearman and Cyril Burt of the University College London. When the Second World War broke out, English psychologists thought that they would simply continue with this same selection test approach, but circumstances worked against it. The world had seen immense technological advances, such that many specialized skills were now required to operate the new machines of war. There were not enough 'natural' operators possessing these abilities to fill the number of positions required. Moreover, specialized skills that could be identified were quickly made obsolete in a context of rapid technological change. In contrast to this, "The ideal situation for psychological testing is one that is rather static in which there is so large a pool of possible test candidates to draw from that a large number of rejections can be tolerated, and in which the standards of accuracy required need be only moderate" (Bartlett, 1956, p. 53).

Thus, as the Second World War progressed many psychologists in Britain began to shift their emphasis from selecting the person for his machine to designing the machine to fit the person – a discipline that would later be known as *ergonomics* (see e.g., Bartlett, 1962). In Cambridge this task was supported by the *Medical Research Council*, on which Bartlett had been a committee member since 1935. These investigations aimed to understand the basic characteristics of complex skill, so as to discover principles to design machines in such a way that the majority of people could be taught to use them accurately and with success. Skill appealed to Bartlett as a topic partly because of his own love of sport, especially cricket. He had earlier described it using the concept of schema (Chapter 4), but by this time he was elaborating it with a different language, though there was clear conceptual continuity. From the beginning, he lamented the artificiality of methods available for this study, which focused on simple and isolated responses to stimuli repeated over and over again. In contrast to this, Bartlett emphasized that skill was an ongoing and flexible activity:

The operations involved [in highly skilled work] are marked by complex, co-ordinated and accurately timed activities. The stimuli in response to which these activities are set up are neither simple nor do they usually fall into an order of fixed succession. They have the character of a field, or a pattern, which has become very highly organized, and may retain its identity in spite of a great diversity of internal arrangement.

(Bartlett, 1941, p. 718)

Prior methods had only looked at isolated reactions, measuring the time between stimulus and movement (i.e., the reaction time) and the time the movement itself takes – for example, having the participant make threshold discriminations over many repeated trials. This method might study a *succession* of fixed events but not how they operate as an organized *sequence*. Among other things, these methods missed the interval between the end of one movement in a chain and the start of another, which Bartlett (1955b) called 'timing.' Timing involves the fitting of a sequence of movements to each other and to the environmental requirements, anticipating the next signal and movement in a sequence. It turned out to be the most interesting and variable feature of skill: it could be greatly modified through training and effort, and was most affected by environment stress, such as fatigue following extended activity. For example, after prolonged flying pilots' attention would lose the total field and become narrowed to single instruments and peripheral signals would be lost. Such stresses could be managed up to a certain threshold, but beyond these 'human tolerance limits' (Bartlett, 1950a) the whole activity would quickly break down. Donald Broadbent (1970), a member of the Cambridge laboratory, offers a succinct summary of this new field of research taking shape at Cambridge during the Second World War:

The views [Bartlett] was putting forward have been published only ... in articles, and probably never formed a complete system. Indeed that was their strength, because they were a flexible method rather than a rigid dogma. The key concept was that of skill: the ability of men to produce for each new situation a fresh and yet perfectly adapted sequence of movements. No prewar model comparing the brain to a telephone switchboard could cope with such facts. Rather they required a subtle hierarchically organized system which could predict the future, launch actions at appropriate times, handle local difficulties by peripheral closed-loop sub-systems, remember for brief periods the stage reached in a continuous process, monitor its own level of performance and adjust to inadequacies, and so on. When such a system is stressed, it would yield first by errors of timing or of integration between sub-units of a performance, rather than by crude forms of breakdown. (p. 6)

There were two key influences on this work that should be mentioned. The first was Norbert Wiener (1894–1964), who had been a close friend of Bartlett since 1913 when he came to Cambridge to study mathematical logic with Russell. Bartlett (1958, p. 144) even credits him with the idea of the method of serial reproduction. Wiener invented an original approach to the problems of 'information theory,' systems of communication and control. Wiener (1948) later named the approach 'cybernetics,' coming from the Greek word for 'steersman,' 'governor,' or 'pilot.' The aim of this approach was to understand the functions and processes of goal-directed self-regulating systems, whether they be machine or animal. Such systems do not operate according to linear causality but rather participate in circular causal chains, in which *feedback* from the environment is crucial. For example, steering a ship involves making a series of small corrections, in relation to changes brought about by the environment and earlier movements, to keep the ship on course. Similarly, in the Cambridge laboratory, Bartlett (1947c) saw the human operator as coordinator of information between 'displays' (signals) and 'controls' (levers, switches, and knobs) in an ongoing activity, such as piloting an airplane. Through controlled experiment, the psychologist might be able to discover principles that could improve this information flow and better manage the stress limits of the system. Wiener visited the Cambridge laboratory in the spring of

1947 and described the work being done there as 'the human element in control processes' (Wiener, 1948, p. 23).[16]

The second key influence on Bartlett at this time was Kenneth Craik (1914–45), who came to Cambridge to study with Bartlett in October 1936. Craik had hoped to begin experimental work on his theories about self-regulating machines that could model human processes, but Bartlett convinced him to write his dissertation on 'visual adaptation' instead. His only published book *The Nature of Explanation* (Craik, 1943) spells out the argument he originally intended to make: put bluntly, the human mind and body operate according to the same mechanical principles of complex machines. If machines could be built that were able to flexibly solve problems in a variety of situations that humans can handle, this he believed would prove that they work just as human minds and bodies, which could then be explained by mechanical principles. This position was also taking root in America at around the same time and would become central to the information processing approach in psychology that followed shortly afterward. In his otherwise warm obituary to Craik, Bartlett (1946a) stated that these arguments were dubious because human beings do not act in a mechanical fashion. Craik's fascination and savvy with machines would nevertheless prove invaluable to the Cambridge Laboratory and the whole war effort. He was one of the early proponents of the idea that the machine might be made to fit the man and developed predictive anti-aircraft gun controls by applying his mechanical model idea (Craik, 1948). In addition to this, Craik designed the famous 'Cambridge Cockpit' (Figure 1.1), which was used to study and train air force pilots and set in motion the experimental research on human skill. Bartlett describes the day it happened:

Kenneth and I had been out to look at some new anti-aircraft equipment. We were being driven back to Cambridge ... I thought something was needed which would show clearly and exactly how skill, long continued, may change and perhaps disintegrate. So I asked Kenneth whether perhaps it would be possible to design an experimental cockpit, so that the essential control responses of the aircraft-pilot, flying on instruments, could be accurately recorded, if necessary for long periods, and we should know, not only whether less or more work was being done, but also by what changes in the coordinated activities these, and other variations, were brought about. He jumped to the idea ... The very next day he was in the Laboratory workshop fashioning the experimental controls for the first Cambridge cockpit. The design was his. He and George Drew together did the work. The whole thing was a very brilliant and beautiful application of calculating machine principle to a complex psychological problem. It was built in our own workshop, with slender resources and at trifling cost. It was to stand up to years of hard work, and ... open up what may well be a new chapter in experimental psychological development. For not only did it show that

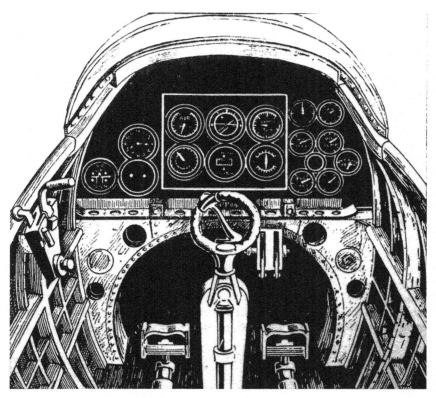

Figure 1.1.   The Cambridge Cockpit

'skill fatigue' is in many ways different from that deterioration which long spells of work may impose upon simple muscular and mental tasks, but also it demonstrated that it is possible to submit highly complex bodily and mental processes to exact and illuminating measurement.

(Bartlett, 1946a, pp. 457–8)

Tragically, Craik died in a bicycle accident on V-E Day. This was particularly hard on Bartlett. Not only did he lose a friend and colleague, but also his chosen successor. In 1944, the Medical Research Council had agreed to establish the *Applied Psychology Unit* (later renamed *Cognitive and Brain Sciences Unit*) at the Cambridge laboratory with Craik as director. With Craik's death, a year later, Bartlett took charge of this position until 1953. When Bartlett retired from his Professorship in 1952, Oliver L. Zangwill (1913–87) was elected to the Chair of Experimental Psychology. He led the department in the direction of information theory, which Bartlett and Craik had earlier advocated. However, whereas Bartlett was clear that the human being is not a machine and thus should not be approached in mechanical terms, many of Bartlett's successors made exactly this move – Craik would probably have continued to do so as well, despite Bartlett's (1946a) suggestions to the contrary. There is thus a subtle conceptual shift in the Cambridge laboratory from the idea of information flow *between* humans and machines to considering humans *as* machines within this interaction. This was the beginning of cognitive revolution in psychology, which took as its root metaphors 'mind as a machine' and 'cognition as information processing.'

In the postwar years, Bartlett received a stream of awards, honorary degrees[17] and was knighted in 1948 for his research efforts during the war. He remained incredibly active even after his retirement in 1952, serving on various committees, as a consultant for the Laboratory, attending intellectual meetings and continuing to write. His last book *Thinking: An Experimental and Social Study* was published in 1958 and is very much a continuation of *Remembering*, but with the research on skill added on to it (Chapter 6). Thinking is approached as a complex and high-level kind of skill: like bodily skills "every kind of thinking also claims that it is based upon information or evidence which, again, must be picked up directly or indirectly from the environment and which is used in an attempt to satisfy some requirement of the occasion upon which the thinking takes place" (Bartlett, 1958, pp. 11–12). The investigation aimed to see to what extent characteristics of bodily skills (discovered during the war) extended to thinking processes. The first part of the book was devoted to how people solve traditional logical problems or what Bartlett calls 'Thinking in closed systems.' The later part of the book on 'thinking in open systems' includes two chapters on 'the thinking of the experimental scientist' – one is a historical analysis of scientific discoveries and the other is a personal account of the development of his own scientific ideas. Bartlett here makes the argument that "experimental thinking ... is fundamentally co-operative, social, and cannot proceed far without the stimulus of outside contacts" (p. 123), which had been the focus of *Psychology and Primitive Culture*. In general, however, the social and cultural emphasis of his earlier work was pushed into the background. The chapter on 'everyday thinking' comes closest to the earlier focus and was itself based on research done in the late 1930s (see earlier). The last chapter of the book describes artistic thinking, connecting back to Bartlett's interest in literature. Although *Thinking* had a rather minor impact when compared to *Remembering*, it was still an important source for some early cognitive psychologists (e.g., Neisser, 1967).

Conclusion: Bartlett's Life Course and Legacy

When Bartlett died on September 30, 1969, he left behind a rich but also controversial legacy, which reflected contradictions in his own life experience and in the framework he inherited from his mentors. On the one hand, he celebrated scientific freedom, adventure, the breaking of methodological conventions, and the interdisciplinary development of ideas. On the other hand, he increasingly emphasized the importance of 'exact methods' training and as an institutional leader severed psychology from the social sciences. The tension between these two attitudes would manifest itself in how Bartlett's work was itself remembered, as being either cognitive or social–cultural: cognitive psychology allied itself with the natural sciences and valorized highly controlled experimentation as method, while researchers working at the boundary with other social sciences set themselves in opposition to this. In what follows, I will briefly highlight how this tension developed through Bartlett's life course and then outline how it set the stage for the divergent developments of his ideas, which will be further elaborated in the chapters that follow. To do the first, I build on recent theories of life-course development, which see it as a process of accumulating and integrating experiences from different social contexts through time (Zittoun et al., 2013; Zittoun and Gillsepie, 2015). This focus on 'integrating experiences' of the past with an orientation to the future in fact comes close to Bartlett's notion of constructiveness, although he never explicitly elaborated his ideas in terms of life-course development.

Bartlett's 'constructive' attitude to intellectual and practical issues was developed during his childhood. Not only was he raised in the liberal and progressive Cotswolds, but he was also given a free hand to follow his own interests in educating himself through independent reading and other activities. Cambridge must have appealed to him because of the similar constructive atmosphere in which ideas from different disciplines were in exchange and development. As a teacher there he tried to create an informal, free conversational space for ideas to be developed. At the same time, the Cambridge context put new constraints on him: Bartlett had wanted to study anthropology but was convinced to do a degree in moral sciences and after finishing was again persuaded to get a rigorous training in the laboratory methods of psychology, in preparation for a career in anthropology. Rivers and Myers fought hard against the University's conservatism to get psychology accepted as a legitimate discipline. To persuade others of its 'scientific' status they emphasized strict methodology, and progressively moved psychology closer to the natural sciences and applied domains, while remaining interdisciplinary in their own work. When Bartlett became professor of psychology and director of the laboratory, he must have felt the same institutional pressure and continued to successfully steer psychology in the same line of development, physically moving the department to the biological sciences. This must be juxtaposed with Bartlett's considerable amount of reading and publishing of material on social and cultural topics up until the 1940s.

On the development of his ideas, Bartlett (1958) stressed the key role played by social contacts with particular others (most notably with Ward, Rivers, Myers, Head, Wiener, and Craik) as well as different fields of knowledge (e.g., anthropology, philosophy, sociology, and engineering).[18] This was very much in line with his theory of cultural dynamics: "The main, if not the only, general condition of mental and social development is that the individual or the group should come into contact with other individuals or other groups: The resulting clash of feelings, actions, ideas, customs and institutions is the great stimulus to change" (Bartlett, 1926, p. 769). His own approach can be seen as progressively weaving together different social influences through time. Bartlett very much started in philosophy but increasingly became disenchanted with its speculative ways of thinking, abstracted from the facts on the ground. His earliest orientation to psychology had been through the analytic works of Stout and Ward, who taught him how the mind was active. Rivers, Myers, and Head added a methodological orientation in both experimentation and clinical sensitivity, as well as key concepts such as 'conventionalization' and 'schema.' Later, information theory of Wiener combined with Craik's engineering savvy provided a fertile base for the applied research done during the Second World War on complex skill. The two world wars were themselves major factors that shaped the development of the Cambridge laboratory toward applied research, especially in military and industrial efforts (Bartlett, 1957).

The two kinds of psychology that Bartlett promoted – as research scientist and institutional leader – are reflected in the way his work is remembered. Only his book *Remembering* has been discussed with any depth.[19] It is certainly his most important work, but to fully understand it we need to see it as part of a broader development of his ideas. *Remembering* sits at a midpoint in his career, where the focus on social and cultural processes had already begun to play a less pronounced role, yet still held an important place. When psychologists remember Bartlett, he is considered *either* as a cognitive psychologist *or* as a social and cultural psychologist, rarely as both. In 1992, Costall pointed out that in the 1968 and 1985 editions of *The Handbook of Social Psychology* edited by Lindzey and Aronson five chapters see Bartlett as a conventional cognitive psychologist and six chapters see him as a cultural psychologist; there is one chapter that recognizes Bartlett as being both, but these are juxtaposed rather than integrated (Costall, 1992). The situation has improved somewhat with the publication of *Bartlett, Culture and Cognition* (Saito, 2000a), the only book (before the present book) on Bartlett. The title, editorial introduction (Saito, 2000b), and some chapters[20] explicitly aim to reconnect the cultural and cognitive in Bartlett's *oeuvre*. Nonetheless, the majority of chapters tend to continue to describe Bartlett as a researcher of 'culture' (e.g., Bloor, 2000; Douglas, 2000) *or* 'cognition' (e.g., Baddeley and Gregory, 2000; Brewer, 2000; Roediger, Bergman, and Meade, 2000). These two are in fact deeply connected in Bartlett's life course and only become separate because of the institutional role he felt obliged to play. In the following chapters of this book, I aim to go beyond this division and show that Bartlett in fact aimed to develop an integrative approach to psychological *and* social-cultural processes.

Notes

1. Although Bartlett's primary influence has been in psychology, his ideas have also entered anthropology, ergonomics, and sociology.
2. This chapter focuses mainly on the Cambridge context. For a general overview of the history of psychology in Britain, see Hearnshaw (1964) and Bunn, Lovie, and Richards (2001).
3. Quotations without references come from Bartlett's unfinished autobiography titled "What's the use of psychology?," which can be found in the Cambridge University Library archives. In this chapter, I am also indebted to the thorough historical research of Campton's (1978) doctoral thesis, *The Cambridge School: The life, works, and influence of James Ward, W. H. R. Rivers, C. S. Myers, and Sir Frederic Bartlett*.
4. Originally, Bartlett wanted to study anthropology or medicine but was advised to do an undergraduate degree in moral sciences with neither anthropology nor medicine.
5. The Bloomsbury group included Keynes, Virginia Woolf, E.M. Forster, Clive Bell, and Roger Fry, among others.
6. This is, however, a rather arbitrary date for the founding of psychology. Disciplines emerge over a period of time; they are not born on a single date (Danziger, 1990; Valsiner, 2012). Much had been done since the beginning of the century to develop the discipline. In fact, Wundt (1907) even spoke of his approach as the 'new psychology' (see Cornejo, 2016).
7. This was a further development of his famous article 'Psychology.'
8. This instrument enabled the experimentalist to flash images to subjects for brief intervals and was used frequently in psychology around 1900.
9. Bartlett thought that it had its place as a form of literature.

10. 'Shell shock' was used by Myers (1915) to describe the reactions of soldiers psychologically traumatized in the First World War. However, Shephard (2003) has argued that it was the soldiers themselves who first coined the term. Like Myers, Rivers became highly skilled at treating shell-shocked soldiers during the war – events memorialized in Pat Baker's novels, the *Regeneration Trilogy*.

11. Myer's other protégé, Tom Hatherley Pear (1886–1972), in fact published a book titled *Remembering and Forgetting* (1922) who like Bartlett critiqued Ebbinghaus's approach and widened the concept of memory to encompass emotional and personal qualities but did so a decade before Bartlett (see Costall, 2001).

12. Not long before his own death, in his last publication, Bartlett (1968a, pp. 159–60) described his final encounters with Rivers in almost supernatural terms:

> On the Saturday I was off to play in a cricket match on the College ground and just as I went by the steps to the paddock from the New Court, Rivers came down then. He was going for a walk. We went to the backsgates together. He seemed cheerful, energetic and well. I was married then and lived out of College. On Whit Monday I came to St John's to go to my rooms. The flag was flying half-mast. I called in at the Porter's Lodge and said "Who's dead?" I was told "Dr Rivers." Everything seemed suddenly silly. The sun shone, decorations were out, holiday makers were all over the place. There seemed no sense in it, for Rivers who was my friend and counselor had gone, and I should see him no more.
>
> But this was wrong. A fortnight or so later I met him again, for the last time. I was in the College Combination Room, at the end where the Council meetings are held. The table was set for a meeting. All the members of Council were there but one. There was one vacant chair. Then he came in, erect and quick as usual. He went to the empty chair and sat down. He had no face. Nobody else knew him, but I knew him. I tried to say "Rivers! It's Dr Rivers," and I couldn't utter a word.
>
> Then I woke up. I was in bed, at home. It was pitch dark. For what seemed like several minutes I was absolutely sure that he was there, in the deep darkness, close to me. It was a dream. We had talked many times about death. He had said that if he should die before me, as seemed likely, if he could he would try to get through to me. So, it was only a dream.
>
> One night when G. G. Coulton was already an old man, and on the verge of his final journey to Canada, as we were coming out of dinner in Hall together, he said "Do you think there is a life after death – I mean a personal life?" I had to say that once I had thought so, and now I did not know. He said "I am sure there must be, though we are unable to tell the form of it: we can't just stop."
>
> When I think now of Rivers, it is in a double kind of way. I know that he died, swiftly and painfully, 45 years ago. But as I have said his power was in himself and not in what he said or wrote alone, and so it matters little if what he left in print is ignored or forgotten. There is something in St John's today which he brought to it and something also in many of us who knew him, and though I cannot find the words properly to tell of this, I think of him also as still alive.

Bartlett's remembering in this passage can clearly be interpreted within his own reconstruction theory: His memories here feed-forward into his own anticipation and reflection on death, which came to him shortly after this was written.

13. Interestingly, this tension in where to institutionally place psychology in Cambridge continued to be debated from Bartlett's time until the present day. In 1970, a new Tripos in Social and Political Sciences was opened up offering psychology, such that students interested in psychology could choose between two different programs, representing the social science and natural science approaches to the discipline. During a further reorganization of the Faculty of Social and Political Sciences in 2004, the Department of Social and Developmental Psychology was created. However, in 2012 it was decided that the two departments of psychology would merge by placing them within the biological sciences, as Bartlett had done long before. Thus, we see a more social psychology opening up elsewhere and later being incorporated into the department Bartlett made.

14. This is available for inspection in the Cambridge University Library archives.

15. For example, we find in Bartlett (1937a) a strong early critique of IQ tests and their failure to take into account cultural differences. In later articles, he focuses on other limitations of such tests (see e.g., Bartlett, 1944, 1954). More recently, Gould (1981) has demonstrated in detail how such tests have been manipulated to support racist ideologies.

16. It is also noteworthy that Gregory Bateson (see Chapter 5) encouraged Wiener to devote a large part of his energies to the application of cybernetics to the social sciences in his book.

17. Bartlett received doctorate *honoris causa* from Princeton (1947), Louvain (1949), and London (1949).

18. Cf. The focus of life-positioning analysis on relations with significant and generalized others (Martin, 2013)

19. Interestingly, early reviewers and Bartlett's own students did not seem to think *Remembering* would have the enduring impact that it in fact has had.

20. Some chapters of the book do explicitly reconnect the culture and cognition. Two notable examples are Rosa's (2000) chapter on 'Bartlett's psycho-anthropological project,' which analyzes his early work up to the early 1920s, and Cole and Cole's (2000) chapter that explicitly aims to bring anthropology and psychology back together.

2   Experiments in Psychology

> If ... human reactions had been built up to meet a series of unchanging environments, emphatic insistence upon rigidity of [experimental] conditions would be justifiable. Obviously, they are not so built.
>
> (Bartlett, 1930, p. 64)

> It is vastly important to realize how much experimental thinking is controlled by experimental method and by experimental instrumentation and how hard it is, once methods and instruments have become accepted and established, to break away from their use.
>
> (Bartlett, 1958, p. 127)

Bartlett's early experiments have been praised for their originality and have continued to exert a considerable influence on memory research and other fields of inquiry. At the same time, contemporary experimental psychologists have often criticized them as methodologically loose pseudo-experiments. This critique comes in part from psychology's current understanding of an experiment as the manipulation of an independent variable while holding all other variables constant, and inferring a relationship between variables through statistical analysis of a large sample of subjects. This definition was not, however, dominant in Bartlett's time and only became so in the 1960s; the natural sciences, in contrast, still tend to use a much more open definition of an experiment (Winston and Blais, 1996).[1] In the first-half of the twentieth century what counted as an 'experiment' in psychology was still quite permissive, and included many qualitative and idiographic approaches, as can be seen in the classic experimental studies of Jean Piaget on children's development, Wolfgang Köhler on gestalt laws, and Lev Vygotsky on language and thought.[2]

The aim of this chapter is to re-examine Bartlett's experimental approach in light of the earlier understanding of an experiment. First, I present the historical context in which he developed his methods, by reviewing the experimental studies of Hermann Ebbinghaus, the Würzburg School, and Jean Philippe. This choice of figures is necessarily selective, but will suffice to draw out the general background of

Bartlett's approach through an exploration of what he accepted and rejected from each of them. Second, I will review the procedures and findings of his earliest experiments conducted between 1913 and 1916. These innovative studies will also be used as examples to illustrate Bartlett's theoretical ideas in the chapters to follow. Third, I will highlight some of the distinctive features of his methodological approach, which shares much in common with the German–Austrian approach of the time but diverges in significant ways from contemporary understanding. Lastly, I will discuss the numerous replications and extensions of Bartlett's experiments by psychologists. This will help to illustrate the transformations in experimental practice from Bartlett's time to today.

From Elements to Wholes: Experimental Psychology, 1885–1910

Bartlett conducted his most well-known experiments at a time when psychology was beginning to move away from the traditional model borrowed from psychophysics toward a more holistic approach. Bartlett (1932/1995, chapter 1) argued that psychological processes involve an active mind and therefore one cannot only use a methodology that simply looks for cause–effect relationships between variables. Traditional experimentation involved isolating and itemizing responses in order to identify how a stimulus directly *causes* a sensation in the organism. For example, Gustav Fechner (1801–87) had used experimental methods to discover a nonlinear mathematical relationship between a stimulus's physical intensity and the psychological sensation it produced in a subject. It was Fechner's *Elements of Psychophysics* (1860/1912) that inspired Hermann Ebbinghaus (1850–1909) to apply this methodology to 'higher mental functions' in order to discover the quantitative laws of memory.

To apply the psychophysics model, Ebbinghaus needed to find stimuli that were simple and homogeneous, so that they could be treated as constant and interchangeable units. This was found in his famous 'nonsense syllable,' a consonant–vowel–consonant combination, such as SEH or RUP. Ebbinghaus (1885/1913) prepared all possible syllables, which were then mixed together and pulled them out by chance to construct series of non-syllables of varying lengths. He looked at each syllable in the series for a fraction of a second, keeping the order of syllables constant and pausing for 15 s before going through the series again. This was repeated until he could recite each syllable in the series without error. Ebbinghaus then measured, for example, the number of repetitions it took to learn a list as a function of the number of syllables in the list, and

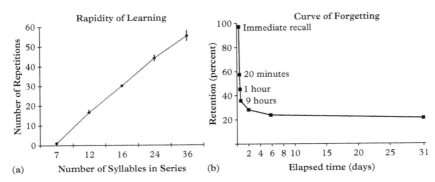

Figure 2.1. Relationship between length of the list and the number of repetitions it takes to learn it (a). The amount of time 'saved' relearning a list at different time intervals from when it was first learned (b)

in another study the amount of work 'saved' in relearning a list as a function of the time that had passed since it was learned – this was measured by subtracting the number of exposures to relearn the list from the number it originally took. The former is a near-linear relationship (i.e., it takes about twice as long to learn a list with twice as many syllables, once the first seven immediately memorized units are accounted for), whereas the latter is a nonlinear relationship (i.e., most forgetting occurs in the first 20 min after having learned the list; as more time elapses the rate of forgetting decreases) (see Figure 2.1).

Bartlett (1932/1995, chapter 1) critiqued Ebbinghaus by arguing that it is impossible to fully remove meaning from stimuli that require a human response and that attempting to do so creates artificial conditions with little generalizability to everyday life. Ebbinghaus wrongly assumed that he could eliminate meaning from the laboratory and in doing so study memory in its simplest and purest form, uncontaminated by other influences. In fact, in attempting to do this, he lost the very phenomena he set out to study in his pursuit of greater experimental control. Moreover, this method ignores other important aspects of remembering, such as imagination, emotion, and context. What is most essential about remembering, as it normally occurs, is that it is done through previous experience, in a social context and activates a person's interests. These factors are precisely the ones that Ebbinghaus tried to remove from his investigation.

The above critique applies to all forms of experimentation in psychology that take psychophysics as their model and attempt to rigidly control conditions by stripping complex processes down to their simplest elements. According to Bartlett (1932/1995, p. 6), "In it all is the tendency to overstress the determining character of the stimulus or of the situation, the effort to secure isolation of response by ensuring simplicity of external control." In short, these experimentalists come to worship the stimuli. This causal method may have been successful in psychophysics but its application to psychological processes is questionable, because psychology must deal with the whole person making a response within a particular context, not just how some stimulus causes an isolated reaction. Bartlett advocated a methodological holism, in which whole organisms are seen as being actively involved with their environment. In other words, he is much more interested in what the organism itself contributes to a reaction than how it is caused by some external factor.

The analytic focus on an active person was found in the Würzburg School's experimental method, which was being fervently debated in Cambridge when Bartlett was conducting his own experiments (Chapter 1). The Würzburgers were critical of the tendency to think of the mind as mechanically reacting to stimuli. In one early experiment, Külpe and Bryan (1904) presented subjects with a series of nonsense syllables, but unlike Ebbinghaus's lists, their cards were of different colors, letters, and arrangements. The subjects were instructed to remember one of these aspects (e.g., the color). They found that subjects could easily remember the task-specified aspect but remained oblivious to other aspects of the syllables, even though they impinged on their sense organs just as the apprehended features had. To explain these differences, a passive mind mechanically responding to stimuli would not do; instead the mind would need to be conceptualized as possessing 'intentionality.'

Intentionality is a technical word borrowed from the philosopher, Franz Brentano (1874/1973). The term should not be confused with the common language usage of having an intention; rather it describes how every mental act (in contrast to the physical) has 'aboutness' – it points beyond itself to an object. This idea became an essential part of James Ward's (1918) psychology, which played a major role in Bartlett's thought (Chapter 1). Bartlett (1916b, pp. 10–11) himself draws a parallel between Brentano's notion of 'intentionality' and his own key notion of 'an effort after meaning,' which characterized all psychological processes. He defined effort after meaning as "a very constant general tendency on the part of the subject to link on that which is now being experienced with something that has been experienced already, so that a present object is given a setting." The Würzburg psychologists further elaborated the notion of intentionality to develop a theory of consciousness that emphasized mental directedness over mechanical association. For instance, Ach (1905) and Watt (1905) experimentally demonstrated that subjects could easily give synonyms or superordinate associations of words, over more strongly associated words, if the task demanded it (Boring, 1950, p. 403ff).

Subjects in Ach and Watt's experiments also reported the experience of task orientation and monitoring of progress toward a goal (e.g., experiences of doubt, hesitation, and confidence). These were characteristics of consciousness that the Würzburgers claimed could not be reduced to either sensations or images. Würzburg psychologists, Mayer and Orth (1901), had earlier labeled this new mental content *Bewusstseinslage* (literally 'position of consciousness'). The word has been used to describe both goal-directedness (e.g., a state of readiness and monitoring of progress toward a goal) and a general impression or summary feeling of some material (e.g., 'this is familiar' or 'this is foreign'). The Würzburg psychologists that followed developed similar concepts to describe this directed and diffuse characteristic of mind, such as 'determining tendency,' 'task,' 'conscious attitude,' and 'awareness.' In all cases, directedness was considered the principle 'motor' of mind, rather than passive associative laws (see also Chapter 6).

Bartlett used the concept of 'attitude' in a manner similar to the Würzburg concepts, in order to describe both a subject's monitoring of progress toward a goal as well as a summary feeling or *general impression* of some material (see also Larsen and Berntsen, 2000). In fact, Titchner (1909) first (mis)translated *Bewusstseinslage* as 'attitude of consciousness.' Bartlett (1916b) himself explicitly recognized the similarity between his concept and the Würzburg psychologist Betz's (1910) term *Einstellung* (attitude or mental set). The early concept of attitude should not be confused with the way it is used in contemporary psychology as a static evaluation of some object, which is easily measured on a rating scale. Instead, an attitude here is a holistic orientation to the world which occupies a moment or position within a serial process (elsewhere described as schema – see Chapter 4). Some attitudes named by Bartlett are 'surprise,' 'astonishment,' 'suspicion,' 'doubt,' 'indifference,' 'anticipation,' 'expectancy' (Bartlett, 1952, p. 88).

Bartlett applied the concept of attitude to his own experimental methodology in carefully observing and listening to his subjects as they performed his experimental task. From the Würzburgers's research as well as from his brief clinical experience (see Chapter 1), he knew that inner conditions of a response were just as important as the external, and thus simply keeping the environment constant was not enough to ensure objectivity in an investigation.

[T]he external environment may remain constant, and yet the internal conditions of the reacting agent – the attitudes, moods, all that mass determining factors that go under the names of temperament and character – may vary significantly. These, however, are precisely the kind of determinants [of experience and behavior] which are pre-eminently important for the psychologist. (1932/1995, p. 10)

Bartlett notes, for example, that on entering the context of an experiment an 'analytic' attitude tends to arise in subjects, such that they become more concerned with details and accuracy than they would be in their everyday life.[3]

Although Bartlett borrows key features from the Würzburg psychologists, he is also critical of their reliance on retrospective data. This is not to say that introspection should not be used in psychology – he is clear it should – but rather it should be caught on the fly, so that the beginning and end of a process are not privileged, as tends to happen when subjects are asked about their thinking retrospectively. We know from Ebbinghaus's (1885/1913) experiments that the first and last items in a series are remembered with a much higher frequency than those in the middle – what is called 'serial position effect.' Moreover, Bartlett's primary data is always subjects' (re)construction of some given material, which can then be interpreted in light of introspective evidence. Thus, introspective data tends to be used by him more as a resource to interpret objective constructions.

The most important and direct methodological inspiration for Bartlett's method, by his own account, was French psychologist Jean Philippe's (1897) experimental study of mental images, which James Ward had encouraged him to explore (Bartlett, 1932/1995, p. 63). Philippe (1897) had his subjects close their eyes and handle a small object, so as to obtain a mental image of it. Subjects were then to draw the image they formed immediately and at intervals of one or two months. From the series of drawings subjects produced, Philippe identified three different types of changes occurring in them: (1) the image tends to *disappear*: its details drop out one by one or become so confused that the subject will not even be able to indicate it verbally; (2) while certain details drop out, others grow and become dominant in the whole which in turn fosters new details being *substituted* for those in the original; or (3) the image becomes *generalized*: it conforms more and more to a general type for which it belongs, such that specific details of the object disappear and those that are most central remain.

The above analysis of qualitative changes occurring through a series of reproductions comes very close to the one Bartlett used in his 'experiments on remembering.' In his *fellowship dissertation*, Bartlett (1916b, p. 9) even accepts the qualitative changes Philippe identified as the starting point for his inquiry and modestly aims to extend them in his own study. Thus, Philippe provided Bartlett with a holistic method to study the mind as active, affective, and most importantly, in the process of development. Against the traditional view of images as static remnants of sense perception, Philippe (1897) argued, "images are mobile, living, constantly undergoing change, under the persistent influence of our feelings and ideas" (quoted in Bartlett, 1932/1995, p. 15). Bartlett (1932/1995) approves of this point and adopts a similar view of images when he later articulates a 'theory of remembering' (see Chapter 4). However, from the very beginning, he rejects Philippe's account of images as things hiding in the unconscious, coming up occasionally to be seen in mental life. Instead, Bartlett adopts a 'functionalist view,' exploring the conditions under which images arise.

There is another important difference between the thinkers worth pointing out. Philippe (1897) makes a sharp distinction between 'images' and 'memory.' According to him, memory describes those mental features that are 'lifeless' and 'fixed,' while images are just the opposite, though the two lie 'side by side.' This division perpetuates the view of memory as a distinct faculty that is isolated from total organismic functioning (the same fallacy committed by Ebbinghaus). Thus, while Philippe provided a powerful new method for studying holistic transformations, his analytic distinctions led him back into old ways of thinking. Bartlett is more consistent in his holism, recognizing that it is the whole person involved in a particular setting who makes a response. The mind cannot be divided into separate faculties, each to be studied in isolation from the others. Any sharp distinctions made between perceiving, imagining, remembering, and thinking will always be arbitrary; these processes differ in *degree* rather than *kind*. Thus, we find studies focused on perceiving and imagining directly contributing to the study of remembering in Bartlett's work.

In summary, Ebbinghaus's study was instructive to Bartlett in that it showed the dangers of overly simplifying psychological reactions to obtain greater experimental control. A psychophysics method would not do if one wanted to study truly psychological responses. In contrast, the Würzburgers helped to analyze factors that the persons contributed to a reaction, such as their dynamic attitude to the stimulus material and experimental task. The objectivity of the experimenter thus required knowing the inner conditions of a response as well as the outer. Philippe then provided Bartlett with a method for accessing and analyzing qualitative transformations in experience, though Bartlett rejected his distinction between images and memory. From these influences Bartlett developed a holistic methodology that neither isolated human responses from the person who makes them, nor did it try to artificially separate these responses from the environment in which they occur and the material they work on. Instead, Bartlett aimed to show how a situated person actively responds to a meaningful situation with the help of previous experience.

Experiments on Perceiving and Imagining

According to Bartlett's (1932/1995, p. xvii; 1958, p. 139) own account, his experimental program began on the day of the official opening of the Laboratory of Experimental Psychology at the University of Cambridge, on an afternoon in May 1913. The founder and then director of the laboratory, C.S. Myers, asked Bartlett if he would carry out a variety of routine visual perception experiments on the visitors to the laboratory. Bartlett was fascinated by the variety of interpretations that people made of the same diagrams and pictures. This event inspired him to invent his own study for "demonstrating experimentally those parts particularly of the complex perceiving response for which the observer himself was responsible" (Bartlett, 1958, p. 140). This led to an investigation of imagining, to some extent thinking, and eventually to remembering.

To study perceiving, Bartlett used a tachistoscope to present subjects with visual material for intervals of 1/15 to 1/4 of a second and then asked what they had seen. The material presented was highly diverse, progressing from simple designs and patterns to concrete picture material, including paintings. Bartlett noted that subjects immediately set up an *attitude* or *general impression* to the material. From it, they constructed a unified interpretation out of the limited information that they took in during the brief interval; this in turn helped to 'fill in the gaps' in what they had seen. With regards to designs and patterns, the general impression was the 'plan of construction' and with picture material it was a feeling for the kind of situation depicted. One fairly confident subject described his experience doing the task with complex designs thus: "In every case ... I kept my gaze fixed on the screen for a few seconds after the window had shut down. I was trying to get a clear image of what I had seen, and in doing this I usually felt part of the design escaping me, while the rest set into a firm enough shape to be transferred to paper" (Bartlett, 1916a, p. 233).

From the beginning, Bartlett noted subjects' spontaneous act of *naming* the material. This functioned to render their attitude toward it more 'definite and contented.' With the simplest designs, naming was done immediately but did not change their reproduction; however, with the slightly more complex designs this did occur. For example, one design was given pointed prongs by a subject who called it a 'pick-axe,' a rounded blade by a subject who called it a 'turf-cutter,' a larger ring at the top of the shape by several subjects who called it an 'anchor,' and the blade was correctly reproduced by a subject who called it a 'prehistoric battle axe.' This finding directly foreshadows a famous experiment by Carmichael, Hogan, and Walter (1932) that showed the way a design was remembered depended strongly on the name given to it. Carmichael et al.'s experiment differs in that they provided the name for their subjects, whereas subjects spontaneously generated it in Bartlett's perceiving experiment. However, in Bartlett's *method of picture writing* (see later), he also provides his subjects with names for the material to be remembered.

Bartlett often presented the same or similar material multiple times, so as to *slow down* the process of perceiving to capture early and the intermediate phases.[4] Some designs progressed in a series from simple to complex. For these, subjects got an impression of the whole and its symmetry, while readily 'feeling' changes from one design to the next. Their perception also included an *anticipation* of what was to come in the next design.[5] When their expectation of changes did not pan out, their reproductions suffered. When a painting was presented multiple times, subjects tended to add details but hold fast to their first impression. For example, every person made something different out of a well-known painting of 'Hubert and Arthur' by W.F. Yeames.[6] One commented on the first trial: "It is a woman in a white apron with a child standing by her knee. She is sitting and has her legs crossed. She is on the right of the picture as I see it, and the child is looking at her." On a second showing, the subject decided that the woman was standing up but on the following 36 presentations the interpretation did not change much.

Subjects got a feeling for the material 'as a whole' but some *dominant details* also stood out. The most easily apprehended figures were those in which there was a dominant detail in the center around which other features were organized. Details that seemed out of place in the whole were also often recognized, such as the missing corner in a square with dialogues, although what corner was missing was not easily identified. For complex designs (like figure 6.1. on page 177) subjects noticed the circles in the design and often tended to multiply them in their drawing, particularly when they did not comprehend the plan of construction.[7] Finally, with picture material many subjects attended to and claimed to be able to read the nearly illegible writing on a sign next to a gate: Amazingly, 80 percent of his subjects saw 'trespasses will be persecuted' (p. 27), while others saw very different letters but words with similar meaning – for example, 'No road' or 'keep off the grass' (ibid), which is a sign still commonly seen today in front of Cambridge College lawns.

In perceiving, we already find the rudiments of imagining. A study of imagining was thus a natural next step. Bartlett gave subjects ($N = 36$) a series of 13 inkblots on cards and asked them to "see what you can make of them, as you sometimes find shapes for clouds and faces in the fire" (p. 252). To do the task subjects quickly developed the habit of holding the cards at arm's length so as to better observe the whole situation, and as such, outstanding details played a lesser part in these reactions. For particularly complex inkblots, however, some subjects adopted the method of breaking the inkblot into parts and dealing with each separately. These subjects tended to develop less fantastical images than subjects that did not adopt this analytic attitude. In all cases, subjects had to find something to link the material to: one person described the process as 'rummaging around' in his mind to find the appropriate image.

One of the most striking general results of the imagining study was the enormous variety of interpretations subjects came up with. The same inkblot suggested entirely different things for different subjects. For instance, one blot evoked the following images for different subjects: a 'camel,' a 'tortoise,' 'a dog worrying[8] a tablecloth,' 'two dead ducks and an ostrich,' an 'octopus,' 'a baby in a cot with a doll following out,' 'a picture of Sohrab and Rustum in a book of Arnold's poems' (p. 36). To say interpretations were varied is not, however, to say that they are random, without consistency or constraint. A number of factors influenced the interpretations. First, Bartlett observes that the majority of interpretations concerned dynamic animal life and that inanimate objects were rare. Second, images tended to be related to an active *interest* in the subject. For example, a woman saw a series of clothing items (e.g., 'bonnet with features') and fabrics (e.g., 'furs' marabout'); a minister of religions saw scenes of the biblical King Nebuchadnezzar; while the same blot reminded a physiologist of the 'basal region of the digestive system' (1932/1995, p. 38). Third, Bartlett noticed that an interpretive stance or *attitude* set up toward one inkblot often persisted through the series. For instance, one subject saw '"ghosts," "more ghosts kissing," "more kissing," "green ghosts"' (p. 38). This occurred independently of any conscious effort on the part of the subject, further confirming Würzburger's observations about attitudes.

In the last step of his analysis, Bartlett classified his subjects into two general types: a *particularizing* type, who tend to form images of a definite character, and a *generalizing* type, who imagine an object of general kind, outside of a specific situation or time. Particularizers made up 59 percent of subjects, generalizers 24 percent, and mixed only 17 percent.

Bartlett further subdivides particularizers into those whose images are mostly reminiscent and those whose are not. Reminiscent particularizers tended to get a strong personal feel of an earlier experience from the blots which was accompanied by distinct visual imagery. One subject even turned her face in disgust from an inkblot that reminded her of an incident many years before in which she suffered a shock on finding a snail crawling along a bread plate. Particularizers who were not dominantly reminiscent were generally amused with the strangeness of their suggestions. All particularizers tended to form detailed and lively images at a rapid pace. In contrast, generalizers reacted slowly, without visualization and often no interpretation came for an inkblot. They approached the task analytically, impersonally, disinterestedly, as a problem to be solved. These subjects often had highly specialized scientific interest.

Taken together, these studies demonstrate the importance of interests, values, feelings, and previous experience in psychological acts, such as perceiving and imagining. All subjects related to the material given by connecting it to some previous experience; as such perceiving and imaging are already infused with memory. From this observation, Bartlett argued that psychological acts involve what he calls 'an effort after meaning.' This refers to the general tendency "to connect what is immediately given with something else not actually present" (1916b, p. 14). The 'something else' is later referred to as a 'setting,' 'scheme,' or 'schema,' which he defines as an active organization of past reactions and experience (see Chapter 4). Moreover, by 'effort' he does not mean to imply strain but rather the work of an active mind. 'Effort after meaning' comes very close to Brentano's notion of 'intentionality' with its analytic focus on the transitive character of psychological acts and the Würzburg notion of mental directedness (see earlier). Bartlett (1932/1995) also makes an analogy with Rubin's insight that a figure (e.g., the face-vase) only stands out against some background, the background here being the active organization of past experience. This framework would be essential to interpret his experiments on remembering.

Experiments on Remembering

Bartlett's most famous experiments on 'remembering' were in fact first framed as 'a contribution to the experimental study of the process of conventionalization' in his 1916 *St. John's Fellowship Dissertation*. 'Conventionalization' was coined by Bartlett's mentor W.H.R. Rivers (1912a) to refer to the process by which foreign cultural elements are transformed toward familiar patterns when they enter a recipient group (see Chapter 3). Bartlett designed his studies to explore some of the psychological aspects of this process. He says, in his *dissertation*, that the studies will additionally contribute to the psychology of imagining (by extension of Philippe's work) and lead into a study of thinking. Remarkably, the issue of remembering is only ever peripherally mentioned in his early write-ups. There is, nonetheless, much consistency in his analysis of these experiments from their discussion in his *dissertation* through their publication as articles in the 1920s to his book *Remembering*. The methodological strategy of these experiments will be our focus here.

The four methods found in Bartlett's *Dissertation* (1916b), and in *Remembering* (1932/1995) under the heading of 'experiments on remembering,' follow the same general form: subjects were shown some stimuli (i.e., images, stories, or other prose passages), which they were to reproduce from memory at increasing time intervals. The interval of reproduction was carefully selected to capture the emergence of qualitative changes in reproductions: if the intervals were too short the reproductions would become fixed[9] and if too long the research would not see the intermediate phases of change. The four methods differ mainly in the conditions under which reproduction takes place. Bartlett purposely varied conditions to explore different aspects of reconstruction. Let us consider each method in turn.

In the *method of description*,[10] subjects ($N = 20$) were shown five faces[11] of military men consecutively for 10 s each. These experiments were carried out during the First World War and as such these kinds of images were familiar to subjects. After an interval of 30 min subjects were asked a series of questions about each face, regarding its details and direction of view.[12] A slightly different set of questions was used in the second reproduction, which occurred after a week or two, and additional reproductions were done after longer intervals. Some of the questions asked suggested details not present in the particular face discussed. The suggested but inaccurate detail was either to be found in another face in the series or else simply in the subject's broader knowledge of faces.[13] This allowed Bartlett to compare 'transferences' of detail from one face to another within the series and 'importations' of details into a face from without the series. Importations were about twice as frequent as transferences. Regarding the latter, Bartlett finds that *dominant details* in the series, such as a pipe, a mustache, and cap badges, were most frequently transferred. We are told that cap badges were of general public interest during First World War, which also helps to explain why familiar cap badges that were not in the original series were commonly imported into reproductions. Two other frequent transformations were confusions concerning the order of faces (occurring in 35 percent of subjects by the first reproduction) and change in the 'direction of regard' (by 60 percent of subjects).

In addition to categorizing the changes introduced into reproductions, Bartlett also analyzed the influence of the attitudes, interests, and methods used by subjects to recall the faces. As with his experiments on perceiving, he emphasizes subjects' reliance on a *general impression*, partly formed out of dominant details, selected based on the subject's interests. Faces are described as 'with a smiling look,' 'good humored,' 'with a broad grin,' or "He has a grave expression," "He is about fifty, stern, serious and unattractive-looking," "He looked very well-feed and groomed" (p. 53). Bartlett further noted the power of affective attitudes to shape the subject's image. One subject had the impression of a face as being 'serious and determined.' Compared to the original, the image that she developed "was very much more serious; his mouth was firmer, his chin more prominent, his face more square" (p. 54). This effect was even more striking when subjects were reminded of a conventional representation of a face, such as British drawings of a common soldier (i.e., 'the Tommy Atkins'[14]) or a sailor. These images tended to conform more to this general type, as Philippe's (1897) study had also shown.

As with his experiment on imagining, Bartlett concludes his analysis with a typology of subjects. Here he identifies two methods of remembering used by subjects – *visualization* and *vocalization*. Visualizers are those

Figure 2.2.   Faces used in Bartlett's method of description

who rely primarily on visual imagery, while vocalizers rely more on linguistic cues. These describe the preferred persistent method used by a subject in dealing with an experimental task, which he identifies through participants' reports. Through these reports, he finds that visualization carries certainty with it whereas vocalization is accompanied by doubt. This is the case because of visual images' vivid, rich, and exciting expression in consciousness. Due to these characteristics, when a subject is torn between a visual and vocal memory of an object they will choose the former. This, however, does not mean that visualizers reproduce the material more accurately; demonstratively they do not. Secondly, vocalization is a direct expression of meanings, while meanings have to be developed out of visualization. For this reason, remembering through visualizing appears 'jerky' in comparison with vocalizing. Bartlett also comments that subjects tend to prefer the use of one of these modes in their engagement with his experimental tasks, which he can say because he used some of the same subjects in multiple experiments.

The other three methods deal more directly with the question of "the way in which conventional modes of representation and behaviour are developed within the social group and transmitted from group to group" (Bartlett, 1932/1995, p. 95). In other words, these latter methods were meant to directly model the psychological processes involved in conventionalization. To do this, Bartlett borrowed the majority of stimuli material for these experiments from his wide anthropological readings – in particular, from Taylor's (1883) comprehensive study of *The Alphabet*, Mallery's (1894) study of North American petroglyphs, and Boas's (1901) study of Native American Folklore. All these studies demonstrated a variety of ways in which culture is 'simplified' and 'elaborated' in systematic directions by receiving groups (see Chapter 3). Using unfamiliar material also helped to make visible social psychological processes that normally operate unnoticed. The dramatic changes introduced into a foreign story or image when it is reproduced foreground the social background through which these processes occur. Bartlett also used more familiar material to compare with, such as a journalist's description of a croquet match, selections from Emerson's 'Self-Reliance,' and a drawing of a house.

The *method of picture writing* was designed to explore the transformation of written language signs, as one finds in petroglyphs. Subjects were required to learn 80 signs, each standing for a specific word, which they did by grouping the signs together by representativeness, association, common reference, or principles. Fifteen minutes after the subject had finished learning the signs, Bartlett told them: "I am going to dictate to you a short story in which some of the words that had signs will be used. Whenever a sign-word comes, write the sign for it. Write as quickly as you can, and don't worry too much about exact accuracy. I shall keep you writing as fast as you can go" (p. 97). With this method, Bartlett was intentionally setting up conditions in which subjects are unable to make a directed and laborious effort to secure accuracy of reproduction. This was for him a great virtue of the method, because in everyday life accurate reproduction is incidental to our main purposes. In contrast, when subjects in an experiment are directly asked for a reproduction they generally adopt a careful and diligent attitude. Finally, as with the *method of description*, the method of picture writing allowed Bartlett to explore *cross-modal* dimensions of memory – here between word and image.

In subjects' reproductions, *omissions* were common and tended to occur when the form of the sign had no representative significance in relation to the word, to some signs in a sign-grouping that were similar in form, and where there was a simple sign in an easy series. Of the 920 total test words reproduced by his subjects, just over half (i.e., 466) were significantly transformed (Bartlett, 1916b, p. 153). To give an example, consider the series of successive attempts one participant made to reproduce the sign for 'king' shown in Figure 2.3. The four signs that get blended together in the reproductions are also included above. In his first attempt the subject seems to transpose details from the sign for 'strong' but remains unsure of his efforts. Further changes within the same general form are added in the second and third reproductions. In the fourth attempt, the subject makes a sign similar to that for 'head' but adds a detail suggesting a 'crown.' The details of this feature get elaborated in the fifth attempt, after which the sign settles into a stable form going through no further changes in subsequent reproductions.

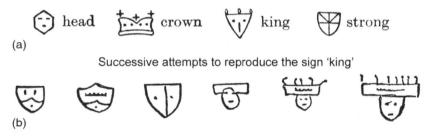

Four original signs from series I (out of 23 total signs)

⬡ head   👑 crown   ♔ king   🛡 strong

(a)

Successive attempts to reproduce the sign 'king'

(b)

Figure 2.3. Original signs (a) and their progressive transformation in reproduction (b)

Speaking of general changes, there was widespread *blending* and *confusion* of details for signs after a week (as in the above example of 'king'), especially among those that were similar in form but unlike in assigned significance. Signs were frequently given a different direction, but this change did not seem to follow any given rule. Some other common changes were signs that were taken to be representative lose details which are not essential to their significance (e.g., an eye sign loses its eyelashes) and those with a similar conventional representation changed to look more like the familiar form (e.g., a squiggle changes to look more like lighting). As in the other methods, odd and novel details were often retained and exaggerated, while unrepresentative signs containing repetition of some features frequently multiplied them further. Moreover, signs grouped together tended to be assimilated to a class of signs and lost their distinctive features. Finally, *naming* an unrepresentative sign strongly influenced how it was reproduced.

Bartlett is perhaps most famous for his *method of repeated reproduction*. He used many different written texts with this method but in *Remembering* he confined himself to an analysis of participants' reproductions of the Native American folk tale *War of the Ghosts*, while keeping in mind throughout corroborative detail from the use of other material. The story is particularly apt to the task because it involves numerous narrative disjunctures, seeming lack of logic, strange and vivid imagery, among other puzzling elements. French anthropologist Lévy-Bruhl would have interpreted the story as a good example of 'primitive mentality' (see Chapter 3). For Bartlett, the striking difference to British ways of thinking provided a powerful illustration of the process of conventionalization. He says, "I wished particularly to see how educated and rather sophisticated subjects would deal with this lack of obvious rational order" (Bartlett, 1932/1995, p. 64).

Interestingly, the story itself had already gone through a number of transformations before finding its way into Bartlett's experiment. Bartlett's source for the story was a book *Kathlamet Texts* (1901) published by the American anthropologist Franz Boas, who learned it from one of the last remaining Kathlamet speakers. Boas transcribed two versions of the story, told to him on different occasions, and then translated them into English with his informant's help. Before publishing it, Boas smoothed the language out to make it more readable. Bartlett then 'slightly modified' one of these stories, removing phrases such as 'blood came out of his anus' – apparently to make it more palatable to his British participants.[15] In this way, the story had already been partially conventionalized before it had even been shown to Bartlett's participants. Here is the version of the story he used in his experiments:

War of the Ghosts
One night, two young men from Egulac went down to the river to hunt seals and while they were there it became foggy and calm. Then they heard war-cries, and they thought: "Maybe this is a war-party." They escaped to the shore, and hid behind a log. Now canoes came up, and they heard the noise of paddles and saw one canoe coming up to them. There were five men in the canoe, and they said:
"What do you think? We wish to take you along. We are going up the river to make war on the people."
One of the young men said, "I have no arrows."
"Arrows are in the canoe," they said.
"I will not go along. I might be killed. My relatives do not know where I have gone. But you," he said, turning to the other, "may go with them."
So one of the young men went, but the other returned home.
And the warriors went on up the river to a town on the other side of Kalama. The people came down to the water and they began to fight, and many were killed. But presently, the young man heard one of the warriors say, "Quick, let us go home: that Indian has been hit." Now he thought: "Oh, they are ghosts." He did not feel sick, but they said he had been shot.
So the canoes went back to Egulac and the young man went ashore to his house and made a fire. And he told everybody and said: "Behold I accompanied the ghosts, and we went to fight. Many of our fellows were killed, and many of those who attacked us were killed. They said I was hit, and I did not feel sick."
He told it all, and then he became quiet. When the sun rose he fell down. Something black came out of his mouth. His face became contorted. The people jumped up and cried.
He was dead.

Bartlett had Cambridge students, colleagues, and townspeople read the story twice at regular reading speed.[16] After a period of usually 15 min, participants wrote the story down by hand as best they could remember it on a sheet of paper. This was repeated several times at increasing time intervals – in one case 10 years later. The reproductions produced by each participant were analyzed as a *series* or *chain*, exploring what was added, deleted, and transformed from the original to first reproduction and from one reproduction to the next. In his analysis, Bartlett first provides readers with a full series of reproductions for particularly illustrative cases and a detailed analysis of the changes introduced and secondly elaborates on the general trends found across his sample. As mentioned earlier, his analysis incorporates participants' introspective reports in order to understand the interpretive and affective processes that lead to the transformations introduced into their reproductions. One participant provided the following detailed account (abbreviated here) at the first reproduction:

When I read the story ... I thought the main point was the reference to the ghosts who were went off to fight the people further on ... I wrote out the story mainly by following my own images. I had a vague feeling of the style. There was a sort of rhythm about it I tried to imitate. I can't understand the contradiction about somebody being killed, and the man's being wounded, but feeling nothing. At first I thought there was something supernatural about the story. Then I saw that Ghosts must be a class, or clan name. That made the whole thing more comprehensible. (1932/1995, p. 68)

This participant is typical with regards to the changes Bartlett identified within his sample – namely, missing the point of the story, moving the ghosts up earlier in the story, remembering the story based on visual images, the attempt to reproduce the style and rationalize the incomprehensible.

Bartlett notes that strict accuracy of reproduction is the exception rather than the rule. The most significant changes to the story were made on the first reproduction, which set the form, scheme, order, and arrangement of material for subsequent reproductions.[17] However, as more time went by there was a progressive omission of details, simplification of events, and transformation of items into the familiar. Some of the most common and persistent changes were 'hunting seals' into 'fishing,' 'canoes' into 'boats,' the omission of the excuse that 'we have no arrows,' transformations of the proper names (i.e., Egulac and Kalama) before they disappeared completely, and the precise meaning of the 'ghosts.' Whenever something seemed strange or incomprehensible, it was either omitted completely or rationalized. For example, the 'something black' that comes out of the Indian's mouth was frequently understood as the materialization of his breath and in at least one case as 'his soul' leaving his body. The second meaning given to an item often appeared only in participants' introspective reports on the first reproduction but in subsequent reproductions it took the place of the original. In other cases, 'rationalization' of the material happened without the person's awareness, as when 'hunting seals' became 'fishing.'

Rationalization operates by giving the material in question a setting and an explanation within one's own frame of reference, and thereby rendering it "acceptable, understandable, comfortable, straightforward; rob[bing] it of all puzzling elements" (p. 89). It is directly related to the 'effort after meaning,' whereby the presenting material is connected to something else the person is already familiar with. This happened for both the particular details of the story and the story as a whole. Hardly ever was there ready acceptance of the story as it was first presented. Bartlett noted that participants needed to first *label* the story – for example, as a 'dream,' 'like what I read when I was a boy' or simply 'not English.' He stresses that the unfamiliar makes us uneasy and that rationalization helps us to cope with this. The process of remembering starts with an attitude or general impression of the story (e.g., 'not English') and proceeds in order to justify it. The end of the process is primarily affective in that it produces an attitude in which 'no further questions are asked.' Furthermore, rationalization was at work in participants' efforts to link together the disjointed events of the story. Bartlett made an analogy with a silent film in which the explanatory tags connecting one sequence of events with another was removed. In making sense of the story, participants supplied the tags themselves without realizing they were doing so.

The *method of serial reproduction* followed the same procedure as that of *repeated reproduction*, except that the first reproduction was shown to another participant to read and reproduce after 15–30 min. Like the party game 'telephone' or 'Chinese whispers,'[18] this was then repeated such that each link in the chain of reproductions was made by a different participant. Bartlett got the idea for this method from Norbert Wiener, the inventor of cybernetics, on one of their walks in Cambridge together (Bartlett, 1958, p. 144). In his *Dissertation* and *Remembering*, Bartlett devotes as much space to the method of serial reproduction as he does to the other three methods combined. Thus, we can assume that he saw it as particularly important and certainly the closest analog to the process by which popular stories, designs, and rumors circulate within and between groups. Furthermore, he notes that many of the same changes seen in the method of repeated reproduction appear in even more dramatic form using this method.[19] His analysis follows the same logic as that of the method of repeated reproduction, which involved providing full reproductions for the reader to scrutinize. The major difference is that he presents data from a much wider range of material, including folk stories, newspaper clippings, argumentative passages, and picture material.

Let us begin by further illustrating his analytic strategy by presenting a chain of reproductions for the ending of *War of the Ghosts*. The original reads, "When the sun rose he fell down. Something black came out of his mouth. His face became contorted." Here is a striking example of progressive changes in a serial reproduction chain:

When the sun rose he fell down. And he gave a cry, and as he opened his mouth a black thing rushed from it.

When the sun rose he suddenly felt faint, and when he would have risen he fell down, and a black thing rushed out of his mouth.

He felt no pain until sunrise the next day, when, on trying to rise, a great black thing flew out of his mouth.

He lived that night, and the next day, but at sunset his soul fled black from his mouth.

He lived through the night and the following day, but died at sunset, and his soul passed out from his mouth.

Before the boat got clear of the conflict the Indian died, and his spirit fled.

Before he could be carried back to the boat, his spirit had left this world.

His spirit left the world.

('Nonsense,' said one of the others, 'you will not die.') But he did.

(Bartlett, 1932/1995, p. 127)

Through the chain the vague but vivid 'something black' becomes an increasingly more concrete entity, before it finally disappears. To understand this transformation, we must read it as an unfolding process toward a stable conventional form. First, something black becomes the slightly more tangible 'black thing.' This image is eventually linked with 'flew' from his mouth, which is a transformation from the original 'came out of his mouth.' This change in turn facilitates the shift from the ambiguous 'thing' to 'soul' and later to the 'spirit.' At this point, the story is still supernatural but in the conventional and familiar form of "His spirit left this world." However, by the end of the series there is no mention of spirit or even the 'ghosts,' which were left at the heading of the story by Bartlett in an attempt to keep these supernatural elements in the story.

The analysis of changes was done holistically. Bartlett noted how the story is *simplified* through omitting parts of it that seem irrelevant to the whole. Omissions and later transformations of the story are intertwined: "In a story series of this type, any omission from an individual version is liable to become significant and to account for a succession of connected changes in subsequent versions" (Bartlett, 1932/1995, p. 125).[20] There was also a tendency for some incident or incidents to become *dominant*, such that all the details of the story are grouped around it. This 'unwitting selection of central facts' could be frequently seen in events connected with the wound and death of the Indian in *War of the Ghosts*. When elements do not fit the central grouping they are omitted or rationalized, the latter leads to an *elaboration* of the story. The combined effects of these changes fashion 'a more coherent, concise and undecorated tale' (p. 127) which becomes a conventional form within the group of subjects concerned. Bartlett also compared a chain of reproductions from an Indian and English group. In both cases, he found the story takes on a distinctive 'group stamp or character' (p. 173), but he notes a stronger tendency to elaborate in the Indian group.

Speaking of general trends seen across the serial reproduction experiments with a variety of texts, Bartlett highlights that proper names and titles tend to be omitted; the concrete tends to be preserved and emphasized; many stories tend to be given a 'moral'; argumentative passages 'tend to be reduced to bald expression on conventional option' (p. 173); and while stories tend to gain explanatory links through rationalization, argumentive texts lose them.[21] He further emphasizes the 'radical nature of changes' in the serial reproduction chains: "Epithets are changed into opposites; incidents and events are transposed; names and numbers rarely survive intact for more than a few reproductions; opinions and conclusions are reversed – nearly every possible variation seems as if it can take place" (p. 175). Bartlett also was at pains to point out that Ebbinghaus's approach is wholly inadequate to understand these changes. For example, material is not preserved based on its position within a text – according to Ebbinghaus, items coming at the beginning or end of a list are remembered at a higher frequency (i.e., the 'serial position effect') – but rather based on what is deemed meaningful to the subject or group of subjects. Furthermore, 'preservation is in no way a guarantee of accuracy' (p. 175).

As a final illustration of the versatility of the method of serial reproduction, consider a reproduction chain using visual material, which according to Bartlett affords elaboration and invention. In the following series, an Egyptian hieroglyph, conventionally representing an owl, was used as a stimulus to begin the chain (Figure 2.4).

Figure 2.4.   Serial reproduction chain with images

Bartlett highlights the progressive elaboration occurring through the chain of reproductions until the figure reaches a conventional English form:

The reversal of the direction of the wing curve by subject 3, and its doubling, at once suggested a tail, and thereafter the tail drops lower and lower until it assumes its proper tail position, and is greatly emphasized, in which process it is reversed twice more. The apparently disconnected lines in the original drawing are all worked into the figure, and the original beak mark is elaborated into a ribbon with a bow. Whiskers are introduced in due course, and the small lines of the back are multiplied and become shading ... A rather unusual figure, carrying a fairly strong suggestion of a realistic representation, becomes greatly elaborated into a familiar whole. (p. 181)

Two kinds of the elaboration are mentioned here, which were also pointed out in Bartlett's experiments on perceiving: first, there is the elaboration of individual details into recognizable features – for example, the elaboration of certain items into a tail, whiskers, and a ribbon. Second, there is elaboration by multiplication of different parts. This happens with the duplication of the wing in the third reproduction and the inner shading in the ninth. The Cambridge anthropologist Haddon had described this second type of elaboration as the 'characteristic device of the decorative mind' (quoted in Bartlett, 1932/1995, p. 182). As with the textual material, elaboration goes hand in hand with *simplification*, in which disconnected details tend to be either omitted or worked into the general pattern. Often unfamiliar material will be elaborated until it is recognizable to the group it enters, at which point it will be simplified to a conventional form – a black cat in the above chain of reproductions. If simplification goes too far, elaboration may take over again, leading to the development of a new figure or of a decorative motif without representational character. One can also see the importance of *naming* or *labeling* in this process, which may be applied to the figure as a whole or to its different parts. In either case, the figure(s) will be transformed toward a conventional representation, as Bartlett had also found in the method of picture writing.

Reflections on Methodology

Having described Bartlett's early experimental studies, we will now take a step back to consider the methodological assumptions that guided them. These assumptions were a key to the German–Austrian tradition of the time, as described by Watson (1934) and Toomela (2007). As we will see, Bartlett (an Englishman) fits squarely within this methodological tradition. This is not entirely surprising given that Bartlett's

Cambridge mentors were all highly influenced by this tradition, several of them even studied in Germany. In what follows, I will describe the methodological assumptions coming out of the German–Austrian tradition of the time in relation to Bartlett's experimental studies, namely the focus on (1) psychological qualities over quantitative scores, (2) psychological controls over physical controls, (3) human reactions as wholes, (4) single cases over probabilities in groups, (5) type over trait differences, (6) insight over prediction, (7) a systemic approach to theory building, and (8) thinking over the accumulation of facts.

One of the most surprising features of Bartlett's methodology, from the standpoint of contemporary experimental psychology, is the scarcity of quantitative scores. He rarely counted how many items were remembered, forgotten, or changed, as is routinely done in memory experiments today. This is not to say that Bartlett never used quantitative scores, but rather he used them to further illustrate a qualitative tendency – for example, he reported over half his subjects changed 'canoes' to 'boats' by the second reproduction of *War of the Ghosts*. Bartlett's main strategy is to bring his readers close to the phenomena under investigation by offering individual subjects' full reproductions and his detailed qualitative analysis of them. Readers use the 'raw data' to decide for themselves whether they agree with his interpretation, which becomes impossible once the data has been coded, quantified, and aggregated. Gaskell and Bauer (2000) call this strategy of assuring data quality 'thick description.' According to it, the context, meanings, and interpretations that illuminate the research process should be made available for greater transparency.

For Bartlett 'thick description' also involved describing the subjective conditions of response, which his concept of attitude highlighted: "Subjective attitudes and orientations are an important part of every response at the psychological level" (Bartlett, 1936, p. 43). Attitude, in Bartlett's sense, is a dynamic and holistic orientation and thus an unquantifiable psychological quality. His concept sensitizes us to the fact that participants interpret the 'same' situation and experimental materials in a variety of ways, and these interpretations have real effects on the way in which they respond to it. Therefore, the experimenter needs to carefully attend to participants' attitude as they enter the laboratory and perform the experimental task. For Bartlett, this involved both observation and conversation with his participants. Bartlett's experimental reports are in fact filled with participants' comments on the task and material. This is even more evident in his *Dissertation* (1916b), where he often includes introspective protocols over a page in length. One has the feeling that the experimenter–participant relationship is close and dynamic, as it was in the Würzburg School.[22] Bartlett (1936) said "very often the most valuable information can be given in terms possible only to the person himself who responds" (p. 42).

The concept of attitude points to Bartlett's treatment of human responses as wholes rather than as isolated reactions. It is the whole active person embedded in a particular context that makes a response. As described earlier, this contrasts sharply with Ebbinghaus's approach, which aimed to isolate and itemize a response by stripping it down to its simplest elements and studying it without regard to context or meaning. Bartlett is emphatic that a simplified stimulus does not necessarily lead to a simplified response. In addition, by attending to a subject's holistic attitudes, Bartlett also embraces holism in his efforts to make the experiment closer to everyday life conditions. In contemporary parlance, he was concerned to retain 'ecological validity' (Neisser, 1976). This is done first by using meaningful materials, such as images and narratives (rather than nonsense syllables), which subjects can engage with through their interests, personal history, and social conventions, and secondly by making the experimental situation itself more like an everyday activity.

An experiment is a social situation that tends to create a guarded and analytic attitude in those who enter it. Bartlett considers this a problem and invents strategies to mitigate it; he always justifies his methods in relation to everyday life conditions (even if remembering a strange Native American story is far from the everyday life of his subjects). From his perspective, it is impossible to isolate 'pure memory' from other factors; there are no 'experiments in a vacuum' (Tajfel, 1972) where the context can be stripped of meaning so as to neutralize its effect. Participants make guesses about what the experimenter is up to and what he or she wants them to do. For the experiment to work, the participant has to 'play along.' Context is then part of the subject's *normative* framework of action and understanding, not another *causal* variable that can be externally controlled. This prohibits the inference of a direct *causal* relationship between independent and dependent variables; instead, context normatively regulates the meaning of both (Brinkmann, 2010). In contrast to this holistic concept of an experiment, psychology has often employed the experiment in order to identify a central processing mechanism that is a transcendent, abstract, fixed, content-free, and universal property of the mind (Shweder, 1991). This search has frequently led experimentalists to consider processes taking place in the laboratory as somehow more real than what goes on outside. In contrast, Bartlett is clear that psychological processes cannot be isolated from the context in which they occur and the material they work on.

Another part of Bartlett's holistic methodology is his analysis of single cases over probabilities in a group. He is especially critical of the analysis of aggregates by inferential statistics, which he refers to as 'scientific makeshifts' (1932/1995, p. 7). According to him, they have the opposite problem to Ebbinghaus's method that aims to identify direct causal relationships, in that they show there is some relationship between variables without shedding light on what it is.[23] Bartlett's critique is a particularly controversial aspect of his methodology for many experimental psychologists today, as it runs against contemporary research norms. Kintsch (1995) says in his introduction to the latest edition of *Remembering*: "There are no statistics, and little data aggregation. What we get are selected examples. In my opinion, this is the weakest aspect of the book" (p. xiv). In his review of the new edition, Roediger (1997) is even more critical: "Not one true experiment appears in the book; he never systematically manipulated an independent variable to determine the behavior of a dependent variable, with extraneous sources of variation held constant or randomized" (p. 489).

When Bartlett's experiments were conducted (in the 1910s), the application of inferential statistics to populations of subjects was still fighting for its legitimacy, and only became the dominant approach in the 1950s through an appeal to the general public and applied areas of psychology, not to research scientists (Danziger, 1990; see also Gigerenzer et al., 1989). Statisticians in the first decades of the twentieth century were careful to point out that one cannot make claims about individual processes from group averages.[24] A 'scientific' methodology at this time worked with single cases: the second, third, and fourth subjects in an experiment served only to validate what was found with the first subject. There was only one subject in Ebbinghuas's (1885/1913) experiment, himself! Generalized models of some phenomenon were developed through one single case being tested against other single cases. An idiographic methodology thus allows one to explore the complexity of single cases and attend not only to normal but also to outlier cases (Salvatore and Valsiner, 2010). For example, only one out of twenty subjects remembered the proper names in the story *War of the Ghosts*, and was able to do so after 10 years. Rather than ignoring the bizarre case as an outlier, Bartlett (1932/1995) not only acknowledges it in the discussion of his results (p. 82), but also explores and uses it to elaborate his theory (p. 208ff). Today qualitative researchers call this methodological strategy 'deviant case analysis.'

Bartlett also explored and systematized the variability of responses by creating typologies of subjects in his analysis. For example, in his study of imagining he identifies 'particularizers' and 'generalizers,' and in his *method of description* he distinguishes 'visualizers' and 'vocalizers.' According to his approach, a person is of a particular type if he or she has a persistent and preferred tendency to respond in a certain way. Because Bartlett used some of the same subjects across different experiments, he could often say that these persisted beyond a single situation. Types are different from traits in that they are concerned with the whole person and acknowledge that the same outcome might be reached by different processes. They are also visible processes rather than abstract qualities projected into people by psychologists – a tendency William James (1890, p. 196) called 'the psychologist's fallacy.' Bartlett's interest in identifying the 'methods' used by subjects is consonant with a type focus. Traits, in contrast, are treated as sets of static and isolated variables a person has. They are typically analyzed through inferential statistics at the level of the population.

In all this, we see Bartlett's methodology is aimed at insight over prediction, the systemic development of complex theory and thinking over the accumulation of facts (see also Chapter 6 on 'experimental thinking'). In contrast, experiments today are often seen as a strict sequence of procedures for research design and analysis which if carefully followed will lead to objective knowledge. These procedures have generally been statistical exercises in null hypothesis testing, which the statistician Gerd Gigerenzer (2004) has referred to as 'mindless statistics.'[25] Within this approach, who the experimentalist is makes no difference as long as the proper steps are taken; the subjectivity and expertise of the researcher are given little place. Daston (1992) has pointed out that the earlier notion of objectivity was precisely the opposite of this aperspectival understanding in currency today; it stressed the scientist's accumulation of experience in research and thereby the refinement of his or her methodological perspective over time. Similarly, Bartlett (2010[1959]) is clear that "to separate psychology from the psychologist is an entirely artificial procedure" (p. 988). He goes on to outline a number of personal characteristics that make a good experimental psychologist, including 'having a number of lively interests outside of psychology,' 'loyalty to evidence,' 'know[ing] where and how to look for evidence,' recognizing the limits of statistics particularly with regard to the study of process, and effective collaboration with different disciplines (see also Bartlett, 1958, 1959).

For Bartlett, the experimenter's own subjectivity plays a key role in the research process (cf. Branco and Valsiner, 1997). He practices a more open interpretive process, in which the experimenter is likened to a clinician. "If the experimentalist in psychology once recognizes that he remains to a great extent a clinician, he is forced to realize that the study of any well developed psychological function is possible only in the light of consideration of its history" (Bartlett, 1932/1995, p. 15). This is why Bartlett makes a virtue out of knowing his subjects prior to the experiment (see Bartlett, 1916b, p. 32). If he had not known their background, he would have missed many important insights about their reactions in the course of the experiment. The clinical perspective thus cannot be removed from rigorous experimentation (Bartlett, 2010 [1959]): a clinician must attend to subjects' history, as well as develop sensitivity to knowing where and how to look for evidence in the clinical encounter. The latter requires an open conversation with the patient. Along these lines, Edwards and Middleton (1987) point out that Bartlett engaged his subjects in a 'task-oriented dialogue' in which they answered questions, explicated, and explained their mental processes to him. This data was essential for constructing a holistic picture of the processes involved.

Thus, Bartlett's focus was on building a general picture of psychological processes through a consideration of a range of different sources of evidence. This range was found by attending to different sides of an experiment as well as by finding common patterns across partially overlapping studies on what would often be considered entirely different areas of research today, such as perceiving, imagining, thinking, and remembering (cf. Kleining, 1986). Bartlett is clear that these processes differ in degree not kind. A study of perceiving is a necessary complement to one on remembering and vice versa. Bartlett's goal was to develop general theory to describe and explain the mind as a whole, rather than a mental process taken in isolation. This requires an open approach to research that weaves together insights from different studies, rather than one bound to rigid procedures that produce isolated facts. Although the method is more open, we should not assume that these studies lack research standards. Bartlett was clear that the experimenter must be 'loyal to evidence,' 'honest about his assumptions,' and 'willing to give and to take incisive criticism' (Bartlett, 2010[1959], p. 989). I have also discussed strategies that he used for assuring research quality, such as 'thick description' and 'deviant case analysis.'

Replications and Extensions

Since the publication of *Remembering*, Bartlett's experiments have inspired innumerable other studies. In what follows, we will focus on those that have reported to replicate and extend his experiments using the methods he developed. Within this corpus of studies, his *methods of repeated* and *serial reproduction* have been widely used, while to my knowledge only Nadel (1937) has used a technique resembling the *method of description* and no one has taken up the *method of picture writing*. In the history of appropriations of his experiments from the 1930s to today, there has been a general shift in the understanding of what it means to replicate these experiments, which in large part corresponds to a move away from the methodological assumptions outlined earlier. Many of the earliest replications and extensions had some direct personal contact with Bartlett and focused on the function of social group membership in remembering.[26] For example, Northway (1936) explores how 'social background' of the children in different Toronto schools shapes their remembering (see Chapter 4); Maxwell (1936) compares the memory of priests, soldiers, students, boy scouts, among others; and Nadel (1937) contrasts how children in two Northern Nigerian tribes remember a story and a picture based on their groups' distinctive cultural patterns (see Chapter 5). Moreover, all three of these researchers constructed a novel story tailored to their research site, presented single cases in discussing their results, and focused on qualitative changes introduced into the story in their analyses.

A transition away from this early focus on how membership in distinct social groups conditions remembering can already be seen in the 1940s. Participants in most Bartlett's inspired studies became mostly undergraduate students, though there is still an acknowledgment of 'cultural influences' on the process. For example, Taylor (1947) compares Indian and English students' reconstructions of the *War of the Ghosts* and is also the second Bartlett inspired study to only provide aggregated data (the first was Klugman, 1944).[27] In contrast, the serial reproduction studies of Allport and Postman (1947), Ward (1949), and Hall (1950) focused on qualitative changes in single cases, as Bartlett had done. In fact, both Allport and Ward had direct contact with Bartlett and Hall studied with Bartlett's former student R.C. Oldfield.[28] Ward's (1949) experiment is interesting in that it is the only study until recently that has aimed to reproduce changes of some material that could be observed historically in the laboratory. He finds similar changes in the serial reproduction of coin designs to those that actually occurred in Macedonia between the fourth and first centuries BC. This result probably involved a bit of luck; at least Bartlett thought so. In contrast, Hall (1950) aimed to further Bartlett's study of the relation between signs and words. He found giving a name or title to images and stories could *enhance* certain features of the material or *impede* their assimilation, depending on the 'fittingness' of the name or title to what it refers.

Allport and Postman's (1947) classic study was aimed at exploring the conditions leading to the transmission and transformation of

Figure 2.5.   Subway scene used in Allport and Postman's serial reproduction study

rumors, which was a major topic of interest after the Second World War. To do this, they showed a picture to a subject, who then had to orally describe it to another. The second subject then described it to a third and so on. Figure 2.5 is one of the most famous images used in their study. In one chain, the last reproduction reads: "This is a subway train in New York headed for Portland Street. There is a Jewish woman and a Negro who has a razor in his hand. The woman has a baby or a dog. The train is going to Deyer Street, and nothing much happens" (pp. 65–73). Their analysis is faithful to that of Bartlett's focus on qualitative transformations; however, to describe the nature of changes they use the gestalt terms of *leveling, sharping,* and *assimilation.*[29] Similar to Bartlett's notion of simplification, *leveling* refers to the tendency to change the story toward a version that is shorter, more concise, more easily grasped and told. The complementary process of *sharpening* describes how certain items are selected and emphasized, and thus it overlaps with Bartlett's notions of dominant details and elaboration. In the chain of reproductions for the image below, 'the Negro,' whose size and unusual appearance invite attention, often became 'four' or 'several,' or of a 'gigantic stature.' Also, the razor was always retained and sharpened. Furthermore, in more than half of the experiments, the razor moved from the white man's hand to the African American's hand. This is a striking example of *assimilation* to conventional prejudices.

The next phase of Bartlett inspired studies in the 1950s and 60s aimed at testing his theory of remembering through the use of strictly controlled procedures for data collection and analysis. These researchers were critical of Bartlett's flexible style of experimentation preferring instead what they considered 'definitive experiments (those that yield a yes–no answer)' (Paul, 1959, p. 5). This led to a number of interesting shifts in the studies during this period. First, Bartlett's focus on how social and cultural processes shape remembering completely disappears as a topic of investigation.[30] Second, an attempt to code replications for kinds of changes (e.g., simplification, elaboration, condensation, sharpening, normalizing) or different levels of change (e.g., individual words, information units, themes) is gradually replaced by coding simply for accuracy and distortion at one level of analysis – I say 'gradually' because there is an intermediate period in which particular kinds of changes are coded for but they are used as indicators of distortion. Third, there is an increasing reliance on inferential statistics, at the expense of qualitative analyses of story reproductions. Finally, the idea that memory is reconstructive is progressively taken to mean that it is distorted or inaccurate. I will consider each of the major studies at this time to trace the shifts in theoretical focus and mode of analysis more clearly.

Kay's (1955) repeated reproduction study aimed to better understand why the 'general form' of the first reproduction persisted in later reproductions,[31] and by extension whether subjects would be able to amend errors after they had changed the story in memory. To test this, he re-read the original story to his participants after each time they had reproduced it (over six reproduction sessions), so that they could see their mistakes. Kay coded reproductions for both general content and specific verbal phrasing, as well as included a qualitative analysis of general changes found across his sample. In all cases, he found that once the first reproduction had been made it was not easily modified; in other words, despite the repeated rereading of the story, each subsequent reproduction of it remained strikingly similar to the first reproduction. This lead Kay to argue that the constructive nature of memory emphasized by Bartlett applies mainly to the initial perception and reproduction – where the person's stable tendencies of interpretation and the story material first establish a relationship – and less to subsequent reproductions.[32] However, Kay says nothing more about the specific nature of the changes in question.

While Kay (1955) explicitly ignored interests, attitudes, affects, and goals in his investigation, Paul (1959) gave them central place. This is a result of Kay's interest in learning processes versus Paul's background in personality psychology and psychoanalysis – Paul was a student of the psychoanalyst David Rapaport, author of the classic book *Emotion and Memory* (Rapaport, 1942). Paul's (1959) study is one of the most extensive replications of Bartlett's serial reproduction experiments – it is only after it that *War of the Ghosts* became the choice text for replications of Bartlett's experiments. The aim of the study was to understand to what extent 'the distortions and fragmentations in recall' (p. 6) that Bartlett had found could be explained by 'gaps and ambiguities' (ibid) in a story, on the one hand, and unfamiliarity of the material, on the other. To test the role played by gaps, he prepared an *explicated* version of *War of the Ghosts*, adding links to make the story less disjunctive, and found that it was more easily and accurately remembered than the original. With regards to familiarity, he created a story about secretaries with familiar actors and actions, which fared better in reproduction than both versions of *War of the Ghosts*. Following his training in personality psychology, Paul also identified two general types of rememberers which he called *importers* and *skeletonizers*. While *importers* added material for purposes of integration, *skeletonizers* stripped, fragmented, and segregated the material. These types turned out to be 'stable and general individual difference parameters' (p. 7), as they were able to predict the direction of story change in an additional serial reproduction experiment, in which the groups were composed of people belonging to either solely importers or skeletonizers.

Much like Kay (1955), Johnson (1962) adopted a more restricted focus with the aim of determining "whether learned material which is qualitatively changed [in memory] from the original material is retained better than learned material which is not qualitatively changed" (p. 218). Using the method repeated reproduction and *War of the Ghosts*, he compared the retention of items between the first and second reproduction. Items were coded as *duplicates* (of those in the original text), *omissions* (items absent in recall), *sharpenings* (where an item is given greater emphasis), and *normalizations* (where an item was changed toward existing conventions). According to Johnson, if Bartlett's theory was correct then we would expect items qualitatively changed on the first reproduction – by being *sharpened* or *normalized* – would be better retained on the second reproduction than those that were *duplicates* of the original on the first reproduction. This is because items that better fit existing schema were thought to be better retained (see Chapter 4). Johnson, however, does not account for the fact that items might also be retained on the first reproduction *because* they fit existing schema. In any case, he found that *duplications* were better remembered than modified items.

Following this general trend of studies, Gauld and Stephenson (1967) set out to show that the 'distortion' in remembering found by Bartlett could be explained by his lenient experimental instructions. This study is particularly interesting for our purposes because it clearly demonstrates how the assumptions about remembering and how to study it had completely shifted by this time: first, memory is now seen as a mental faculty which can be isolated from other processes, and second, reconstruction now means that memory is distorted. Gauld and Stephenson's (1967) description of Bartlett's experiments is revealing:

Bartlett's theory that remembering is a 'reconstructive' process is based largely upon the ways in which subjects change and distort prose passages when reproducing them from memory. If such changes and distortions are to serve as the foundation for a theory of remembering it is clearly desirable to be quite certain that the persons who make them really are trying to remember, and are not deliberately inventing material to fill in gaps in their memories. (p. 1)

As described earlier, Bartlett deliberately understressed accuracy in order to bring the experiment closer to everyday life conditions. In contrast, Gauld and Stephenson (1967) thought that 'the memory' functions to reproduce facts and could be separated from context. They aimed to show that reconstruction of the material entered only under the pressure to create a more convincing narrative through guesses, inventions, and inferences. They hypothesized that memory would not be prone to error if in the place of Bartlett's 'loose instructions' participants were told to only write down what they were sure they remembered 'fact for fact' (p. 41).

They used Bartlett's method of serial reproduction and *War of the Ghosts* as their stimulus but had the participants reproduce the story *immediately* after they heard it. Given their interest in showing that reconstruction is not characteristic of remembering, it would have been worthwhile to provide a longer interval before reproduction or preferably they could have used the method of repeated reproduction to see changes after increasing time intervals. Moreover, Gauld and Stephenson (1967) operationalized 'reconstruction' by counting only extreme deviations from the original – what they called 'errors.' These did not include many of the changes that Bartlett attended to, such as omissions, word substitutions (e.g., 'boats' to 'canoes'), time order changes, and place name mistakes. With their strict instructions, the limited time interval before reproduction, and the narrow definition of 'errors' as a mark of reconstruction, it is little surprise that they found few 'errors.' Yet errors were produced in their study. To account for this, they showed that there was an inverse correlation between a person's *conscientiousness* and his production of *errors*. Again, the assumption is that memory is pure until contaminated by other influences; where the loose instructions do not explain errors, it was assumed to be the fault of an unconscientious personality. Unfortunately, the results are only presented as aggregate data and thus we have no way of knowing the kinds of errors that did occur (see 'think description' as a method of quality assurance earlier).

Gauld and Stephenson (1967) concluded that "We feel that our experiments to some extent undermine Bartlett's theory of the reconstructive nature of remembering" (p. 48). They proposed that 'errors' in remembering are mainly the result of "pressure to produce something completed and coherent" (p. 48). Their study shows that under particular social conditions – in this case, strict task instructions – remembering can be done with high accuracy. However, these results can be seen to further confirm Bartlett's theory of remembering, rather than disprove it. In an unpublished reply to Gauld and Stephenson (1967), Bartlett commented, "I did not say, I think I did not imply that literal retrieval is impossible, but I did imply that it requires special constricting conditions" (Bartlett, 1968b, p. 3). In fact, Bartlett gives several examples in *Remembering* (1932/1995) of exceptional memory for details, such as the 'prodigiously retentive capacity' of Swazi herdsman for their cattle (see Ost and Costall, 2002; chapter 5).[33] Rather than understanding memory as an isolated mental faculty, he saw it as domain-specific process that was socialized by the group. Social and contextual conditions are always present, some of which promote literal recall and others construction. Furthermore, Bartlett positively valued 'construction' as demonstrating flexibility and creativity in remembering, while Gauld and Stephenson (1967) saw it only as 'error.'

Gauld and Stephenson's (1967) experiment had the effect of putting an end to replications of Bartlett's experiments for over two decades.[34] It also led memory researchers in the 1990s to believe that Bartlett's experiments had never been replicated (see, e.g., Bergman and Roediger, 1999[35]; Schacter, 1996, p. 320[36]). All the earlier replications, discussed in this section, had apparently been forgotten. Furthermore, a study by Wynn and Logie (1998) seemed to also disconfirm Bartlett's theory in relation to remembering 'real-life' situations rather than folk stories: they had first-year undergraduate students repeatedly reproduce events from the first few days of orientation and found little forgetting over time and very few errors. Within this context, Bergman and

Roediger (1999) aimed to provide a demonstration that Bartlett's repeated reproduction studies could be replicated. Their study is much more convincing than Gauld and Stephenson (1967) in two respects: first, they used the method of repeated reproduction (with reproduction intervals after 15 min, 1 week, and 6 months). Second, they adopted a more refined coding scheme that classified items as 'accurate,' 'omitted,' 'major distortion,' or 'minor distortion' (i.e., surface level changes that do not change the meaning of phrase). They also had experimental conditions for 'loose' and 'strict' task instructions. While the loose instructions did seem to have an effect on the first reproduction, on the second reproduction a week later there was no difference when compared to the strict instructions. In both conditions, they found that over time significantly less was remembered and of what was remembered a growing percentage was 'majorly distorted.' Thus, they could not find support for Gauld and Stephenson's (1967) claim that loose instructions were the cause of reconstruction. At the same time, they demonstrated Bartlett's experiments could be replicated within contemporary quantitative conventions of experimentation.[37]

Although more convincing, Bergman and Roediger's (1999) study continues to follow Gauld and Stephenson (1967) in the assumption that reconstruction means 'distortion' and that it should be studied through a comparison of group averages. A study of 'accuracy' and 'distortion' can lead to conclusions about failures of memory against the standard of strict reproduction – that is, what memory is not, not what it is. Likewise, the methodological problem with simply comparing aggregate scores across the three time conditions is that one cannot see holistic changes occurring in the series. This requires attending to a particular participant's series of reproductions as Bartlett had done. A recent study by Wagoner and Gillespie (2014) brought back the focus on qualitative transformations and took it a step beyond Bartlett by not only comparing qualitative changes through a series of reproductions but also exploring the process by which reproductions were produced at each reproduction. They had dyads remember *War of the Ghosts* together so as to externalize some of the spontaneous processes of remembering. Participants did not simply output fully formed memories but constructed them through an extended process of making suggestions and evaluating them, posing questions and answering them. Importantly, this constructive process need not lead to inaccuracy. Consider the following example:

Henry: Ok, so, there were two guys hunting
Bill: No, no, no. There were two guys looking for seals
Henry: They were hunting seals.

It is only through disagreement and mutual suggestion that the dyad arrives at what was in the original. The participants do not passively take over the other's suggestion but rather use it to construct a counterpoint. The process is constructive because it involves actively cajoling and managing remembering as it unfolds. The study also found new ideas being added to the story, but importantly these were not coded simply as 'errors'; rather they were analyzed as revealing something about the process of remembering. For example, several participants added the idea that the protagonist of the story was himself a ghost. There is nothing to directly suggest this in the original and it does not show up in Bartlett's data. The authors conjecture that participants remembered using a narrative template taken from recent Hollywood films about ghosts (such as the *Sixth Sense* and *The Others*[38]), in which there is a surprise ending where the main character realizes he or she is a ghost. Applying this narrative template to *War of the Ghosts* helps rationalize and explain some of the puzzling elements of the story. Thus, 90 years after Bartlett's studies we find participants using different cultural resources to help them remember the story and in doing so they change story in a new direction. This points to the importance of situating an experiment within the broader social and cultural world to which the participants belong.

The twenty-first century also brought renewed interest in Bartlett's method of serial reproduction as a powerful tool to study cultural transmission and transformation. Kashima (2000a) used a story of a man and a woman to explore gender stereotypes in a five-person reproduction chain. He found that participants in earlier positions of the chain tended to reproduce stereotype-inconsistent information, but toward the end of the chain stereotype-consistent information was better retained. This shows important differences between individual and collective remembering (where information is transmitted through several individuals). Similarly, Bangerter (2000) used a scientific description of sexual reproduction to explore how science is transformed into common sense when it is passed through the general public – a central topic of the social representations theory, itself inspired by Bartlett's work (Chapter 3). Through the chain, sperm and egg cells became increasingly anthropomorphized: sperm were described as active and the ovum as passive. In other words, the text was transformed to conform to gender stereotypes of male and female roles in courtship. This study brings back an analytic focus on the *direction* of change introduced into reproductions rather than simply coding for accuracy and distortion. Mesoudi and Whiten (2004) used the method to show how everyday events tend to be described at higher levels of abstraction as they were transmitted through the chain, and in another study Mesoudi, Whiten, and Dunbar (2006) demonstrated a bias for social over nonsocial information in serial reproduction. Finally, Nahari, Sheinfeld, Glicksohn, and Nachson (2015) set out to answer whether there was a qualitative difference in chains starting off with low accuracy versus those starting off with high accuracy. They found the first reproductions influence inter-chain trends but not their end points. Their study is also interesting in that they aimed to develop an integrative methodology (i.e., 'trend analysis'), which was quantitative but at the same time sensitive to holistic, dynamic, and process changes.

Conclusion: Rethinking the Experiment

Bartlett's experimental methodology started from the principle of complexity: we cannot adequately study human responses by stripping them down to the simplest possible elements, as Ebbinghaus had done in his method of nonsense syllables. Instead, the experimentalist must work in a systematic way with whole complex human beings, which includes their history, interests, feelings, group affiliations, aspirations for the future, etc.[39] His metaphor of the experimentalist as a clinician nicely highlights this orientation to the whole human being. Moreover, he wanted to capture qualitative changes in reactions over time as a result of new experiences and to account for how social context shaped the results. This holistic focus is lost when responses are itemized and aggregated in order to discover relationships between variables in a large sample of subjects.[40] Bartlett (1923, p. 23) distinguishes his own approach from this when he says, "[t]he man who knows intimately but one mental life will the sooner enter others, than the man whose observation has grasped the external form and movements of thousands of people, but has gone no further." According to the earlier assumptions about experimentation, the road to general knowledge about human beings is through the detailed analysis of contextualized single cases rather than group averages (cf. Salvatore and Valsiner, 2010). Given the differing assumptions about methodology, it is not entirely surprising that contemporary experimentalists have referred to Bartlett's studies as pseudo-experiments. In the first decades of the twentieth century whether these were experiments would not have been doubted. To turn the issue around, early twentieth-century psychologists would have found contemporary methods problematic because they questioned the application of inferential statistics to a large sample for the investigation of individual functioning (Danziger, 1990).

The progressive transformation of Bartlett's experimental methodology (and by implication many other early experimental studies) can be clearly seen in the replications and extensions of his studies. These changes can themselves be analyzed as a serial reproduction study which powerfully illustrates Bartlett's theory of reconstruction: each replication assimilates Bartlett's studies to their own preexisting understandings and highlights a particular aspect of the original, which leads to major omissions and transforms of the whole when it is reproduced. While early replications and extensions focused on the role of group membership in remembering, by the 1950s the focus shifted to individual memory as a cognitive process. Moreover, aggregate statistics replaced the presentation of the particular qualitative changes introduced into reproductions. Although the initial studies at this period coded for a number of different kinds of qualitative changes (e.g., leveling and sharpening), these became subsumed under the more general and abstract category of 'distortion' or simply 'error.' Around the same time, this was also happening in research on thinking (see Chapter 6). This change coincided with a reinterpretation of 'reconstruction' to mean that memory was prone to error. As such it became negatively valued, whereas for Bartlett it was linked with flexibility and creativity. At a methodological level, Bartlett's notion of 'reconstruction' implies the need to study the process of remembering rather than simply its outcomes, as is typically done in memory experiments today. Error and distortion are outcome measures done against the standard of literal reproduction; they can tell us what memory is not, but not what it is.

Contemporary experimental psychology need not exclude studies like Bartlett's from its remit. The automatic labeling of Bartlett's experiments as 'pseudo-experiments' is what Bartlett (1918) called 'conventional criticism,' whereby something is rejected simply because it does not fit familiar conventions. Qualitative and idiographic experiments in fact have a rich history in psychology, and as such can offer valuable methodological insights today (Wagoner, 2009). What these approaches provide is the possibility of systematically probing the different sides of a contextualized and concrete phenomenon in order to reveal its structure. Bartlett did this by varying the conditions and tasks of his experiments (e.g., drawing, interrogation, written or oral recall), employing a diversity of materials (e.g., abstract shapes, concrete objects, ambiguous material, faces, representative signs, folk stories, and newspaper texts), and using different data sources. For example, Bartlett's task-oriented dialogues with his participants provided him with their affective–interpretive background against which their written reproductions were made. He was frequently able to anticipate a change that would happen in the next reproduction based on their comments. Furthermore, his open analysis of reproductions enables him to explore a range of different kinds of transformations and what conditions them. In this logic of discovery, the analysis becomes an *abductive* process, whereby data and theory continually enrich one another through the insight of the researcher. Rather than simply confirming or disconfirming some hypothesis, this research strategy allows a broader range of factors to be brought in and thus novelties to emerge in the analysis.

To include this flexible and qualitative investigation of a research object, we can redefine a psychological experiment in an open way: an experiment is a social intervention into a person's life for the purposes of systematic exploration of an underlining structure (cf. Bartlett's own description of 'experimental thinking' – Chapter 6). Within this definition, an experiment need not involve manipulation or strict control of conditions to uncover causal relations. In fact, the experimenter can control only some aspects of the situation (Valsiner, 2000). Participants arrive in the experimental situation with a certain history, mood, and character, and are themselves constructive in making sense of the experiment and deciding how to be involved in it. A qualitative experiment, as practiced by Bartlett and others, attempts to explore the role of all of these kinds of factors by structurally varying them and observing the results on the research object (Kleining, 1986). In this way, it combines the systematic setting variation of quantitative studies with the observation and near-to-subject, phenomenologically rich insights typical of qualitative research. This open approach has informed some of the classic experiments in psychology, such as those done by the Würzburg School, Gestalt psychology, Piaget, and Bartlett; its rediscovery by psychology today is long overdue.

Notes

1. Winston and Blais (1996) demonstrate that natural science textbooks tend not to define an 'experiment' at all.
2. Kleining (1986) has earlier described 'qualitative experiments' in relation to the Würzburg School, Gestalt psychology, and Piaget's developmental studies. According to him, this form of experimentation operates by a logic of systematic variation in a controlled setting while at the same time remaining close to the phenomena of interest through exploration of single cases; this allows the experimentalist to discover the underlining 'structure' of the research object. Bartlett's own experimental methodology fits squarely within this definition.
3. Middleton and Edwards (1990b) also demonstrated this by leaving a tape recorder running after the experimental task was completed by participants. During the experiment, participants focused on accurately describing and ordering events of a film, whereas their post-experiment discussion shifted to their feelings and evaluation of it.

4. This technique was later mastered by the Second Leipzig School of psychology, which they called *Akualgenese*. Interestingly, their key phrase 'striving for the whole' comes very close to Bartlett's own 'effort after meaning.' However, I have not discovered any evidence of a direct influence between them. Instead, these ideas seem to be a part of the *zeitgeist* of early twentieth-century psychology.

5. The notion of 'anticipation' in perception would become central in Bartlett's study of complex skill (Chapter 6).

6. In the painting, we see young Arthur, the rightful heir of the throne, plead with Hubert not to blind him, as he has been instructed to do by Arthur's usurper uncle King John.

7. This tendency toward multiplication of a particular feature had been identified by Haddon as a key mechanism of cultural *elaboration*, and as the characteristic device of the decorative mind.

8. He may have meant to write 'wearing' instead.

9. There is a phenomenon called 'hypermnesia,' in which memory will actually improve when reproductions happen at short intervals from one another (see Wheeler and Roediger, 1992).

10. This experiment was first published as 'the functions of images' (Bartlett, 1920b) and thus was originally conceived by him to be focused on the process of imagining, though the boundary with remembering was an arbitrary one for him.

11. Interestingly, Bartlett (1916b) opens his *Dissertation* with this quotation from R.L. Stevenson on memory of faces: "Faces have a trick of growing more and more spiritualised and abstract in the memory until nothing remains of them but a look, a haunting expression, just that secret quality in a face that is apt to slip out under the cunningest painter's touch" (p. 1).

12. For example, for one face he asked: "(1) Which way does he look? (2) Was he smiling? (3) Was he getting old? (4) Did you see both ears? (5) Had he a square chin? (6) Did you notice the cap? (7) Was it round, without a peak? (9) Did you notice the ribbons? (10) What was the name on the cap in black or in white? (11) Was the cigarette half-smoked? (12) Had he an open front to his uniform?" (Bartlett, 1916b, p. 43).

13. As such, this could be seen as an early experiment on memory suggestibility (see, e.g., Loftus, 1975).

14. This was the colloquial name for a common soldier during the First World War in Great Britain.

15. See Beals (1998, pp. 19–24) for a comparison of Bartlett's and Boas's versions of the story.

16. Bartlett also tried presenting the story orally to subjects.

17. Kay (1955) later tested whether participants could correct their mistakes by allowing them to see the original after their reproductions. He found that even under these conditions participants continue to reproduce the story as they had on the first reproduction.

18. The game has been given different names in different countries, which itself illustrates the process of conventionalization. It has also been called 'Russian scandal.'

19. Recently, Roediger, Meade, Gallo, and Olson (2014) has quantitatively compared results of repeated and serial reproduction of word lists. Unsurprisingly, they found much greater forgetting and distortion of the material with serial reproduction than with repeated reproduction.

20. This principle also partly explains how his own experimental work was transformed by others after him (see 'replications and extensions' later).

21. Social representations theory has also described how expert theories are introduced to the lay public when they are transformed in such a way that they lose connections they had in the original (see Chapter 3).

22. Bartlett saw friends as preferable subjects than strangers: "Many of the subjects who submitted to the tests were personal friends, with whose manner of life, and general outlook I was pretty well acquainted. This I consider to be not unimportant, for it frequently helped me to interpret results with fair certainty of accuracy ... Often a few trials with well-known subjects afford more suggestive and reliable material than a great deal of indiscriminate experimentation upon strangers" (1916b, p. 32).

23. Later Bartlett (2010[1959]) says statistics may provide a *structural description* but do not address problems of *process*.

24. Billig (2013) has recently critiqued experimental psychology's rhetorical use of aggregates by pointing out the frequent slippage between what happened on average for a group of subjects and what happened for each subject in the group, which was Bartlett's interest. Molenaar (2004) has recently made the same arguments.

25. Gigerenzer (2004) argued that null hypothesis testing has more in common with ritual than scientific thinking.

26. The extent of Bartlett's (1932) systematic social group comparisons is confined to two reproduction chains of Indian participants, which he analyzes in light of what he has found with English participants (pp. 138–46). He finds that the Hindu subjects are more likely to adorn and elaborate the story as well as give it a characteristic moral as found in Hindu tales. Although this cultural comparison is limited, Bartlett is constantly stressing the influence of group membership and conventions on reproductions.

27. Klugman (1944) used the method of serial reproduction to study 'memory for position, among children' by having them copy the position of a dot on a sheet of paper. He compared "boys and girls; the white and coloured children; older and younger subjects; and those of higher and lower mental ability (as measured by I.Q.)" (p. 23) but found no significant differences between these groups.

28. As part of a 2-year traveling scholarship received upon finishing his Ph.D. in 1922, Allport worked with Bartlett in Cambridge, as well as with Stern and Koffka in Germany. His research on rumors clearly synthesizes Bartlett's approach and Gestalt psychology. Ward was a member of Bartlett's laboratory.

29. Other serial reproduction studies also used Gestalt terms to describe the changes seen through a series of reproductions (see, e.g., Tresselt and Spragg, 1941; Talland, 1956). Johnson (1962) also used the term 'sharpening' in his repeated reproduction experiment (see later).

30. In finishing this chapter, I discovered one exception to this. In 1956, Talland published a study on 'cultural differences in serial reproduction,' in which he compares how different national groups (viz. France, Britain, Italy, the Netherlands, Sweden, and the United States) changed a range of texts representing different interests. As with the earlier studies, Talland (1956) analyzes both qualitative and quantitative changes. He uses a varied terminology from Bartlett and Gestalt psychology in analyzing changes (e.g., assimilation, sharpening, leveling, reversals).

31. Bartlett (1932/1995, p. 83) earlier said, "The most general characteristic of the whole of this group of experiments was the persistence, for any given subject, of the 'form' of his first reproduction."

32. This is in line with Gomulicki's (1956) study of the immediate reproduction of short passages, which was being done at the same time in the Cambridge laboratory under the supervision of Zangwill. Contrary to Bartlett's theory, Gomulicki argued that abstractive processes could explain selective omissions.

33. In his reply to Gauld and Stephenson (1967), Bartlett (1968b) adds that "Apart from laboratory experiment, moreover there are a number of well-known special circumstances in which accurate remembering is demanded, for example, in 'learning by heart,' in many school, university and technical examinations, of witnesses in a court of law, and in other cases not difficult to identify" (p. 3).

34. One exception to this was Haque and Sabir's (1975) small serial reproduction study of national stereotypes in the context of the Indo-Pakistani conflict.

35. Bergman and Roediger (1999) claim, "Bartlett's (1932) famous repeated reproduction experiments, in which he found systematically increasing errors in recall from the same person tested over time, have never been successfully replicated" (p. 937).

36. Gauld and Stephenson (1967) themselves had made the much more modest argument that no one had reproduced Bartlett's experiments in such a way to eliminate the production of 'errors' through guess work.

37. Other studies have since been done along the same lines: For example, Ahlberg and Sharps (2002) used the method of repeated reproduction to compare long-term memory in young and older adults.

38. Find descriptions of the films on Wikipedia: https://en.wikipedia.org/wiki/The_Sixth_Sense and https://en.wikipedia.org/wiki/The_Others_(2001_film) (Accessed: July 23, 2015).

39. This is not to say we should have a loose, 'anything goes' attitude to an experiment; rather it is to be always aware that we are dealing with whole human beings rather than isolated reactions. The feature of systematic variation and testing of boundaries remains an important characteristic of an experiment.

40. Danziger (1997) describes in detail how the notion of 'variable' became the new 'meta-language' for psychology around the 1950s, at which time aggregate scores were shown in the majority of research reports in psychology.

3   Cultural Diffusion and Reconstruction

> Every normal man's activities are to a large extent socially determined,
> and whether he is aware of it or not, are directed towards the perpe-
> tuation and development of the complicated systems of culture charac-
> teristic of social groups. Consequently, the psychologist is as interested
> in culture problems as the ethnologist and the sociologist and he has
> his own special contributions to make towards the study of the growth,
> distribution, maintenance, and transformation of culture patterns.
>
> (Bartlett, 1926, p. 769)

Bartlett's experiments powerfully demonstrated the psychological dimensions of cultural diffusion, but largely left aside the role of social interaction and group dynamics. Being well aware of this limitation, he began
to sketch out a broader social psychological theory of the conditions and
processes through which culture is reconstructed and diffused within
and between social groups. His approach differs from the majority of
contemporary approaches to cultural transmission (e.g., memetics) in
that it (1) focuses on an investigation of the complex dynamics of concrete single cases, (2) aims to explore the transformation of culture rather
than simply predicting the likelihood of transmission, (3) highlights individual and group agency in this process, as well as (4) focuses on the
history, traditions, and norms particular to different social groups.[1]
His holistic approach builds primarily on the ideas of early diffusionist
anthropology. In this framework, culture is conceptualized as heterogeneous, systemic, and changing patterns of activity mediated both by individual and group processes as well as by material objects. Furthermore,
any society must be conceptualized in time, existing in a state of tension
between stability and change, conservation and construction. A major
catalyst for change is 'culture contact,' whereby new cultural elements
are introduced into a social group from outside, stimulating constructive
efforts to integrate them into its ways of life.

As with the study of cultural dynamics itself, to understand early
diffusionist ideas they must be placed in historical and social context.
Thus, this chapter begins by providing some background in Cambridge

anthropology between 1890 and 1912. It was in dialogue with this background that Bartlett developed his own diffusionist approach that he presented in his first book in psychology, *Psychology and Primitive Culture*. This chapter proceeds to outline Bartlett's framework for exploring cultural dynamics, according to which the investigator should focus on the systemic conditions that shape individual and group responses; these conditions include a whole individual, belonging to a particular social group and acting in a particular social and material environment. This framework is then applied to the study of 'cultural contact' (where groups are in intimate contact with one another) and 'cultural borrowing' (where foreign cultural elements are carried by single individuals to a receipt group). The results of these intercultural contacts will depend on a number of factors, including the symmetry of relationship between the groups concerned and the social organization particular to them. A discussion is then made of how this framework can be extended so as to apply it to contemporary society, focusing on Bartlett's book *Political Propaganda*. Finally, Moscovici's Theory of Social Representations is described as a contemporary extension of Bartlett's diffusionist ideas.

From Cultural Evolution to Diffusion

The cultural evolutionary approach, the predecessor of diffusionism, dominated anthropological thinking from the nineteenth century through the first decade of the twentieth century. This approach aimed to map cultural differences onto a single line of cultural development that progressed in stages from simple to complex culture, culminating in European scientific culture. The collective project of anthropology scholars was to describe the different stages of humanity's cultural evolution. For example, in his *The Golden Bough* (1890), the Cambridge philologist James Frazer (1854–1941) described in great detail similarities in magic and religion in widely diverse 'primitive cultures' around the world, so as to chart societies' evolution from magic through religion to science. Two years earlier, Oxford anthropologist Edward Burnett Tylor (1832–1917) had put forward a statistical method to chart out the stages of cultural evolution from information provided by missionaries and colonial officials. He found advancement from polygamy to monogamy, matrilineal to patrilineal descent, nomadic life to permanent settlement, homogeneity to class hierarchy and role differentiation, and polytheism to monotheism. When a cultural item did not fit the stage at which the society had reached, Tylor argued that it was a 'survival' from an early stage. Moreover, when information was missing about a society he argued that the anthropologist could justifiably fill in the gaps with knowledge of other societies at the same stage of development. This was possible because each stage constituted a holistic cultural 'complex' and all societies progressed in the same direction through uniform stages, though at different rates.

The evolutionary scheme was upheld by the assumption of 'psychic unity': confronted with similar problems, all minds respond in a similar way. Accordingly, elements of culture were to be explained through individual psychological causes. For example, Frazer (1890) traces society's initiation ceremonies back to the individual's instinctual desire for food. Society was here understood in terms of the psychology of the individual writ large. Individual development was a process of socialization that recapitulated the cultural history of humanity up to the stage the group had reached, at which point individual members of the group further advanced its culture. As such, the cultural evolutionists emphasized the everyday inventiveness of humans rather than the spread of cultural innovations from a particular society as the diffusionists would do. Similarities of culture in different societies were understood to be the result of 'independent invention,' though they also acknowledged that diffusion of culture might happen between societies at the same evolutionary stage. Most of the time, however, progress in a society is achieved through the accumulation of small innovations made by individuals every day. This scheme was similar to the small modifications that constituted biological evolution in Darwin's influential theory, although the two theories differed in that the cultural evolutionary scheme was overtly teleological.

The cultural evolutionists' theories were developed primarily from reports made by missionaries and colonial officials. The notion of 'fieldwork' that we are familiar with today had not yet been developed. Frazer explicitly defended the division of labor between those who collect the data and the 'armchair' academic who uses it to construct theory. He was himself the prototype of this model, having hardly ventured out of England and certainly not to do fieldwork. In fact, Frazer played an important role in convincing Alfred Cort Haddon (1885–1940) to collect ethnographic data (which Frazer's theories depended on) during a trip to the Torres Strait to investigate marine biology. Frazer argued that whereas the marine life would be around for generations, the culture of the Torres Strait islanders would soon disappear as a result of European intervention in the region. Haddon followed Frazer's advice and soon after became fully engaged with anthropological research. His books *The Decorative Art of British New Guinea: A Study of Papuan Ethnography* (1894) and *Evolution in Art: As Illustrated by the Life*

Histories of Designs (1895) present a wealth of indigenous art which is organized by classificatory modes analogous to biologists' investigation of the distribution and evolution of different species (Roldán, 1992).

Beyond this, Haddon argued from a cultural evolutionary framework that there was a teleological progression in art from figurative representations of natural objects to geometrical and conventionalized patterns. Figure 3.1 displays variations of alligator designs among the Chiriqui of Central America, where it was a powerful symbol. The top series shows a number of simplifications to the alligator figure that ends in a symmetrical and geometrical pattern. Conventional designs produced by the Chiriqui often feature an alligator head and a tail at each end, giving the design a shape as can be seen in C and D in the top row (Haddon, 1895, p. 168ff). The middle, large figure is an elaborated version of this shape with ends on both sides that curve back into the design.

Figure 3.1.   Derivative alligator designs among the Chiriqui

These ends represent both the alligator tail and mouth. Valsiner (2014) has recently noted that spiral forms, similar to those found here, have been frequently incorporated into designs around the world to give them closure, as one also finds with ionic columns. Finally the bottom series illustrates how these conventional designs have themselves morphed into an abstract triangular pattern in which the part representing the animal's body disappears, as can be seen in the final design of the series (F). The triangles are then 'reduplicated' or 'multiplied,' as Bartlett had also found in his experiments using visual material (Chapter 2).

In 1898, Haddon organized a large Cambridge expedition to the Torres Strait in order to collect a breadth of data on its people and their culture. In the interdisciplinary team of experts he assembled, Haddon stressed the importance of psychologists. The Cambridge polymath W. H.R. Rivers originally declined to participate but on hearing that his two best students, C.S. Myers and W. McDougall, had been recruited he changed his mind. All three were initially trained in medicine but had an interest in psychology (Rivers was considered a leading experimental psychologist at the time for his work on vision and would go on to contribute to a number of other areas, while Myers and McDougall would later become distinguished in organizational and social psychology, respectively). They were to handle the psychological component of the expedition, which aimed to experimentally test the then current European belief in the superior sensory capacities of 'uncivilized' peoples (and by implication of lower intelligence), a belief fashioned from circumstantial missionary reports of native's incredible perceptual feats. This was to be the first rigorous cross-cultural study ever conducted. Responsibilities for investigating each of the special senses were distributed between them: Rivers studied vision, Myers studied audition, smell, and taste, and McDougall studied touch and weight discrimination.

The results of these experiments were somewhat mixed. McDougall found differences in tactile acuity using the 'two point test,' whereby two pin points are applied to the skin and moved further apart until the subject experiences them as two points rather than one. However, there were intermediate qualities between one and two points, such as 'dumbbell'- or 'line'-shaped sensation. This would explain the variation within the Torres Strait islands estimates, and their on-average superior performance could be explained by their interpretation of the experiment as a competitive task, which was different from a European's understanding of the task instructions (Richards, 1998). In contrast to McDougall, Myers found that the Torres Strait islanders, in comparison to Europeans, had inferior auditory acuity. This was probably the result of

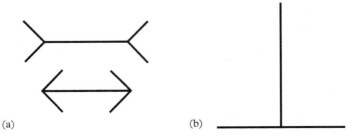

(a)   (b)

Figure 3.2.   Müller-Lyer illusion (a) and horizontal–vertical illusion (b)

their habit of pearl diving. However, it did not seem to interfere with their everyday use of audition. Finally, Rivers found differences in visual acuity but was clear that these differences were too slight to confirm the belief in the natives' extraordinary sensory capacities. With regard to color perception, he found that the islanders were generally more sensitive to red and less sensitive to blue than Europeans, but were otherwise capable of similar color discriminations. This finding was important in that it provided evidence against the notion that the limited color vocabulary of 'primitives'[2] was indicative of an inability to discriminate colors and thus helped to theoretically differentiate biology from culture.

Rivers also tested the natives' susceptibility to visual illusions. It was thought that 'primitives' would either be easily fooled by such illusions as a result of their inferior intellect or not be fooled at all due to their attention to sensory details. In fact, the islanders turned out to be less susceptible to the Müller-Lyer illusion and more susceptible to the horizontal–vertical illusion (Figure 3.2). Clearly, these were two different 'sets' of illusions. Rivers thought that the horizontal–vertical illusion was based on physiological differences and the Müller-Lyer illusion was based on psychological ones. Much later, this difference would be explained by perceptual training to meet the demands of particular environments: those living in 'carpentered' environments (with tables, chairs, and all kinds of corners) are susceptible to the Müller-Lyer illusion, whereas those spending time outdoors with long vistas (e.g., at sea) are susceptible to the horizontal–vertical illusion (see Segall, Campbell, and Herskovitz, 1966).

Rivers's Diffusionism

Rivers greatly enjoyed his time doing research in Torres Strait and afterward devoted himself to the emerging discipline of anthropology through further fieldwork in Melanesia, Egypt, Australia, and southwest

India.[3] Within the course of his investigations, he came to increasingly question the assumptions of cultural evolution. In 1911, he gave a lecture to the anthropology section of *The British Association for the Advancement of Science* explaining his 'conversion' to a diffusionist perspective. The diffusionist approach had itself migrated to England from Germany, where it was first developed by Ratzel, Graebner, and Schmidt. This approach saw a group's culture as a result of contact between different cultural groups rather than as an independent evolution. For instance, a society's transition from figurative to geometric decorative art designs would be explained through the history of contact with another group that had a convention of more geometric artistic designs, rather than by an evolutionary tendency as Haddon had done.

The diffusionists argued that a group's history of cultural contacts provides a better guide to how a culture had developed than a uniform evolutionary norm. The cultural evolutionary approach often led to erroneous conclusions about a group's cultural history. For example, it said that a group believing in *mana* (an impersonal supernatural force) was at the most primitive stage and would progress in the next stage to animism. Rivers (1911) pointed out that in some Melanesian groups he had worked with, it was likely that the earlier religion was animistic and that this was replaced when the natives came into contact with a group believing in *mana*. What cultural evolutionists considered as the more primitive form of religion had in fact been imported from outside replacing what they considered to be the more advanced cultural form. Furthermore, elements of a group's culture may also internally devolve if they lose their functional significance: Rivers (1912b) showed how different South Pacific groups lost the art of making canoes, pottery, or the bow and arrow.

Rivers further argued that cultures were not as unitary as the evolutionists made them out to be. Multiple different cultural beliefs and practices could coexist in the same society. For instance, in Melanesian society, Rivers (1914) found several different customs of disposing of the dead, which for him illustrated a history of diverse cultural contacts. Even more, some cultural forms only arise out of the interaction between two groups – that is, they did not exist in either group before their meeting and interchange. Following psychoanalytic theory, Rivers said that groups developed cultural forms that were 'compromise formations' bringing together two different and often conflicting cultural practices in a new cultural form. A society's culture must then be seen as the result of a 'blending' of different peoples. The question for him becomes what are the factors involved in the transmission and transformation of culture between peoples.

One important conceptual move was to see culture as having different levels, from social structure at the 'deepest' level to material culture at the 'shallowest' level, and language occupying a middle position between the two. Material culture could be easily changed when one group recognized a superior element of culture in the other – a good example is the quick adoption of European firearms by 'primitive' people. This kind of cultural change requires only a few migrants carrying the cultural item with them. In contrast, social structure – including marriage customs, kinship patterns, and group 'sentiments' – has a far more deep-seated character and changes only with the intimate blending of two peoples or the most profound political changes. As such, "it is with social structure that we must begin the attempt to analyze culture and to ascertain how far community of culture is due to the blending of peoples, how far to the transmission through mere contact or transient settlement" (Rivers, 1911, p. 395).

The above emphasis on social structure in Rivers's theory was itself influenced by contact with the ideas of Durkheim and his sociological school. This influence helped Rivers to make a departure from the individualistic psychology of cultural evolutionism. Durkheim argued that out of group interaction emerged social forms that were irreducible to individual processes within the group. He made the analog with the properties of H_2O: hydrogen and oxygen are flammable on their own but together as a molecule they can put out a fire. Just as properties found at the molecular level cannot be predicted from the atomic level, so too properties of groups cannot be predicted from the individuals in them. These group properties (such as customs, values, and traditions – in short, 'collective representations') exert a determinate influence on the thought and behavior of individuals in the group. While recognizing the importance and autonomy of 'social facts,' Rivers (1916) would not separate sociology and psychology as sharply as Durkheim; instead, he saw the two fields as developing a number of connections and mutually enriching one another.

Rivers also retained a more psychological perspective in his belief that individuals would regress to more primitive levels of functioning under certain environmental conditions. The physiological basis for the above was demonstrated in a well-known experiment by Rivers and Head (1908): Rivers severed a nerve in Head's arm in order to observe the process by which sensation returned to it over a period of 5 years. They found that first a holistic all-or-nothing sensitivity returned (i.e., *protopathic sensibility*), which registered blunt pressure on the skin but was completely insensitive to stimulation with cotton wool, pricking with a pin, and all degrees of heat and cold. Later, localized sensitivity (i.e., *epicritic sensibility*) returned and suppressed the influence of the former. Following the neurologist Hughling Jackson, they thought that the former was evolutionarily a more primitive response.[4] Likewise, on the Torres Strait expedition Rivers had recognized that the islanders' performance on a task was worse when they were fatigued or during certain times of day. These studies and others lead him to emphatically reject the more radical Durkheimian position of Lévy-Bruhl who claimed that the thought processes of 'primitives' were entirely different from Europeans (see later).[5] Individuals from any culture could regress to more primitive functioning under certain environmental conditions such as fatigue or in the extreme case of war.

Bartlett's Social Psychological Approach

Bartlett's approach follows Rivers in charting a middle way between different theoretical positions on the creation of culture and the mentality of 'primitives' (or what today would be called 'traditional' people). On the one side, he rejects the cultural evolutionary explanation of culture as originating in the minds of individuals, à la Frazer. On the other side, he accepts Durkheim and his school's stress on the importance of social factors without, as they did, asserting that individual psychological processes had a negligible influence on the shaping and sharing of culture. Moreover, Bartlett sees both similarities and differences between 'primitive' and 'advanced' peoples. According to him, all people have certain fundamental instinctual tendencies, which are universal components of mind. However, these fundamental tendencies operate interdependently with one another, group norms, and material engaged with in an individual's action and experience. Thus, the mental and cultural diversity of humankind has to be explained by how these tendencies are combined and put in relation to different environments and material. The basic unit of analysis in this scheme becomes the active individual embedded within a social and physical environment:

The individual who is considered in psychological theory, in fact, is never an individual pure and simple. The statements made about him always have reference to a particular set of conditions. The individual with whom we deal may be the-individual-in-the-laboratory, or – and in social psychology this is always the case – the-individual-in-a-given-social-group.

(Bartlett, 1923, p. 11)

The job of the psychologist is then to explore the conditions under which certain responses occur. The conditions set up by the social group to which the individual is a member are always present and of central importance. The struggle against the view of individuals as atoms unencumbered by the social-cultural world to which they belong continues to be a major point of critique in the social sciences today (see, e.g., Shweder, 1991; Taylor, 1989). In stressing social conditions, Bartlett was attempting to avoid the pitfalls of the cultural evolutionary approach, which explained culture by speculating about its origin in purely individual psychological processes. For example, the folk story had been explained as the outcome of an individual's contemplation of nature or "like the dream, springs from one or two deep-seated individual needs, or desires, or wishes" (Bartlett, 1923, p. 58). Both Frazer and psychoanalysis adopted this form of explanation. This explanation fails first because it is normally impossible to discover the absolute origin of a folk story and secondly because it ignores inescapable social influences. For a folk story to be transmitted or maintained within a 'primitive' community, it must be performed to an audience. The storyteller must make an appeal to their interests and ways of thinking in order to retain and bolster his own prestige. This dynamic facilitates conservation of the story when it is retold within a particular community. However, when a folk story spreads from one community to another it is usually transformed in order to appeal to new audiences. Bartlett uses Boas's (1901) work on Native American folk tales to illustrate how the 'same' story morphs into different forms as a function of the community to which it enters. He shows how the story's characters, their relations to one another, and the moral conveyed change from one community to the next. In all this we find that "it is not the institution that is derived from the story but the story from the institution" (Bartlett, 1923, p. 61).

Even outside the direct presence of the social group, the individual is unconsciously influenced by his or her group's 'cultural patterns' or 'conventions.' Bartlett gives the example of the Dahomey artist who is convinced that he is creating a new design. In fact, the artist is following a number of conventions, such as the need to put a kink in each curve, rather than to make them smooth, and for the figure to possess a certain harmony of outline and balance of parts, which are characteristics to the social group he belongs (p. 12). Thus, we cannot fall prey to thinking of individual experience and action in pre-social terms, outside the traditions of his or her social group:

It is only if we interpret individual to mean pre-social that we can take psychology to be prehistoric. The truth is that there are some individual responses which simply do not occur outside a social group. To look for these outside such a group is to court failure, and leads inevitably to speculation and guesswork. (pp. 12–13)

The notion of the 'social' used here is markedly different from the one used in contemporary psychology, which tends to focus exclusively on interactions between individuals, ignoring the broader social-historical context. In contrast, social scientists up to the early decades of the twentieth century defined the 'social' as the norms, values, and traditions specific to different social groups; properties that could not be reduced to the individuals in the group (Greenwood, 2003). Thus, when Bartlett speaks of 'the-individual-in-a-given-social-group' as a basic unit of analysis in social psychology, he is arguing for the need to situate individual action and experience within historically existing and developing cultural frameworks (cf. Taylor, 1989). All groups have conventions that are in many cases unique to them. Scientists can use a group's conventions as legitimate starting points in their analysis without having to explain them in themselves, as cultural evolutionists had done.[6] The methodology for such an approach becomes the 'intensive study' of particular social groups and their mentalities. Bartlett (1923) argues that general theory should be developed from the careful analysis of concrete single cases rather than simply from the abstract. He also practices what he preaches: *Psychology and Primitive Culture* is replete with extensive discussions of 'primitive' cultures from the North America, Africa, and Southeast Asia, demonstrating Bartlett's wide reading in anthropology. These studies are worked within their complex uniqueness in order to generate principles for describing and explaining cultural dynamics at a general level.[7] At the core of his general theory is the concept of 'tendency' to which we now turn.

From Instincts to Tendencies

To explore the interdependence of individual and group influences on the creation and diffusion of culture, Bartlett conceptualizes the individual as a dynamic system of 'tendencies.' Tendencies are psychological dispositions that are continuously being reorganized in relation to different contexts and material. Bartlett defines a tendency as,

an active prompting towards a given mode of response – whether cognitive, affective, or expressed in definite bodily movement – which arises when an individual is brought into touch with a situation and attends to it. The tendency must have material to work upon, there must be some definite situation apprehended; while for its part the material must be met by a tendency if it is to provoke a response.

(Bartlett, 1923, pp. 273–4)

The notion of tendency here implies a dynamic relationship between an individual and his or her environment, similar to what other theorists have called a 'transactive' approach (see also Chapter 4). Bartlett's 'tendency' was an extension of McDougall's 'instinct,' discussed in his *An Introduction to Social Psychology* (1908), which for many years was the most widely read source on the subject especially in England. Inspired by Darwin's evolutionary theory, McDougall made 'instincts' the central ingredients of his psychology. For him, instincts were innately determined 'psychophysical dispositions' which provide the drive behind the human mind's 'purposive' character. They should not be understood in terms of a rigid behavior sequence, but rather flexible patterns taking shape in particular environments. Through the instincts, McDougall aimed to give 'motivation' (the active part of the mind) its rightful place in the discipline of psychology.

Bartlett was sympathetic to McDougall's approach but criticized him for his focus on creating an exhaustive list of instincts rather than on emphasizing how they combine in individual and group behavior.[8] Bartlett was content to work with an incomplete set of instincts in his analysis of culture and only add others when it becomes necessary. He extends McDougall's 'instincts' to create a typology of 'tendencies,' which includes:

(a) instinctive tendencies; (b) other tendencies, also innate, but particular to the individual himself; (c) derived or constructed tendencies which, in the course of experience, are built up on the basis of (a) and (b). In the last class perhaps the most important of all are the tendencies to reaction which an individual absorbs or takes over directly from his social group.

(Bartlett, 1927c, p. 198)

Bartlett called the first group 'fundamental' tendencies, because they provide the foundation on which the other tendencies are constructed. The fundamental tendencies are innate and shared by all human beings. Examples are flight, repulsion, curiosity, pugnacity, construction, suggestibility, imitation, feeding, and parental and gregarious instincts. Some fundamental tendencies are immediately social, requiring a group for their expression (e.g., suggestibility), while others are not. Two different classes of the fundamental tendencies are particularly important to Bartlett's approach and will require more detailed explication.

First, 'the social relationship tendencies' include *dominance, submissiveness,* and *primitive comradeship.* When there is asymmetry of power and status in a social relationship, the higher-status individual or group takes on the *dominant* or *assertive* tendency, while the lower-status actor takes on the *submissive* tendency. The *dominant* actor has influenced through command and by making an impression on the other rather than being an expression of their way of thinking. In contrast, *primitive comradeship* is expressed in symmetrical social relationships. Here influence moves freely from both parties without force from either. Elsewhere, Bartlett calls this tendency 'friendship' and 'persuasiveness.' This group of tendencies is distinctly social in that they require a group for their expression. They are present in the relations between groups, between individuals in a group, and between an individual and his or her group (e.g., a leader).

A second class of important fundamental tendencies includes *conservation* and *construction*. "The conserving tendency provides a basis for the continuance of institutions, just as ... constructiveness gives us a basis for the formation of institutions" (p. 42). These tendencies are interesting in that they suggest situating individuals and groups dynamically in time. Stability is maintained through *conservation* which is oriented to the past, while change is brought about through *construction* which is oriented to the future. *Conservation* is supported by a "tendency of preferring the familiar to the unfamiliar" (p. 41).[9] At a group level, it is upheld by collective 'sentiments' toward established group symbols, such as religious objects, titles, uniforms, etc. (see later). In contrast, the *construction* tendency looks forward and is responsible for the creation of new cultural forms and social organization.[10] In short, conservation and construction are the dynamic mechanisms of stability and change.

The last class is the derived tendencies, of which I will only mention a subset that "the individual takes over directly from his social group." This brings into Bartlett's framework the inescapable influence of group conventions. Bartlett says, "[These tendencies] cluster about a group's established institutions and act directly as determining factors of individual social behavior" (p. 29). He calls them the 'group difference tendencies' to make an analog with 'individual difference tendencies' – groups, like individuals, have different mentalities. In *Remembering*, Bartlett renames them 'the group's preferred persistent tendencies.' It is important to note that he does not see these tendencies as necessarily opposed to biological tendencies, but rather as constructed from them. At the same time, he is emphatic that they are not reducible to individual processes. This idea of tendencies taken over from the group is similar to thinkers, such as von Humboldt, Cassirer, and Vygotsky; however, they differ from Bartlett in that they dealt with the issue by invoking some notion of language and symbolic mediation whereas he typically did not.

The typology of tendencies is useful for analytic purposes but it is important to keep in mind that the tendencies always operate together as a dynamic system. For example, if fear is called into play in a social setting in which the prevailing tendency is primitive comradeship it is likely to lead to panic, group disintegration or stampede. In contrast, if the social relationship tendency is that of dominance "the constructive [tendency] is likely to be immediately aroused, and therefore definite social mechanisms of persecution and cruelty, hardening into social institutions will appear" (p. 39). These examples describe the hierarchical organization of different tendencies, but there may also be conflict between them – for example, between the tendencies of curiosity and fear, comradeship and dominance, or conservation and construction, to name a few. On the one hand, when the antagonism among tendencies is strong, the opposing tendencies will have their expression limited to a particular sphere of activity or a recognized period of time. Social limitations on the expression of sexual or violent impulses to certain contexts are obvious examples. On the other hand, weak antagonism between tendencies tends to lead to their integration in new cultural forms, sometimes called 'compromise formations' (see earlier). For instance, friendly discussion between people with different points of view is highly conducive to the construction of new ideas. Lastly, tendencies can mutually reinforce one another in positive feedback loop without becoming integrated into a new form.

Group Organization

Characteristic groups and institutions grow up within the spheres of activity to which specific tendencies are limited within a society. These groups function to maintain the tendencies in question and guide their expression. Bartlett's (1925a) definition of a group puts tendencies at its core:

A group is *any collection of people organized by some common appetite, instinctive or emotional tendency, need, interest, sentiment, or ideal.* The essential character is the organization, and one of the best general ways of differentiating one group from another is by reference to the different typical organizing tendencies that are at work. (p. 347)

This definition includes broad social groupings, often referred to as 'cultures' or 'societies,' as well as differentiation within these groups, which he tends to refer to as 'special groups.' In both cases, a group is more than a half hazard collection of people; it is an *organization* of people around a particular tendency or set of tendencies. For example, several people sitting in the same compartment of a train are not yet a group, but if they start a conversation around a topic of mutual interest they become one. Tendencies constitute the group's *psychological* possessions.[11] These in turn create an interpretive background through which meaning can be given to its 'cultural elements' (e.g., objects, ceremonies, dances, decorative designs, and all kinds of institutions). Cultural elements then tend to function to reinforce the group's tendencies.[12] The particular set of tendencies that differentiate a group from others and the group's cultural elements together constitute its culture.

Bartlett (1925a) distinguishes between three types of social groups: *instinct*, *sentiment*, and *ideal*. These three types form a developmental sequence from which the new emerges out of the old, and the old continues to abide together in the new. At the most basic level is the *instinct* group, such as the food seeking group for satisfying hunger, the war group to express pugnacity, or the religious group which Bartlett believed is commonly linked with fear. Leaders emerge within the *instinct* group, who express most the tendency in question. For example, the climbers on an expedition to Mt. Everest quickly found themselves in a certain hierarchy based on motivation and ability in that activity.

At the next level is the *sentiment* group. Sentiments are complex and organized sets of emotions. In their social guise, they cluster around group institutions and play a key role in creating group solidarity, an idea that had earlier been articulated by Durkheim (1912). They also help to retain stability through time:

> Even if the group changes its membership, the institutions are maintained, and, being both interesting and persistent, they regularly become the center of sentiments. But sentiments are always turned chiefly toward the past ... They draw their strength from history. They depend on persisting features in group organization, and are apt to be the stronger, the more peculiar and clearly differentiated the group's special functions are. They help to stabilize all kinds of devices – uniforms, hidden formulae, catchwords, flags, symbols of every sort – for maintaining the past. Feelings are mental parasites. They must attach themselves to something, and preserve that to which they attach themselves with as little change as possible. Thus in a world which is in general ceaselessly moving, they constantly weaken their own hosts. The sentiment-governed individual and the sentiment-organized group both lose in adaptability what they seem to gain in inner cohesion. (1925a, p. 362)

Out of the sentiment group a third type of group can develop, called the *ideal* group. This group is practical and intellectual in its workings, though it retains a basis in feeling. Bartlett saw an example of this type in expert scientific groups and the League of Nations (renamed The United Nations). Unlike the *sentiment* group, which looks to the past, the *ideal* group is oriented primarily to the future. In other words, it is more *constructive* than *conservative*. "The sentiment maintains what has been and is, the ideal seeks to determine what will be. Nearly all vigorous and effective groups within the modern nation are mainly ideal groups; all nation groups are at present mainly sentiment groups" (p. 365).

The *sentiment* and *ideal* groups also differ in the type of leadership they support. The leader in the *sentiment* group garners his or her prestige through the *institution*. This is done with the use of institutional symbols, such as uniforms, titles, badges, and modes of address, which elicit group sentiment. These leaders have difficulty in deviating from the traditional requirements of their role and thus lack flexibility. In contrast, the leaders of the *ideal* group acquire their position as a result of their practical insight and ability to weave different factions into a common pattern. In short, they are of the *constructive* and *comradeship* type.

Every group in a society develops its own institutions which express and maintain the tendencies that differentiate it from other groups. The group receives a certain 'reputation' and 'prestige' within the broader community that is passed onto its members – thus, we need to consider the relations between groups. A reputation means that certain abilities and qualities immediately spring to mind when persons of that group are seen. This in turn makes members of the group more likely to display and exaggerate the abilities and qualities in question, such that they become *conventionalized* attributes of the group. Leaders within the group tend to most strongly display these attributes. A feedback loop emerges between the expectation of the community and display by its members, especially the leader. Such a stabilized social organization will be resistant to change. Even if the broader community tries to drive the group's tendencies out of social life altogether, the group's tendencies will simply go underground and only come to the surface again in moments of crisis, as can be seen in sudden religious revivals and outbursts of persecution. In the next section, we will consider what happens when two cultures come into contact and how these group dynamics shape the result.

Diffusion by Contact and Borrowing

Bartlett's primary interest was to explore the changes that ensue when two cultures come into contact with one another. Contact was the greatest stimulus of change for him, particularly when the groups concerned have radically different forms of social organization. He outlines three different kinds of contact, each of which set up distinct conditions for cultural diffusion: *contact*, *borrowing*, and *intercommunication*. *Contact* involves the migration of whole groups across long distances, carrying their cultural possessions with them. They settle in a new environment where they have a considerable influence on the culture of the indigenous group. This generally leads to the blending of two formerly distinct groups. In the case of *borrowing*, individuals travel from their home, where they become acquainted with the culture of another group. On returning home they bring with them foreign cultural elements, which they often try to introduce into the life of their home community. Finally, *intercommunication* involves two neighboring groups that are in regular contact with one another, assuring the steady flow of culture between them. It thus occupies an intermediate position between *contact* and *borrowing*. Bartlett does not elaborate on it.

Diffusion of culture by *contact* takes different directions depending on a number of factors, such as the social relationship tendency of the group (e.g., being inclined to peace or war), the groups' numerical proportions, differences in physical and cultural endowment (i.e., whether one group is perceived to have a superior culture), and the proportion of the sexes. The most important of these are the social relationship tendencies. When the two groups share an attitude of *primitive comradeship*, the result is likely to be the blending of culture. Knowledge gained of the other's culture will tend to lead to parts of it being adopted. For example, Rivers (1914) described how Melanesian society had incorporated a number of different ways of disposing of the dead through the various waves of contact with other people. In contrast, *dominance* of one group tends to lead to the displacement of the other.

There are, however, different types of dominance that need to be differentiated. The most extreme form of dominance is due to force of numbers leading to the extermination of the other. A more psychological form of dominance is when one group is perceived to have the more superior culture, in which case the other group will readily adopt it. However, the adoption tends to happen at the surface level of culture (i.e., material culture, ceremony, and designs) and not to the deeper level of social organization and the interpretation of these different elements, which will be resistant to change. Moreover, this adoption will be selective; it will depend on the particular tendencies in operation in the group, which are expressed as the group's distinctive 'cultural patterns.' These patterns grow and adapt to incorporate the new: "It is because the group is selectively conservative that it is also plastic" (Bartlett, 1923, pp. 151–2). Thus, the group retains stability through its flexibility.

Finally, one group might force the other to relinquish its culture to be replaced by the culture of the dominant group, which the other does not see as superior. This has generally happened with European efforts to convert 'primitive' groups to Christianity. In this process, the primitive's culture does not altogether disappear, but is driven underground or the old is retained by becoming the backdrop upon which the new cultural material (e.g., Christianity) is superimposed. For example,

Years after the Spaniards had conquered New Granada ... when the native Indians were all accounted Christian, and had taken over the religious paraphernalia of their conquerors, secret Indian shrines were sometimes found. In one of these was discovered, offered to the 'overthrown' idols, the cap of a Franciscan friar, a rosary, a priest's biretta, and a Spanish book of religious precepts. The new material had been assimilated, but its predominant, though hidden significance preserved the past.

(Bartlett, 1925b, p. 5)

These processes lead to the formation of symbols. Symbols are different from signs in that they have double or multiple meanings (Bartlett, 1924). They carry both a 'face' and an underlying 'hidden' value. The latter is generally characterized by sentiment, which helps to give symbols whatever stability they possess. In the above quotation, "the cap of a Franciscan friar, a rosary, a priest's biretta, and a Spanish book of religious precepts" stands for the hidden value of old religious beliefs.

Diffusion by *borrowing* takes a different route. Here an individual travels to another group and assimilates elements of that culture on the basis of his or her particular personality. The personality of the individual borrower is itself the result of a combination of different tendencies, including those taken over directly from the social group to which the individual belongs. Diffusion by borrowing is more influenced by individual psychological processes than diffusion by contact. It is personality that determines which aspects of the foreign culture are lifted out and brought back to the individual's own group, as well as how the individual borrower relates with his or her home group once he or she has returned to it. When the individual tries to introduce the new element of culture to his or her group, a new 'special group' will typically develop around the new item. This group then often comes into conflict with the wider community as it attempts to extend its sphere of influence. Bartlett gives the following example of a Native American man, who in 1901 started a religious cult within his own tribe after having encountered peyote on his travels to Oklahoma:

John Rave, a member of the Winnebago group, was a man of strong religious bias. Travelling eastwards from his home he came into touch with a new religious cult centering about the eating of the drug peyote. He took over many of the new practices, and returned to his home, where he introduced them amongst his friends. Subsequently the cult spread widely throughout the community, with Rave as a ceremonial leader. Outwardly novel, the cult represented in the main the persistence of the old. A fire mound was used. It was called Mount Sinai; it took the place of the old sacred mound of the Buffalo Dance.

The Bible was introduced. On the face of it the Bible was new, and carried the prestige of a higher civilisation. In actual fact it was treated exactly as any item of the old Winnebago ceremonial regalia had been treated. Rave's religious interest had been attracted by the new customs; his strong conservatism had placed them in close relation to the old practices. And his interpretations then became current owing to his position in the community.

(Bartlett, 1924, pp. 281–2)

Rave's personal interest in ceremony was the mechanism that 'lifted' the peyote out of the foreign group and brought it back to his home group. In his home community, Rave formed a special group around the peyote. Conflict with the community started when Rave wanted to expand the borders of the peyote cult. The expansion of the group required increasing its prestige within the wider community, which involved incorporating old cultural patterns into it and thus leading to the formation of symbols. For example, the fire mound took the face value of 'Mount Sinai' and the hidden value of the old sacred mound of the Buffalo Dance. When the community rejected the new cult Rave become more hostile to the old traditions, which paved the way for a more aggressive innovator named Hensley, who introduced the bible into the cult. The growth of the cult into a new cultural pattern was not planned by any single individual, rather it involved the unconscious weaving together of a number of scattered influences.[13] Bartlett (1923, 1928b, 1932/1995) calls this complex process 'social construction' or 'social constructiveness,' which we will return to later.

Some Principles of Cultural Change

Bartlett outlines a number of general principles that hold when cultural elements diffuse from one social group to another, most of which we have already encountered. First, elements of culture tend to travel much more quickly than their significance and thus while the elements themselves come from outside a group their interpretation typically grows up from within. Second, for a new element of culture to diffuse in a community it must be attached to existing tendencies or demands already widely found in the community. These tendencies will likely be different from the community from which the cultural element originated. Third, material culture tends to be adopted as a whole, while ceremonial culture is split up into separate pieces. Fourth, special social groups tend to grow up around new elements of culture (e.g., the peyote cult). Fifth, a group will develop its culture in such a way as to increase its prestige within the wider community and as such is constantly being influenced by the wider community. Sixth, diffusion involves processes of *elaboration* and *simplification* – these had earlier been discussed by Haddon (1894) – which are particularly important to Bartlett's argument (see also Chapter 2 for their use in interpreting Bartlett's experimental data).

Elaboration refers to the increasing complexity of culture, and thus the constructive side of diffusion. This can occur through the repetition of certain patterns, and by conscious or unconscious invention. Ornamental designs are good illustrations of this principle at work, often incorporating patterns of a foreign group into those of the home group. The opposing but complimentary process of *simplification* refers to the disappearance of details through their absorption into a more dominant detail, as has generally happened with the evolution of alphabets.[14] The best condition for *elaboration* is where a special group has a position of moderate dominance within the community and a close working relationship with it. *Simplification* tends to occur through either isolation or popularization. The former typically happens with ceremonial culture and the latter with material culture. In decorative arts, for example, expansion of the group with new members creates conditions for unskilled and careless copying of designs. Isolation may occur when the group secures a position of dominance in the community and makes little effort to widen its influence within the community.

In *Remembering*, Bartlett returns again to the issue of the general principles of cultural transformation in diffusion and provides an altered list of the processes involved, namely *assimilation, simplification, retention of apparently unimportant elements*, and *social constructiveness*. The first three in the list are primarily conservative processes. *Assimilation* refers to the part played by the existing cultural background of the group concerned. Any new cultural element must be linked to the cultural patterns of the receipt group if it is to be adopted. In this process, the new element is transformed to fit the group's cultural patterns while the patterns themselves flexibly adapt to the new content. Earlier, we saw how the natives of New Granada assimilated Christian objects to their old religious beliefs. Bartlett's (1932/1995) description of *simplification* remains the same as in his earlier discussion. He notes again that a process of *elaboration* often precedes and works in consort with it. Changes seen in decorative art and alphabetic script through time are prototypical examples. As with *elaboration* and *simplification, retention of apparently unimportant elements* was frequently found in Bartlett's (1932/1995) own experimental results (see Chapter 2). These retentions tended to exert a decisive influence on the direction of change the material underwent. Again, close parallels can be made with the diffusion of decorative art described by Haddon (1894).

Perhaps the most interesting in the list is the process of *social construc- tiveness*, which we have already encountered in the discussion of diffusion by borrowing. Social constructiveness points to the fact that groups not only have a past but also a *prospect* (i.e., a future orientation). Culture is transformed not only in the direction of already existing cultural patterns but "also positively *in the direction along which the group happens to be developing*" (Bartlett, 1932/1995, p. 275). The general outcome is usually the welding together of cultural elements from diverse sources into a new cultural form or social organization. This is what happened with the peyote cult described earlier, and is how Bartlett (1925a) characterized *ideal* groups, which become particularly important in modern society (see later). Bartlett (1932/1995) even characterizes sports teams as socially constructive in their creative and dynamic response to new chal- lenges in the game. The concept of *social constructiveness* thus synthesizes diffusionism's focus on spread of culture and cultural evolution's focus on the progressive growth of culture from within (see Bartlett, 1928b).

From Primitive to Modern Culture

Although Bartlett advances his argument through examples of primitive or traditional culture, he thought that his framework could also be used to study modern culture, though with certain modifications. At the end of *Psychology and Primitive Culture*, he attempted to describe the rela- tionship between primitive and modern culture. Bartlett wanted to avoid the radical separation of primitive and modern mentality famously described by Lévy-Bruhl. Lévy-Bruhl had argued that in contrast to the modern mentality, primitive thought is characterized as pre-logical, emotional, mystical, and self-contradictory. Primitives do not sharply distinguish themselves from other objects, but rather emotionally *parti- cipate* with them.[15] He famously described how members of a Brazilian Borono tribe claimed to be simultaneously a type of parrot and a human being. From a modern point of view, they were committing the logical error of contradiction. However, this does not mean that we should think of primitive mentality as inferior to modern. Following Durkheim and contra Frazer's notion of 'psychic unity,' Lévy-Bruhl argued that both primitive and modern mentality have their own inter- nal standards of thought and thus it is illegitimate for the modern anthropologist to privilege their own standards in the evaluation of pri- mitive culture. Each mentality is a distinctly *social* form of thinking, irre- ducible to individual psychological processes.

Bartlett accepts Lévy-Bruhl's Durkheimian argument for the need to include social causes in one's analysis but is critical of his way of doing this. First, Bartlett (1923, p. 289) comments, "the error ... is not that the primitive or abnormal are wrongly observed, but that the modern and normal are hardly observed at all." He goes on to say that Lévy-Bruhl compares the primitive to the scientific expert or philosopher rather than the everyday thinking of modern people. Secondly, primitive societies contain a variety of different thought styles (see Chapter 6), which change in relation to the topic (e.g., death, war, food, art). In other words, the same tendencies found in primitive society can also be discovered in the modern society, though not necessarily in the same contexts and in relation to the same material.[16] The notion of causality illustrates this point: "'Causal links' says Lévy-Bruhl, 'which for us are the very essence of nature, the foundation of its reality and stability, have no interest' for the primitive man: he is swayed by a 'kind of *a priori* over which experience exerts no influence'" (quoted in Bartlett, 1923, p. 289). Examples of establishing links and not establishing links in a causal chain can be found in thinking of both primitive and modern people. The range of thinking styles found in both cultures makes the sharp distinction between them untenable. As such, Bartlett argues that the basic processes of thought are the same for both primitives and moderns but their differing life conditions lead to the greater influence of certain tendencies:

There are ... two great differences between primitive and modern mental life. First the contents dealt with are different, and secondly the tendencies which deal with them are differently arranged. We, at our level, are perhaps less closely dominated by immediate vital needs, for the means of which these are to be secured have become to a large extent a part of the regular organisation of society ... we less readily yield ourselves to the sway of freely associated images, more often try to use some formulation which claims general and objective validity. But when the savage thinks, he thinks as we do. When we follow the flight of images our progress has the same characteristics as his.

(Bartlett, 1927c, p. 202)

Instead of a sharp qualitative difference between primitive and modern culture, Bartlett argues for a quantitative one. In his words, "we come from complexity [in primitive society] to yet greater complexity [in modern society]" (Bartlett, 1923, p. 256). The increase in complexity is mainly due to two factors: "the multiplication and division of specific groups, together with immense improvements in the mechanisms of inter-communication" (p. 256). As mentioned in the quotation, the differentiation of groups and their functions frees the individual from the need to focus on securing basic vital needs. Both the differentiation of groups and improvements in the means of communication between groups place the individual within a number of different groups which are in effective contact with one another. For the different groups to which the individual belongs the same element has different meanings, any of which can be pursued by the individual. This gives the individual a more independent status, increasing the possibilities of thought and behavior. Likewise, cultural material can be easily lifted out of one group and brought into another. These processes are already found in primitive groups but are further accelerated in modern society, creating new conditions for the free movement of thought, social constructiveness, and greater individual independence.

Bartlett also mentions the ascendency of a particular kind of leader in the modern world, which he calls 'representative man.' This leader stands in for his group in the negotiation with other representative men over policy that affects all their groups. Representative men are necessary in modern society because of the ever-larger social groups that must be coordinated. The representative man tends to be of a diplomatic type, who "expresses his group rather than impresses it" (p. 261). He is generally of the *comradeship* rather than *dominant* type in his relation with other representative men and members of the group he represents. Any decision or contract arrived at by the group of representatives is binding for all the groups to which they stand. Often a group breaks these contracts leading to accusations of deceit and immorality by others, but this outcome can also be explained from a social psychological perspective. Bartlett (1923) points out that "the behaviour of the representative man in the group which concludes the bargain, and his behaviour in the group which has elected him, are conditioned by different sets of factors" (p. 260). The traditions regulating the group of representative men are not the same traditions regulating their behavior with regard to their own group, and being of the *comradeship* type they are highly swayed by both influences.

Modern Culture and Political Propaganda

Bartlett continued to be actively interested in problems surrounding the contact of cultures throughout his life, though social and cultural aspects of his work took an increasingly more subordinate position after *Psychology and Primitive Culture*. Over his career technology improved rapidly, providing conditions for wider and faster intercommunication between groups. Individuals could more easily travel to distant parts of the world and cultural elements moved even faster through radio, film, and television. "The development of swift and easy forms of locomotion, the rise of a popular Press, the invention and universal use of the cinema, of wireless and of television, mean that no group can live to itself" (Bartlett, 1940, p. 3). These forces greatly accelerate diffusion, particularly diffusion by *borrowing*, where cultural elements are 'lifted' out of one society and dropped into another. As we saw earlier, while these cultural elements come from outside a group their interpretation grows up from within.[17] Bartlett's discussion of these broad social changes, however, remained in general more suggestions to follow up than fully worked out analyses. One exception is his book *Political Propaganda*, published in 1940 shortly after the start of the Second World War.[18] It offers an illustrative example of how Bartlett applied his approach to modern society as well as an interesting reflection on propaganda at the moment it was becoming a major political tool.

Bartlett's (1940) social psychological approach to propaganda is note-worthy in that it gives equal weight to both intelligence and emotion. He is critical of the assumption that modern mind is simply governed by intelligence as well as the assumption that the public is primitive, inferior, prone to forgetfulness, and ruled by emotions. The former position was widespread when he published *Psychology and Primitive Culture* and was his point of critique there. By 1940, the latter position had become ascendant and would be the primary focus of criticism in *Political Propaganda*. Bartlett develops his argument against Hitler and Goebbels's belief that the masses were unintelligent and should be con-trolled by a *dominating* elite – the word 'mass' itself comes from the metaphor of a potter shaping an inert piece of matter.[19] Bartlett points out that if the German public has these qualities it is only because the ruling political party keeps them in this state through censorship and coercion, and by requiring uniformity of opinion. This contrasts sharply with democratic propaganda, a point I will elaborate later.

This book begins with an exploration of the emergence of propa-ganda, which Bartlett (1940) traces to advances in mass media and education:

> The rapid development of effective contact between groups in contemporary society means that no important political, economic or other cultural change can take place anywhere which will not swiftly be treated as affecting the desti-nies of distant groups. The rise of popular education means that any major poli-tical, economic or other cultural change must be explained, or justified, to an ever-increasing number of people. These two movements together provide the setting and the fundamental conditions which have led to a terrible outburst of political propaganda.
>
> (Bartlett, 1940, p. 4)

With regards to education, Bartlett describes the efforts made by the Bolsheviks to make the largely illiterate masses literate so that they would be in a position to replace old habits with new ones deemed correct by the Communist Party. As Bartlett's theory of groups would predict, these efforts resulted in stimulating intellectual curiosity beyond the Party ideology. Thus, in the interests of retaining uniformity of opinion, totalitarian regimes combine education with strict censorship, dramatic persecution, and many forms of repression. Ultimately, Russia began to prefer more visual propaganda, such as film, picture posters, and art, which according to Bartlett (1932/1995) are less likely to stimulate analysis and critical distance than words. Italian and German Fascists developed similar tactics for totalitarian education, rewriting schoolbooks, controlling the press, and pitching their message to the lowest intellectual level. These efforts were particularly systematic in Germany.

In any social organization, the propagandist must pitch their message so that it connects up with the public's already existing tendencies if their efforts are to be successful, although education might be put in the service of creating new tendencies. There will always be certain aspects of a group's beliefs that are highly resistant to change while others are more open to it – Bartlett (1943, 1946b) called these the 'hard' and 'soft' features of culture, respectively. A thorough understanding of the particular cultural background of the audience is needed to identify where propaganda can be successful. This makes it much easier to create propaganda for the home group than a foreign group as currents in the culture can be much more easily 'intuited' in the former case. Even in the home group, the message will often be transformed in the process of communication. An extreme case of this is where the propagandist spreads rumors within a population (i.e., 'a whisper campaign'). The problem with this is that while rumors are easy to start, they are difficult to control; they readily transform in their transmission, often in surprising directions, as Bartlett's (1932/1995) serial reproduction experiments themselves show (Chapter 2). In the end, they may have the opposite effect to the one intended by the propagandist.

In addition to whisper campaigns, Bartlett analyzes a number of different methods used by the propagandist in order to shape public opinion. Some of these are of general utility when used in a certain way but nevertheless come with limitations. For example, humor can be successfully used if the propagandist is sufficiently acquainted with currents within the culture of his audience. For it to be effective the message must be pitched just beyond what has already become a routine joke, so as not to bore or offend the receiver. Another frequently successful method is the use of statistics. Even though the assumptions made about them are usually wrong, the use of statistics succeeds because numbers operate as symbols that have the aura of scientific fact. Symbols of all kinds can be highly potent in that their hidden value produces effects without the person ever becoming fully aware. For instance, the Italian fascists put images of a club, fist, or particularly square jaw next to verbal content in order to convey authority. There are other methods of propaganda, however, that often completely fail because of their assumption that the public is of low intelligence and forgetful. For example, lying and distortion generally only produces the desired effect in the short term, as it is likely to be called out by counter-propaganda, destroying the credibility of propagandist's group in the future. Other methods that pitch to the lowest intelligence, such as constant repetition and avoiding argument in preference for simple declarations, run the risk of boring their audience, so that they pay little attention to the message.

Bartlett argues that democratic propaganda operates with a different set of principles than totalitarian regimes: it allows for dissenting views, avoids the lie, and focuses on long-term rather than short-term effects.[20] Moreover, rather than keeping the public's intelligence at a low level and trying to get the bulk of people to accept wide generalizations without criticism, democratic propaganda allows for the free interplay of different points of view, so as to stimulate intelligence and independent thought – Bartlett (1923) had earlier described this in relation to modern culture (see earlier). Bartlett finds parallels between democratic propaganda and modern advertising, where multiple different messages are available and thus the sender must *persuade* the receiver. In short, while the democratic propagandist tends to be of the *persuasive* type, the totalitarian propagandist is *dominant* in relation to a *submissive* audience. Bartlett clearly favored democratic forms of propaganda and continued to believe in the power of words "to settle difficulties that arise when interdependent larger groups come into contact" (Bartlett, 1947a, p. 36). It is worth noting that whereas Rivers's social theory had authoritarian elements (of cybernetic hierarchical control) that fit colonial administration, Bartlett's (1923, 1940) social theory is thoroughly democratic in its focus on horizontal feedback loops.

Social Representations Theory as a Contemporary Diffusionist Approach

In contrast to Bartlett's widely discussed experiments on remembering (see Chapter 2), his theory of cultural dynamics has generally not been taken up. This is particularly unfortunate because it provides the broader framework to understand his early experiments – in particular, how 'conventionalization' is part of the wider social and cultural processes that have been described earlier in this chapter. Although Bartlett's theory of cultural dynamics represents the most systematically developed diffusionist theory, anthropology soon after became dominated by functionalism, which had less interest in this kind of diachronic analysis[21] – Bartlett (1946b, p. 154) himself continued to warn against the neglect of time and history in anthropology. Psychology, on the other hand, turned away from issues surrounding culture and society toward a more individualistic approach (Danziger, 2000; Farr, 1996; Greenwood, 2003), which was a far cry from Bartlett's unit of analysis 'the-individual-in-a-given-social-group.' One exception[22] to this trend was Moscovici's Theory of Social Representations, which owes a great deal to Bartlett's thinking. In fact, Moscovici had 'a pleasant conversation' with Bartlett at the *International Congress of Psychology* in Brussels in the fifties, at which time he had begun to work on his classic study *Psychoanalysis: Its Image and its Public*. He recalls,

> Bartlett was more 'social' with respect to thinking than many social psychologists today. During our conversation he made a remark about Lévy-Bruhl, saying that it was wrong to compare primitive man to Kant. Later I found he had already made this remark in the twenties in his book on primitive culture. But this comment impressed me because I thought it was in line with my own scientific method. This encounter prompted me to read his book *Remembering*. At the time I was working on the theory of social representation. And his analysis of conventionalization helped me to grasp the process of objectification [see below] more clearly.
>
> (Moscovici and Marková, 1998, p. 389)

In his book, Moscovici (1976/2008) aimed to revitalize a more 'social' psychological approach through the 'lost concept' of social representation, developed by Durkheim and his followers. Keeping with this tradition, Moscovici (1973) defined social representations as systems of ideas, values, and practices constructed by social groups with the two-fold function of enabling orientation to the world and providing a code of communication for its members. Elsewhere, Moscovici (1984, p. 25) says the primary function of social representations is "to make something unfamiliar, or unfamiliarity itself, familiar," a phrase he takes directly from Bartlett (1932/1995). Like Bartlett (1923) and Durkheim before him, Moscovici characterizes modern societies as increasingly differentiated into different social groups, each with their specific mentalities. But in contrast to Durkheim's relatively static approach, Moscovici shares with Bartlett a focus on the *transformation* of culture as it moves between social groups. Later, Moscovici (1990) refers to his approach as 'genetic social psychology,' which studies the construction and reconstruction of representations through 'Bartlett's way' (in sociogenesis) or 'Vygotsky's way' (in ontogenesis).

In *Psychoanalysis*, Moscovici (1976/2008) specifically sets out to explore how scientific ideas are transformed into common science or public knowledge. Contrary to the current theories that saw common sense as a deficit or vulgarized form of science, he aimed to re-evaluate it on its own terms, within its own logic and functions, as Lévy-Bruhl had done for primitive culture. In doing so, Moscovici remaps Lévy-Bruhl's distinction between primitive and modern thought onto the distinction between scientific and common sense thinking, thus identifying primitive thought in modern society as Bartlett (1923) had done. Jahoda (1988) has also pointed out that Moscovici seems to use Bartlett's (1958) idea of 'everyday thinking' (see Chapter 6) to characterize common sense or 'social thought,' though without giving him credit. According to Moscovici (1981, p. 190), "in social thought, conclusions have primacy over premises, and as Nelly Stephanie so aptly put it, 'the verdict rather than the trail dominates our social relations.'" It is impossible to escape the principle role played by traditions, values, and history in conditioning our perceiving, thinking, and remembering, though various scientific procedures have been invented to temper their influence.

Moscovici identified two principal processes involved in social representation, which he called *objectification* and *anchoring*. Objectification is a process of projecting what is in the mind into the world, and in so doing making what was formerly abstract concrete. The process involves *naturalizing* scientific concepts by turning them into a familiar image – for example, we automatically label someone's linguistic mistake a 'Freudian slip' or forgetfulness as 'repression.' "Objectification saturates the idea of unfamiliarity with reality, turns it into the very essence of reality" (Moscovici, 2000, p. 49). This is why Moscovici said social representations are somewhere between a percept and concept, taking on characteristics of both. Similarly, in his experimental studies, Bartlett (1916a, 1932/1995) pointed out how participants' expectations about *naming* of ambiguous stimuli shaped their perception of it (see Chapter 2). In Moscovici's questionnaire and interview data, he found that participants formed a concrete image of the psychoanalytic self through the metaphor of *depth*: The self is said to be split between conscious and unconscious, mapping onto and extending already existing dichotomies, such as 'visible' and 'invisible,' 'false' and 'authentic,' 'superficial' and 'fundamental,' etc. In this image, 'repression' is an expression of the conflict between these two parts of the self, which leads to 'complexes.' This common sense model of psychoanalysis is a selective reconstruction of Freud's theory. Nowhere in it, for example, do we find the central and unifying idea of the libido – a situation equivalent to leaving gravity out of Newton's theory.

The second major process, *anchoring*, explains how the unfamiliar is brought into a group's familiar symbolic universe, where it is used to model and express everyday social relations. For example, in common sense thinking, sperm and egg are seen as representing gender roles in a romantic courtship (Bangerter, 1997). New objects are *named* and *classified* according to previously existing social knowledge. Moscovici describes *anchoring* as a defensive maneuver, circling around an unfamiliar object to decide what aspects to reject and familiarize ourselves with.[23] In Moscovici's study, psychoanalysis is likened to the more familiar activities of conversation and confession. Anchoring is never neutral, in that social groups use it as a *tool* to advance their own interests. Psychoanalysis became part of a larger 'cultural struggle' between different groups in French society. In other words, it feeds into the group's *prospect* (Bartlett, 1923) or *project* (Bauer and Gaskell, 1999). These social dynamics of anchoring were analyzed through a content analysis of the French press in Part II of *Psychoanalysis*.

In the 1950s, the French media was highly differentiated between *Liberals*, *Catholics*, and *Communists*. This provided Moscovici with an excellent opportunity to compare their respective representations of psychoanalysis and the forms of communication practiced by each group. Moscovici called the liberal press's communication style *diffusion*, because it spreads the idea of psychoanalysis without specifying how individuals should think about it. It should be noted that here 'diffusion' is one of three communication styles, whereas Bartlett used it more generally. The primary goal of the liberal press was to please the public and attract readers, which created a symmetrical (or *comradeship*) relationship between addresser and addressee. The liberal press distanced itself from psychoanalysis through "irony, growing reservations about psychoanalysis, the creation of an aura of humour and references to specialists" (p. 217), which leads readers to develop individual *opinions* about psychoanalysis. This group is linked together through loose affective bonds of *sympathy* toward people who are skeptically minded, against an out-group seen as dogmatic (see Duveen, 2008).

In contrast to the liberal press, both the Catholic and Communist presses developed what Bartlett would call a *dominant* form of communication; however, Moscovici (1976/2008) makes the further distinction between communication that is *authoritative* and *authoritarian*. The Catholic press attempted to *propagate* a particular representation of psychoanalysis that was *authoritative* but not *authoritarian*. The parallels between psychoanalysis and Catholic confession created a situation in which some aspects of psychoanalysis were accepted (viz. the therapy) while also differentiating it from their own practice. Thus, psychoanalytic therapy was separated from Freud's 'image of man' as a violent and sexual being. Propagation thus leads to shared group *attitudes* toward psychoanalysis, but does not try to change group members' behavior toward it. In this way, the group authority imposes limits on its members' intellectual curiosity. The affiliative bonds linking group members are that of a *communion* of believers, while the out-group is characterized by a lack of belief or an alternative belief (Duveen, 2008).

Lastly, the Communist press is *authoritarian* in style, using what Moscovici (1976/2008) calls *propaganda*. The group is defined through exclusive commitment to the party ideology, which is the basis for *solidarity* among its members; the out-group is defined by lack of commitment to this ideology (Duveen, 2008). Instead of engaging with psychoanalysis, it immediately places psychoanalysis into the 'bad' column of its dichotomized view of the world. Propaganda involves referring to psychoanalysis in combination with 'American,' 'bourgeouise,' 'capitalist,' or 'pseudo-science.' With time any word in the semantic cluster simultaneously brings to mind all the others, at which point *stereotypes* have been created. Moscovici's study thus illustrates the heterogeneous nature of social groups: each develops its own representations, communication style, leadership, and ways of defining the in- and out-group.

Conclusion: A Conditional Analysis of Cultural Change

This chapter has looked at Bartlett's framework for exploring the systemic conditions of cultural diffusion, maintenance, change, and invention, as well as its contemporary extension in social representations theory. The focus has been on understanding transformations of culture and what conditions them. This concluding section will highlight how this framework is guided by the principles of conditional analysis (see, e.g., Beckstead, Cabell, and Valsiner, 2009; Cabell and Valsiner, 2014). The different factors, Bartlett identifies, that condition the direction of cultural diffusion do not directly 'cause' cultural elements to be incorporated or ignored, transformed or maintained; rather they 'set the stage' for these processes to occur. These factors can thus not be treated as mere variables that somehow 'interact'; instead, the researcher must consider how they operate as a system through the analysis of concrete and contextualized single cases as they change through time. Thus, Bartlett confronts us with a wealth of ethnographic studies that illustrate particular processes of diffusion and analyzes them with a flexible theoretical apparatus that looks at the *relations* between different tendencies and the material in which they work. This framework necessitates attending to individual and group processes, which dynamically relate with the material and the environment. The unit of analysis is an active individual embedded within an environment that is both physical and social.

The social part highlights a number of important conditions of the transmission and transformation of culture – for example, the forms of relationship (i.e., *dominance, submissiveness,* and *primitive comradeship*), which operate between individuals, between the individual and the group, and between groups. These work in concert with a group's 'cultural patterns' or 'conventions,' which always stand in a dynamic tension between past and future, stability and change, *conservation* (the flexible maintenance of the old) and *construction* (the creation of the new). 'Primitive' or 'traditional' groups tend toward conservation but conditions can quickly change such that construction takes the lead. Although these different factors may appear rather simple from the outset, their dynamics quickly become complex when applied to single cases. 'Primitive' groups are not homogeneous but are differentiated into 'special groups,' which become custodians of certain tendencies and material culture. Conflict between tendencies is managed by separating them in time and space. Special groups develop certain relations with the wider community which in turn create particular conditions for the growth of culture. For example, a group's relative *dominance* and regular contact with the wider community 'set the stage' for the *elaboration* of culture, whereas isolation or popularization creates conditions for *simplification*. Individual acts of *elaboration* or *simplification* are not, however, 'caused' by these social conditions, but rather work *through* them.

There are also complex dynamics between one community and another. Contact with new groups and the introduction of new cultural elements can transform a group's whole culture. This is because cultural elements do not stand alone but form a relational whole. Diffusion between communities takes the route of *contact* or *borrowing*, each of which sets different conditions. *Borrowing* depends more on the personality of the individual, who brings a foreign cultural element into the community and is its promoter, while *contact* depends more on broader societal factors. *Contact* creates conditions for the blending of culture when the communities are in a relation of *primitive comradeship* and displacement when one is *dominate* and the other *submissive*. One can see how a number of factors come into play simultaneously and work as a complex whole in preparing the ground for different processes of diffusion and reconstruction – whether cultural elements are accepted or rejected, assimilated as a package or individually, combined with the old or used to construct genuinely new cultural forms.

The processes of diffusion found in modern societies are not fundamentally different from 'primitive' societies, but do set up different conditions as a function of their differentiation into many special groups and their technologies of transport and communication, which allow for ever wider and faster diffusion. These technologies and education themselves create conditions for the widespread use of propaganda in modern societies. Furthermore, belonging to and communicating with a number of different social groups are necessary conditions for the individual to able to follow different trains of thought, which promote individual autonomy and social constructiveness (i.e., the emergence of genuinely new cultural forms that bring together multiple influences). Totalitarian societies try to stifle this development through censorship, coercion, and repression. This certainly creates adverse conditions for intellectual and cultural growth, but as leaders of a one-party system well know, they cannot completely suppress the formation of new ideas and culture. Instead, repression tends to create conditions for them to simply go underground and only resurface during times of social upheaval, as Bartlett (1923) himself stressed. The Arab Spring and the protests that have followed all over the world confirm his point. The diffusion of a single idea like 'revolution' can have dramatic effects, not just on the transformation of individual nations, but also on the world as a whole.

Notes

1. Bartlett's approach is more compatible with Everett's (2003) *Diffusion of Innovations*, especially in relation to (a) and (d); Bartlett, however, is much more focused on the *reconstruction* of cultural elements in the process of diffusion than is Everett.
2. The word 'primitive' is an unfortunate term which was widely used at that time, even by those who criticized what it originally stood for – I retain the word but keep it in quotation mark. Today theorists use 'traditional' or 'developing' societies largely in the same way as 'primitive' was earlier used.
3. See Slobodin (1997) for a thorough description of his work as well as a useful selection of articles by Rivers.
4. Rivers also used this two-tiered system as a model for explaining social systems, which fit well with the colonial position of the British in many 'primitive' societies.
5. Rivers also rejected the functionalist argument that culture was always beneficial for the society concerned. As a psychiatrist who treated 'shell-shocked' soldiers, he knew that extreme conditions such as war clearly lead to pathological functioning.
6. Compare Wittgenstein's (1958) comments on the nature of customs: "If I have exhausted the justifications, I have reached bedrock and my spade is turned. Then I am inclined to say: 'This is simply what I do.'"

7. In this respect, Bartlett's approach is in step with idiographic principles of theory building (see Salvatore and Valsiner, 2010).

8. Bartlett (1957, p. 73) later put the criticism of McDougall (1908) more sharply: "It was curious that an approach which made out men to be much less rational than had often been supposed should nevertheless appear unusually neat and tidy, so that everything that anybody did could be listed under a limited number of headings, each heading being a name for an instinct and its associated emotion."

9. This phrase is taken over directly from McDougall (1908). In *Remembering*, Bartlett changes it to the more active 'making the unfamiliar familiar.' The revised phrase in turn becomes central to Moscovici's theory of social representations (see later).

10. The concept of construction would later become a central to Bartlett's (1932/1995) theory of remembering, in which memories are not merely registers of the past but are constructed in order to meet current demands (see Chapter 4).

11. Bartlett (1937a, 1943) argued that a group's psychology possessions can best be brought to light with psychological methods, such as his method of serial reproduction.

12. Here Bartlett's approach links up to the recent materiality turn in social sciences (e.g., Boivin, 2008; Gonzalez-Ruibal, 2012; Latour, 2008).

13. Bartlett's method of serial reproduction is to some extent an attempt to simulate this process (see Chapter 2).

14. The exception to this is ancient Egyptian hieroglyphs, which were highly ritualized and changed little over thousands of years.

15. Piaget (1930) characterized the mentality of children in the same way.

16. This argument can also be put to contemporary cross-cultural approaches in psychology, which make generalizations about the mentalities of peoples by placing them into broad categories such as 'Asian' versus 'Western,' 'individualist' versus 'collectivist' (see, e.g., Nisbett, 2005). From a Bartlettian perspective, we need to look for how these tendencies operate in particular social contexts. For example, it is not sufficient that Indian culture is collectivist, when one can point to important practices such as meditation, which have an extremely individualistic focus.

17. This insight has important implications for and parallels with contemporary theories of globalization. Robertson (1992), for example, argues that we need to simultaneously consider 'localization' alongside 'globalization.' He combines the two processes in his invention of the term 'glocalization.'

18. Later in his career, Bartlett did publish a number of other articles and speeches on different aspects of modern cultural diffusion – e.g., national and international social groupings (Bartlett, 1947a, b), globalized culture (Bartlett, 1955a), the cinema (Bartlett, 1960), and again propaganda (Bartlett, 1963).

19. Gustave Le Bon (1895/1966) first developed the notion of the irrational crowd that was used by Hitler and Goebbels.

20. Moghaddam (2013, 2016) points out that Democratic and Totalitarian societies exist along a continuum rather than being exclusive categories; no society is an absolute democracy or dictatorship. This insight is compatible with Bartlett's (1923) theory of society in which opposing tendencies are

relegated to different spheres of influence, though it is not developed in *Political Propaganda*.

21. There are some important counter-examples to this (viz. Bateson, 1936; Nadel, 1937), which I take up in Chapter 5.

22. David Bloor is another social scientist who builds on Bartlett's diffusionist ideas, and was himself a student of Cambridge. His notion of 'social construction' is a continuation and development of Bartlett's concept of 'social constructiveness' (see Bloor, 1997, 2000).

23. This is similar to metaphor theorists' notion of 'conceptual mapping,' where one concept is metaphorically understood through another – for example, 'life as a journey' (Lakoff and Johnson, 1980) – but adds the wider social dynamics of the process.

4   Concept of Schema in Reconstruction

> Remembering is not the re-excitation of innumerable fixed, lifeless and fragmentary traces. It is an imaginative reconstruction or construction, built out of the relation of our attitude towards a whole active mass of organised past reactions or experience [i.e., schema], and to a little outstanding detail which commonly appears in image or in language form.
>
> (Bartlett, 1932/1995, p. 213)

> If this view of remembering as a constructive activity is correct, the whole experimental setting of the problems of recall is changed.
>
> (Bartlett, 1935, p. 226)

No other concept in Bartlett's *oeuvre* has generated as much attention as 'schema,' except perhaps the related concept 'reconstruction.' Psychology is today littered with references to 'story schema,' 'self-schema,' 'gender schema,' 'event schema,' and a wide range of other words combined with schema.[1] Add to these the derivative concepts of 'script' and 'frame' and one begins to get a sense of how widely and variably the concept is used. At a very general level, contemporary psychologists have defined schema as a knowledge structure in the head that is used in the storage of information. This is somewhat ironic because Bartlett (1932/1995) intended to utilize the concept to develop an alternative to the storage theory of memory. For him, schema was to provide the basis for a theory of remembering that was embodied, dynamic, temporal, holistic, and social. Bartlett (1932/1995), however, provided only a hesitant and sketchy account rather than a fully developed theory. This left the concept of schema wide open for reconstruction. Since Bartlett, psychologists of different generations and orientations have assimilated schema into their own frameworks, which Bartlett's reconstructive schema theory would have itself predicted.

This chapter explores the concept of schema's origins, its place within Bartlett's thought, and its successive reconstructions by others after him. First, I present the trace theory of memory, which Bartlett was reacting against in developing his own theory. The memory trace was the dominant metaphor of memory in physiological, psychological, and philosophical discourses of Bartlett's time, and perhaps our own as well. Second, I argue that Bartlett took a functionalist approach to memory, leading him to reject the usefulness of literal recall in an ever-changing world. Rather than treating memory as a *substance*, he explores it as a situated *activity* made possible by a myriad of different processes. Third, I discuss Head's (1920) concept of schema together with Bartlett's critique and extension of it. For Head 'schema' was a purely embodied concept, whereas for Bartlett it takes on social and reflexive significance. Fourth, I outline remembering as a self-reflective process and explicate the phrase "turning around upon one's own schema and constructing them afresh" (p. 206). Fifth, I look at the different waves of reconstructing 'schema' since Bartlett and in doing so make an argument for reconstructing schema as a temporal, dynamic, embodied, holistic, and social process in future research.

Trace Theory of Memory

Bartlett's 'theory of remembering' is explicitly developed as an alternative to the trace theory of memory,[2] which has dominated Western thinking about memory for two and a half millennia (Danziger, 2008). Plato was the first to posit it in his *Theaetetus*, where he had us imagine that there was a wax tablet in the mind called 'the memory,' into which new experiences leave an imprint. When we remember an experience, we simply read off what was impressed on the wax. This sets the stage for regarding memory as just a copy of experience, a faded form of perception. This idea was most clearly developed by British philosophers such as Berkeley, Hume, and John Stuart Mill. For them, old knowledge was represented as a stored collection of distinct mental images. Although contemporary theorists have moved away from the specific metaphor of wax tablet, the root metaphor of memory as individuated marks on a surface has persisted down the ages, such that we now speak of memories as being like code magnetically inscribed on a computer hard disk or physically inscribed in brain as an 'engram' (literally 'that which is converted into writing').[3] Bartlett (1932/1995, p. 198) described the trace theory in general terms as:

When any specific event occurs some trace, or some group of traces, is made and stored up in the organism or mind. Later, an immediate stimulus re-excites the trace, or group of traces, and, provided a further assumption is made (...) that the trace somehow carries with it a temporal sign, the re-excitement appears to be equivalent to recall.

This notion of spatial storage of memories is now so deeply embedded in our thinking that we tend to take the figurative assumptions of the metaphor as literally true. Danziger (2002) has argued that the metaphor leads us to assume memory is a mental faculty literally 'in the head'; that it is naturally divisible into three distinct phases, now called 'encoding,' 'storage,' and 'retrieval'; that memories are stored as individuated 'traces,' now presumed to exist in the brain; and that memories retain the same meaning irrespective of the context in which they take part. Traditional experiments on memory never put these assumptions into question with their use of wordlists, associative pairs, and segmented stories, their analytic focus on counting 'items' remembered, forgotten, or distorted, and their treatment of the laboratory as a kind of social vacuum (see Chapter 2).

This methodological approach is clearly illustrated in Ebbinghaus's (1885/1913) classic study *Memory: A Contribution to Experimental Psychology* (see also Chapter 2). Although Ebbinghaus himself criticizes the memory metaphors of 'stored up ideas' and 'engraved images' (p. 5) in the introduction of his book, he explicitly uses them when discussing his experiments regarding the relationship between the number of times a stimulus is repeated and its retention in memory:

These [experimental results] can be described figuratively by speaking of the series as being more or less deeply engraved in some mental substratum. To carry out this figure: as the number of repetitions increases, the series are engraved more and more deeply and indelibly; if the number of repetitions is small, the inscription is but surface deep and only fleeting glimpses of the tracery can be caught; with a somewhat greater number the inscription can, for a time at least, be read at will; as the number of repetitions is still further increased, the deeply cut picture of the series fades out only after ever longer intervals. (pp. 52–3)

Bartlett strongly opposed treating memory as a thing, as it is described in the above quotation. His criticisms of Ebbinghaus are revealing and as he himself states they apply to a much broader range of theories and methods in circulation at the time. First, he questions the tendency to consider humans as passively reacting to stimuli. Although psychology is now willing to accept that the mind is active, it is still studied by most psychologists using a neobehaviorist methodology whereby some stimulus is varied (independent variable), which *causes* the individual to respond in a particular way (as measured by the dependent variable). This approach is guided by a search for 'efficient causality' (Humean linear cause–effect relationship) rather than 'agent causality' (where the person is considered an active center of causality) (see Harré, 2002).

Second, Bartlett points out that simplifying the stimulus does not necessarily simplify the response. Subjects still tended to give nonsense syllables a meaning. Moreover, this very attempt to use simple and meaningless stimuli, so as to isolate the response, results in wholly artificial conditions with little relation to its workings in everyday life. Lastly, experiments are not social vacuums; they are social contexts that channel human responses in particular directions (see Chapter 2).

From Storage to Action: Bartlett's Functionalism

In contrast to the trace theory that treats memory as an isolated mental faculty, Bartlett starts with a whole organism actively involved with its environment. The mind is taken 'out of the head' and situated in the ongoing transactions between a person and his or her environment.[4] From this perspective, remembering is considered as a situated *activity*, bringing together multiple different processes, to act in the world. Mind and memory here are not separate entities or substances but sets of processes contributing to environmental adaptation. In Bartlett's own words:

> I have never regarded memory as a faculty, as a reaction narrowed and ringed around, containing all its peculiarities and all explanations within itself. I have regarded it rather as one achievement in the line of the ceaseless struggle to master and enjoy a world full of variety and rapid change.
>
> (Bartlett, 1932/1995, p. 314)

A number of theorists from around the world at this time were developing a functionalist approach with similar assumptions (e.g., Dewey, Mead, Vygotsky, Baldwin, Bergson,[5] von Uexkull, etc.). They were all reacting against the tendency to separate mind from activity in the world and describe it simply in terms of its inner contents. Titchener, for example, used a method of self-observation to describe the *contents* of mind. The problem was not the focus on mental contents as such, but rather investigating them in this way, they were removed from the concrete thoughts and feelings of everyday life and the function that they had there. With functionalism, the emphasis shifts to an analysis of the conditions under which a particular psychological or behavioral response occurs (see also Chapter 3). These thinkers likewise rejected the opposing behaviorist approach for its exclusion of mind and its analysis of reactions as simply determined by some external stimulus and artificially separated from the broader context of action.

In applying a functionalist approach to the study of memory, the question of memory capacity or accuracy becomes subordinated to the question of how remembering helps a person function in the environment in which they live. Instead, remembering is considered as a form of pre-adaptation to an indeterminate future. According to Bartlett, literal recall is in most conditions dysfunctional, whereas constructive remembering, which flexibly adjusts itself to the context of occurrence, is of great utility, given that the environment changes.

> So-called 'literal,' or accurate, recall is an artificial construction of the armchair, or of the laboratory. Even if it could be secured, in the enormous majority of instances it would be biologically detrimental. Life is a continuous play of adaptation between changing response and varying environment. Only in a relatively few cases – and those mostly the production of an elaborately guarded civilization – could the retention unchanged of the effects of experience be anything but a hindrance.
>
> (Bartlett, 1932/1995, p. 16)

Bartlett's rather low opinion of literal recall is almost the exact opposite of most cognitive approaches to memory, which focus almost exclusively on accuracy as the ultimate standard for evaluating memory. Thus, 'construction' is considered a vice of memory and has rarely been explored as more than a process leading to memory 'distortion' (see Chapter 2). In contrast, in Bartlett's account 'construction' was indicative of the directedness and creativity of human responses, which could not be adequately studied with a methodology that simply considered the stimulus as determining the organism's response or that removed the organism's response from the environment in which it normally occurs.

Head's Schema Theory

In the 1910s, Bartlett invented a powerful methodology for studying remembering as a more everyday social activity by, for instance, showing how foreign stories (e.g., *War of the Ghosts*) are reconstructed in the direction of familiar social conventions (Chapter 2). Yet it was not until nearly two decades later that he was to articulate a general theory of remembering to account for his results. Inspiration for this theory came from several sources (Northway, 1940a),[6] but it was the work of Henry Head that he most explicitly mentions in elaborating his theory. Head himself borrowed the concept of schema from Immanuel Kant's *Critique of Pure Reason* and breathed new life into it through his rich clinical work. Bartlett frequently met with Head in Cambridge in the 1920s, on which occasions Head had the habit of reading Bartlett drafts of his book *Aphasia and Kindred Disorders of Speech* (1926) and discussing them with him. Bartlett thought Head's research to be extremely important and felt the need to bring his own thinking in line with Head's ideas, although he did this critically as we will see.

Head was a clinical neurologist who worked with brain-damaged patients. As a result of their injury, many of Head's patients were unable to register postural changes in their body, disrupting voluntary movement. Consider this clinical example, which Bartlett (1932/1995) also draws upon in his chapter 'a theory of remembering':

Place the patient's affected arm in front of him on the bed, allowing him to see the position in which it lies; close his eyes, and in most cases he will see a mental picture of his hand. Then change its position while his eyes remain closed and he will continue to see a picture of the hand in its old position. Moreover, if localization is not affected, he will name correctly the spot stimulated but will refer it to the position in which he visualizes the hand. The visual image of the limb remains intact, although the power of appreciating changes in position is abolished.

(Head, 1920, p. 605)

The physiologist Hermann Munk (1890) was the first to pose the question of how earlier movements in a chain are able to continue to exert an influence on latter movements, as happens with bodily skills. He answered that this is possible because mental images of our body movements are stored in the cortex as static and self-contained traces. The brain keeps track of movements by comparing the present image with the previous one. However, Head showed that the image function remains intact even when the ability to seamlessly coordinate serial movements is lost, as in the above example. Head concluded that appreciation of postural change must be separated from the functioning of images. The former is a more fundamental process and operates largely below the level of conscious awareness, whereas images function consciously. Head calls this fundamental unconscious process 'schema,' which he defines as "That combined standard against which all subsequent changes in posture are registered before they enter consciousness." He continues,

By means of perpetual alterations in position we are always building up a postural model of ourselves which constantly changes. Every new posture of movement is recorded on this plastic schema and the activity of the cortex brings every fresh group of sensations evoked by altered posture into relation with it. Immediate postural recognition follows as soon as the recognition is complete.

(Head, 1920, pp. 605–6)

Thus, schema is a holistic and constantly revised record of one's position, which provides the baseline for one's next movement – for example, to make a step forward one has to be aware of the current position of one's leg. Schema is a kind of active and continuously revised memory, providing a 'model of the organized animal,' rather than a memory put away into storage only to be retrieved at a later time. It is an organized generalization but not an abstraction of past experience. Head discusses the phenomena of the phantom limb as a vivid example of the operation of schema. Whereas above we saw the effects of schematic breakdown, the phantom limb demonstrates what happens when schema remains intact while one's body is suddenly dramatically changed by the loss of a limb. Although the limb is no longer there, patients register it as changing position alongside their entire body as they had done before; it remains part of the 'combined standard.' In one clinical case, the patient lost a finger several months before losing his entire arm. As a result, the patient's phantom arm had four fingers rather than five. Head also reports a case in which a patient's phantom limb disappears with a lesion that causes schematic breakdown, as described earlier.[7]

Bartlett's Elaboration of Schema

Bartlett is sympathetic to Head's theory but offers a number of terminological critiques. Reviewing them will help us to understand what he wanted to do with the concept. First, he thinks Head gives away far too much to earlier investigators when he speaks of the cortex as 'a storehouse of past impressions,' thus evoking the storage metaphor. A store is a place you put things in the hope to find them later in same condition they were put there, whereas schema are said to be constantly active, developing, and influenced by the present context. Head rejects the image theory of body movement, whereby present movement is compared to images of past movement, but he implicitly accepts assumptions of the storage analogy. Second, Head (1920) uses the phrase 'rising into consciousness' to describe the workings of schema, whereas Bartlett rejects a strict separation between conscious and unconscious processes. If anything schema operates below the level of self-reflective awareness and as such is not available to introspection. Finally, Bartlett finds the word 'schema' itself to be misleading. He says,

I strongly dislike the term 'schema.' It is at once too definite and too sketchy ... It suggests some persistent, but fragmentary, 'form of arrangement,' and it does not indicate what is very essential to the whole notion, that the organised mass results of past changes of position and posture are actively doing something all the time; are, so to speak, carried along with us, complete, though developing, from moment to moment.

(Bartlett, 1932/1995, pp. 200–1)

In this passage, Bartlett is all too aware of the danger of dividing and fixating a holistic, living, moving process by using technical language to describe it (cf. Billig, 2013). We are told instead that schema should be understood as always operating 'en masse,' 'active,' and 'developing.' In spite of these pre-emptive measures, it will be shown below that early cognitive psychology turns schema into the static structure that Bartlett tried to avoid. Given the problems with the term 'schema,' it is somewhat surprising that Bartlett continues to use it in *Remembering*, although he also frequently uses different terms, reflecting other influences on his thought. His continued use of 'schema' is likely done to express Head's influence on his theory. Bartlett's preferred names for schema are also revealing. He says,

It would probably be best to speak of 'active, developing patterns'; but the word 'pattern,' too, being now very widely and variously employed, has its own difficulties; and it, like 'schema,' suggests a greater articulation of detail than is normally found. I think probably the term 'organised setting' approximates most closely and clearly to the notion required. (p. 201)

Bartlett had previously used the words 'pattern,' 'organized,' and 'setting' in other contexts. In his early experiments on perceiving and imagining, Bartlett (1916a) explained how any psychological response involved an 'effort after meaning,' an active process of connecting given material to a 'setting' or 'scheme.' For example, subjects named a briefly presented ambiguous figure an 'anchor' or a 'pre-historic battle-axe,' thereby rendering their relation to it more definite. This is similar to Brentano's idea of mental acts as always pointing beyond themselves (i.e., having 'intentionality') or the Gestalt idea of figure–ground relations. Thus, as early as 1916 'setting' refers to a self-generated context for action and experience, which itself evolves with the event.

Similarly, in his 1923 book *Psychology and Primitive Culture*, Bartlett frequently uses the phrase 'cultural pattern' to describe folk conventions, such as the distinctive styles of decorative art forms one finds in different social groups (Haddon, 1894). Social groups have the tendency to work any incoming foreign element of culture into their existing 'cultural patterns' (see Chapter 3). Like schema these patterns are 'plastic,' in that they adapt themselves to fit new material while at the same time remaining relatively stable across time. Thus, cultural patterns are to the group as schemata are to the individual (Wagoner, 2013). At both levels, a flexible pattern is imposed on the incoming material, which changes the material but in so doing stabilizes it against additional dramatic changes (Collins, 2006; see also Kay, 1955). The above quote, however, indicates that by 1932 Bartlett was growing dissatisfied with the word 'pattern.'

He ultimately prefers the term 'organized setting,' which better highlights that schema operates at the developing transaction between organism and environment, rather than being a purely cognitive phenomena (i.e., a mental representation). Any reaction utilizes existing modes of relating to the environment but at the same time further develops them, in a fashion analogous to Piaget's (who also used the schema concept) notions of assimilation and accommodation.

Having expressed his terminological objections, Bartlett (1932/1995, pp. 200–1) proceeds to define schema as:

an active organization of past reactions, or of past experiences, which must always be supposed to be operating in any well-adapted organic response. That is, whenever there is any order or regularity of behavior, a particular response is possible only because it is related to other similar responses which have been serially organised, yet which operate, not simply as individual members coming one after another, but as a unitary mass ... All incoming impulses of a certain kind, or mode, go together to build up an active, organized setting.

Driving a car, painting a picture, walking up the stairs, or recalling one's phone number are directed activities that operate as a seamless flow without self-reflection entering into them. They require the unconscious coordination of a series of acts in time and space through a certain attunement to the environment. When we first learn to drive a car, for example, the series of movements needed do not easily flow from one to the other, but with time we learn to do them without reflection. At this point, the activity of driving functions as a 'unitary mass' and cannot be analytically subdivided into separate actions without losing the quality of the whole. It is the massed and unitary effects of previous reactions that provide the basis for a new response while engaged in an activity. This is not a mechanical plan wherein one distinct movement follows another, but rather dynamic relating to the environment against the background of previous experience. In other words, schemata provide an organism with a general orientation to its environment and means of flexibly coordinating action within it. What is given in the environment is unconsciously 'fit' to our changing schemes of action and experience. Bartlett (1932/1995) gives the following example:

When I make the stroke I do not, as a matter of fact, produce something absolutely new, and I never merely repeat something old. The stroke is literally manufactured out of the living visual and postural 'schemata' of the moment and their interrelations. I may say and think that I reproduce exactly a series of textbook movements, but demonstrably I do not; just as, under other circumstances, I may say and think that I reproduce exactly some isolated event which I want to remember, and again demonstrably I do not. (pp. 201–2)

The organism neither responds to nor remembers material with no functional relationship with the active interest of the moment. The above quote describes how the person orients to the environment, with the massed resources of past, to meet the present demands of a game of tennis. This involves not so much separate details of the game but a general impression of the whole activity. Many details of the environment will not have any relevance to the activity and thus will not be attended to. In a later publication, Bartlett (1935) compares remembering a series of cards, as they are played in a game of bridge versus simply dealing them haphazardly.[8] In bridge, there will be an active interest in remembering the cards to meet the needs of the game. In contrast, the haphazard presentation resembles more paradigm of recall demanded by Ebbinghaus's method. Bartlett is emphatic that it is the former's ability to remember, as part of a whole living social activity, that is needed for general functioning in everyday life.

Turning Around upon Schemata

The most fundamental way in which the past influences the present is by the simple action of schemata as an organized stream of activity, as happens in habits and basic skills. This, however, does not describe remembering in the full human sense of the word. For Bartlett, this involves creating a discontinuity in the seamless stream of action, in order to locate specific information from the past. For example, while moving through my routine of preparing to leave the house in the morning, I cannot locate my keys. I suddenly become self-conscious. Bartlett would say an *attitude* (or orientation – see Chapter 2) is set up, which is then directed toward the events of the previous day in order to identify where I left my keys. I begin to create distinctions within my duration of experience – today versus yesterday and here versus there. This enables me to distance myself from the here and now environment, and as such widen my possibilities of action within it. At this point, the environment becomes dual – I become simultaneously involved in a present and past environment. The latter is used to self-reflectively control action in the present. Bartlett (1932/1995, p. 206) calls this "turning around upon [one's] own schemata and constructing them afresh," a process he equates with consciousness.

Turning around upon schemata is involved in any higher mental activity. It points to the fact that we can reflect on our own activity and thereby bring it under our control. Today it might be described with the concept of 'meta-cognition' or 'meta-memory' (see Nelson, 1996).[9] In Bartlett's (1932/1995) words, schema becomes "not merely something that works the organism, but something with which the organism can work" (p. 206). This is done by using one schema in order to check the action of another schema. It is the unique interplay of different schemata particular to a given person that gives memory its *personal* character.[10] Recalling one's phone number or a list of nonsense syllables is a rather 'low-level' response normally relying on a single auditory or visual schema and does not have this experiential quality. Here we have an unbroken chronological sequence, which Bartlett believes is rarely advantageous in a constantly changing world. In contrast, when we recall an event or more complex material, multiple schemata come into play, supporting or checking each other at different points. Bartlett (1935, p. 224) gives the example of an enthusiastic journalist's account of a cricket match: "To describe the batting of one man he finds it necessary to refer to a sonata of Beethoven; the bowling of another reminds him of a piece of beautifully wrought rhythmic prose written by Cardinal Newman." Here different schemata cross and invade one another, causing the organism to turn around upon them. In this process, the material is put into a new setting (in the above music and poetry) so as to further current tendencies (writing a description of the event). It is this building together of different material that makes remembering a constructive activity.[11]

In Bartlett's own experiments, he observed that the setting of an experiment sets up a predominant interest or attitude in the subject. This is the 'attitude' or 'general impression' that the subject then attempts to justify in the act of remembering, and is what makes remembering an affective and emotional process rather than simply a cognitive one. In remembering, the person usually proceeds to chronologically recall the material that is the focus of the task. This may at first move smoothly forward but at some point the subject will pause and ask him or herself "what must have gone here?" At this point, the person enters a self-reflexive mode in which schema are actively manipulated to 'fill in gaps' in memory, analogous to the way the enthusiastic journalist is reminded of Beethoven in describing a cricket match. What is unclear in this account is precisely how this 'turning around upon [one's] own schema' is made possible. Bartlett (1932/1995) acknowledges this when he says "I wish I knew how it was done" (p. 206). Later, he defends the phrase as a 'description' rather than an 'explanation' of the process (see Bartlett, 1968b).[12] In accordance with his functionalist perspective, Bartlett (1937b) does provide a number of conditions through which a rupture arises in one's stream of action and experience: (1) lack of harmony in a cooperative effort; (2) sudden and unexpected change of environment stimulation; (3) clash of testimony about certain practically significant events; (4) swift surging up of some definite sensorial image which conflicts notably with whatever is being done or perceived at the moment.

It is only the fourth in this list (the image) that Bartlett elaborates on in any detail. Therefore, in what follows I focus on explicating it as a mechanism of self-reflection in remembering. Somewhat confusingly Bartlett uses the word 'image' to describe both visual and auditory imagery, though these two have different characteristics for him. In his experiments, he frequently discusses the conditions under which images arise (e.g., when there is ambiguity or ambivalence) and how they in turn shape the process of remembering. For example, he says that the subjects who rely on visual imagery tend to proceed in a jerky or bumpy manner, mix up the original order of presentation, and are often confident of their memories, though objectively unfounded. This is in contrast to those who rely more on 'vocalization' (i.e., subvocal speech). This tend to better retain an order, and proceed more smoothly, because language is a linear medium and meanings are given with it directly, though their attitude is often one of doubt.

Later, when outlining his general theory of remembering he gives a distinctive function to images "to pick items out of 'schemata,' and to rid the organism of over-determination by the last preceding member of a given series" (p. 209). Bartlett (1932/1995) elaborates:

In general, images are a device for picking bits out of schemes, for increasing the chance of variability in the reconstruction of past stimuli and situations, for surmounting the chronology of presentations. By the aid of the image, and particularly of the visual image ... a man can take out of its setting something that happened a year ago, reinstate it with much if not all of its individuality unimpaired, combine it with something that happened yesterday, and use them both to help him to solve a problem with which he is confronted to-day. (p. 219)

Images (both visual and vocal) function to mark salient features (or *dominant details*) of an experience in an organized setting in both the act of perceiving and remembering it.[13] The presence of dominant details and their role in shaping experience of some material was a common theme in his experimental studies (see Chapter 2). Although material is particularized through images it is a mistake to think of them as passively received copies of experience, as in the storage theory of memory. Instead, they are differentiations within organized settings, selected (i.e., 'picked out' or 'unpacked') as a result of the active interests of the subject. They also change according to those interests – they are 'living' rather than 'static.' In an earlier publication, Bartlett (1925c) theorized that images arose when there was a conflict of tendencies to action (i.e., when a reaction is held up) as a way of helping the person to choose between alternatives. But images can also be dysfunctional, as they tend to overly particularize the details of a situation such that the person loses the dynamic whole. For example, forming an image of one's opponent's moves in tennis can often be a distraction in an ongoing game; however, one might later use images of the game to reflect on one's strategy or develop functional images to guide one's performance (Sutton, 2007).

At this point, we are in a position to understand Bartlett's (1932/ 1995) general description of remembering as a reconstructive process:

The need to remember becomes active, an attitude is set up; in the form of sensory images, or, just as often, of isolated words, some part of the event which has to be remembered recurs, and the event is then reconstructed on the basis of the relation of this specific bit of material to the general mass of relevant past experience or reactions, the latter functioning, after the manner of the 'schema,' as an active organised setting. (p. 209)

Despite its sometimes vague and sketchy formulation, it is clear that Bartlett emphatically rejects the trace theory of remembering and wants to replace it with one in which the whole active organism takes central place. 'Attitude,' 'schemata,' and 'image' are all organismic concepts, for Bartlett, which are implicated in a person's dynamic relation to the world. They are functions coordinated within a total system, which must make a unitary response in its environment. Bartlett (1935) bluntly states that his view of remembering fundamentally changes the questions asked by the investigator:

If this view of remembering as a constructive activity is correct, the whole experimental setting of the problems of recall is changed. In the past the problems have been concerned mainly with how millions of individual traces can persist intact in the mind or in the central nervous system; of how those traces, each preserving its own individuality, can nevertheless enter into associations one with another, and of what main forms of association can be discriminated. For us, however, the problems fall into two main groups. First, how are the schemes, the organised patterns of psychological and physiological material formed? We can often watch them in the process of formation and experimentally change and determine their direction. Second, what are the conditions and laws of construction in the mental life? These are urgent psychological problems, not outside the experimentalist's scope.

(Bartlett, 1935, p. 226)

Thus, there is the developmental (or 'genetic') question of how schemas are formed (a long temporality) and a question regarding the processes and dynamics involved in the act of memory reconstruction (a short temporality). The notion of time implied in this framework is one of qualitative, accumulative, and irreversible change, which was also being explored by Bergson, Dewey, and Whitehead around the same time. This notion is very different from the objective clock time of most experimental studies today. In what follows we will explore to what extent these questions posed by Bartlett have been pursued by subsequent generations of psychologists in their investigation of schema.

Reconstruction of Schema, Phase 1: Bartlett's Students

As we have seen earlier, Bartlett put forward a radically new theory of remembering with the help of the concept of schema; however, the concept remained rather sketchy and underdeveloped in his work. Bartlett put it aside and moved on to other projects. In the three decades following the publication of *Remembering*, the sketchy state of the schema concept changed little. There were only a couple sustained attempts to develop it – many memory studies done in Britain did acknowledge the 'schema theory' but did not attempt to elaborate it in any significant way. In a series of articles in the *British Journal of Psychology*, Bartlett's students Oldfield and Zangwill (1942a, b, 1943) did develop a sustained and meticulous theoretical discussion of the concept and how it had been used by thinkers since Head; however, not long after Bartlett's death Oldfield (1972) and Zangwill (1972) publically declared that the concept of schema would best be forgotten. During this first period of reconstruction, perhaps the only substantial methodological development of Bartlett's schema concept was the work of Mary L. Northway.

Northway spent 1935–6 working with Bartlett at Cambridge, and submitted her Ph.D. thesis at the University of Toronto on 'Bartlett's concept of Schema,' which was published in the *British Journal of Psychology* (Northway, 1936, 1940a, b). In the middle article (1940a), she carefully teases apart four different (though not necessarily exclusive) uses that Bartlett makes of the schema concept (viz. as a *force, form, storehouse,* and *apperceptive mass*) and then connects these to different influences on his thought (viz., Head, Ward, and Rivers). To bring clarity to the concept, in such a way that it might lead to methodological innovations, she invents her own definition of schema as "what the subject makes (creates or develops) from the given material (or situation)" (Northway, 1940b, p. 35). This is not a definition that Bartlett himself gives, but is nonetheless closely aligned with his broader theoretical and methodological framework, particularly in his notion of an 'effort after meaning.' With this definition as her guide, Northway develops two clever experimental studies with children in Toronto school classrooms.

In her first study, Northway (1936) uses Bartlett's method of serial reproduction to explore how *age, social background,* and *story difficulty* provide different schemata through which children can 'make something out of the material.' She recruits children from three different schools: (1) a *private* girl's school, run by the Church of England according to long-standing traditions; (2) a *public* school in the slum area of town, whose student body was composed mostly of first- to fourth-generation immigrants; and (3) a *country school*, described as a 'progressive' boarding school for boys on the outskirts of the city. She finds that "the less stable social group [i.e., public school children] gave many more modifications and importations than the comparable age group in a more stabilized social setting [i.e., the private school]" (Northway, 1940a, p. 325). There was also a difference in the kinds of items remembered (e.g., basketball) in different groups. Items with a high value of social meaningfulness in the group tended to be remembered, illustrating once again that remembering is interest and meaning driven, and that these are socially shaped.

In terms of age differences, not only did the younger children (10 years) remember less than the older children (14–15 years), but they were also much more likely to import their own ideas into the stories. Furthermore, they 'recast' the form, setting, and style of the stories much more abruptly and earlier in a reproduction chain. Recasting was usually done by either telling a new story within the same setting as the original, or elaborating some detail in the original into a new setting (e.g., in *War of the Ghosts* the death at the end is selected and used to construct another story about a death). Younger children often created their own 'active centers' to the story based on some interest they had, rather than being constrained by the story's structure. Finally, there were age differences in the kinds of 'modifications' made to the stories: all children *conventionalized* items of the story (i.e., made changes toward common phraseology) but only older children *rationalized* (to create a more reasonable and coherent story), *reversed* (turning phrases into their opposites), and *substituted* (a reason or activity with another).

Northway's (1936, 1940a) first study demonstrated clear qualitative differences in the management of schema as a function of age, social background, and story difficulty. In the second study, also done with Toronto school children, she investigated "the differences occurring in remembering when the learning methods themselves are devised to allow the children more or less freedom in 'making something out of the material'" (Northway, 1940b, p. 22). To do this, she assigns children to one of three different learning methods:

1. *Repetition*: students learn through rote repetition drills.
2. *Repetition combined with discussion*: drills are supplemented with some discussion of the text.
3. *Project-based*: interest-driven learning; for example, making a play or drawing a picture of the material.

Children read a story about a pirate's adventures aloud two times and on the next day they learned it by one of the three learning methods. Three days later, the children were asked to "write a story, pretending you are Don Durk [pirate protagonist] and that you are sitting at home telling your friends of yourself and your adventure" (Northway, 1940b, p. 26). This was meant to create an open context of recall to test children's ability to work flexibly with the material that they had learned rather than simply reproduce it by rote. She finds that children in the project group were much more likely to add a temporal and spatial context to the story, add new nouns related to the story theme, and extend the topic to include new events. In short, these children were much more capable of reconstructing the story material into new forms than those of the other groups. Northway (1940b) concludes,

> It was found that with more freedom and participation in learning the schemata are less controlled by the given material, more adaptable to a new point of view, and more individualistic. When learning is based on definite instruction, the schemata reflect the material as it was given, and are stereotyped. (p. 34)

Comparing Northway's concept of schema to Bartlett's, a number of close parallels emerge. First, both thinkers approach schema as part of an ongoing activity situated within a particular environment – thus the long temporality is included. Northway (1940b) makes clear that she sees her own interventions (i.e., memory tests) with children as being just snapshots of a living process of learning and remembering. Second, schema is understood and studied as a flexible adaption to the environment, rather than imposing the strict accuracy imperative on remembering. Thus, the construction nature of remembering is framed positively as the ability to elaborate material, instead of as a form of distortion. Third, there is a focus on qualitative differences in schematic organization. Northway (1940b) goes as far as to say that quantitative differences actually tell us little about schematic differences. In her second study, she includes a more traditional test of rote recall but finds that this analysis can say very little about what is most essential to "what subjects make of the material." Fourth, like Bartlett, she analyzes remembering as socially embedded and interest-driven. Thus, she finds distinctive patterns of recall for pupils in the three schools and children of different ages. In highlighting these similarities, I do not mean to imply that Northway merely reproduces Bartlett's approach; rather I see her as introducing important methodological innovations (e.g., comparison of different learning styles on schematic organization) and theoretically elaborating it into a highly suggestive form (i.e., "what the subject makes of the material"). Unfortunately, little has since been done to further develop Northway's work. Instead, schema would be brought into the mainstream of psychology in a very different form.

Reconstruction of Schema, Phase 2: Cognitive Psychology

Schema underwent its most significant change with the rise of cognitive psychology. The use of a computer metaphor of mind and methodology of counting units that go in and come out of a generally fixed system changed schema from a dynamic and embodied concept that incorporated affect and interests into a static knowledge structure used to represent information in the world 'out there.' This conceptual change was set in motion in Bartlett's own laboratory, where the metaphor of information flow was already beginning to be used to conceptualize person–machine interactions (Chapter 1). One of Bartlett's former students of the laboratory, Oldfield (1954), translated schema into the new language of information storage on a computer. Unlike the fixed storage on a wax tablet or photograph, he argued that computer information storage allowed for 're-codings' of elements (i.e., binary code) to economize storage and develop new connections between elements. Reconstruction was then a re-coding of elements and schema was the pattern or plan used to do so. This mechanical metaphor of mind spread widely and sets the stage for the rise of cognitive psychology (see also Chapter 6).

In an early foundational book of cognitive psychology, Neisser (1967) drew heavily on Bartlett's (1932/1995, 1958) work but did so very selectively in order to fit Bartlett's ideas into the computer metaphor of mind. For example, there is no mention of an 'effort after meaning' through which schema enters a mental act in Bartlett's account. Instead, Neisser (1967) clarifies schema through a 'program analogy.' Programs, like schema, are said to be 'a series of instructions' or a "recipe for selecting, storing, recovering, combining, outputting, and generally manipulating [information]" (p. 8). With this analogy, Neisser (1967) strictly separates the psychological level of analysis from the bio-functional – the former is the software (program) and the latter is the hardware (machinery) – whereas for Bartlett these were inseparable. Thus, by being defined as a 'recipe,' 'cognitive structure,' or 'organized representation of prior experience,' schema is severed from its location in an active and developing activity.[14]

To describe the process of memory reconstruction, Neisser (1967) famously made an analogy with a paleontologist who must assemble a dinosaur skeleton from a pile of bones. Although this is a colorful example, it leads us to think that there are three separate kinds of entities involved in the process of reconstructive remembering – a central executor (the paleontologist), pieces of information (bones), and schema (plan) – and that only the executor is active (Iran-Nejad and Winsler, 2000). Because schema is already separate from the executor, there is no need for the notion of 'turning around upon one's own schema.' To make the analogy work from a Bartlettian perspective, there would only be bones, which would have to be continuously self-organizing in relation to the changing demands of the museum exhibit.

In the 1970s, a number of new concepts in cognitive psychology were explicitly derived from Bartlett's schema, including Minsky's (1975) *frames*, Shank and Abelson's (1977) *scripts*, and Mandler and Johnson's (1977) *story grammar*. Minsky was a computer scientist attempting to develop machines with human-like abilities. His concept of frame as "a data-structure for representing a stereotyped situation" (p. 212) clearly reveals this starting point. 'A frame' he says,

is a network of nodes and relations. The 'top levels' of a frame are fixed, and represent things that are always true about the supposed situation. The lower levels have many terminals – 'slots' that must be filled with specific instances or data. Each terminal can specify conditions its assignments must meet. (p. 212)

For example, a schema or frame for a graduate student's room (top level) contains items, such as a desk, calendar, pencils, books, etc. (lower level). We are more likely to remember items in the room that are schema consistent than inconsistent and likely to add items to our memory of the room which are schema consistent but were not actually present (Brewer and Treyens, 1981).[15] Shank and Abelson's (1977) concept of *script* has the same general form as *frame* but is organized into a sequence of actions: "A script is a predetermined, stereotyped sequence of actions that defines a well-known situation" (p. 41). A restaurant script, for instance, involves the following sequence of actions: enter, get seated, order, eat, pay, and leave. Each one of these discrete actions can be further divided into simpler actions, such as 'go to table,' 'pull out chair,' and 'sit down' or 'get seated.' Scripts are thus a series of isolated and rather banal actions, with nothing to say about feelings, interests, and rationalizations that one finds in Bartlett's work.

Like *frames* and *scripts*, Mandler and Johnson's (1977) concept of *story grammar* or *story schema* works with the hierarchical network metaphor. They explicitly remove from their consideration of schema Bartlett's notions of "literary style, mood, and various classes of stories" to narrow schema's meaning to "an idealized internal representation of the parts of a typical story and the relationship among these parts" (p. 111). Stories are composed of a setting and an episode, which can be divided into a number of episodes, each with a 'beginning,' 'development,' and 'end.' The development is further subdivided into 'complex reaction,' 'goal path,' and so on. On a horizontal level, these nodes are connected by *and, then*, and *cause* relations. The 'story schema' thus functions as "a set of expectations about the internal structure of stories which serves to facilitate both encoding and retrieval" (p. 112). Analogous to the 'deep grammar' of Chomskian linguistics, story grammar is said to be an innate and universal property of mind. *War of the Ghosts* is shown to deviate considerably from story schema and as such is considered a *bad* story in itself, rather than a story constructed by a culture with different norms, activities, and values. Although Mandler and Johnson (1977) do predict a number of omissions in story recall, they do not attend to the variety of different reproductions made by subjects, which so interested Bartlett. Thus, the social as well as the personal dimensions of schema are ignored in their account.

On the back of these developments, in a well-known paper, Rumelhart (1980) defined schema as "a data structure for representing the generic concepts stored in memory" (p. 34). At this point the concept has turned into a very different framework than the one Bartlett was advocating, though it is not exactly the trace theory of memory either. For one, early cognitive psychologists retain a notion of hierarchical organization as in Bartlett. But whereas for Bartlett schema operated as a unitary mass and could not be broken down into elementary units, the above cognitive theories put their emphases on elements in different slots or nodes of a static structure.[16] Because the structure is presumed to be relatively static or fixed, these psychologists have rarely bothered to do *repeated* reproduction experiments and when they have they merely compared later reproductions against the original material, whereas Bartlett was also attentive to the changes between one reproduction and another (Chapter 2). This is because schemata were said to be always active and developing in relation to interests and the environment. Likewise, Bartlett's focus on functional adaptation to the environment is replaced by a Cartesian view of mind removed from the world. As such there is no need for or mention of Bartlett's notion of 'turning around upon schema,' because schemata are already separated from the embodied organism relating to its environment. Lastly, early cognitive schema theories wholly ignored attitudes, interests, feelings, rationalizations, and a host of other factors, which were central to Bartlett's characterization of reconstruction, which he notably prefixes with 'imaginative.' In short, these early cognitive schema theories are spatial (not temporal), static (not developing), focus on elements or nodes (not holistic), passive (not active), individual (not social), and structural (not functional).

Reconstruction of Schema, Phase 3: Ecological and Discursive Psychology

By the late 1980s, psychologists were beginning to acknowledge again the social and cultural side of Bartlett's thinking. In 1987, Edwards and Middleton published an important article arguing that many important social dimensions of *Remembering* had been unjustly forgotten. In the years that followed, these authors and others at Loughborough University developed a sustained program of research on how discursive norms of different social contexts shape remembering (e.g., Middleton and Edwards, 1990b). Middleton and Brown (2005, 2008) pointed out the similarities between 'organized settings' (Bartlett's preferred name for schema) and their own notion of social context, which like Bartlett's concept is relatively stable but is also always continuously renegotiated in practice. This insistence on situating remembering in social context has provided an important counterweight to the typical belief of experimental psychologists that psychological processes observed in the laboratory are somehow 'pure' and thus more real than those observed in everyday life. A side effect of their emphasis on social context, however, has been to largely leave aside the *personal* experiential dimensions of remembering. This has recently been pointed out by a Japanese psychologist, Naohisa Mori, who in turn has developed a research program that uses insights from discursive psychology about social context, while focusing on the personal experiential aspects of remembering (centered in one's body). Mori (2009) calls his methodology 'the schema approach.'

Mori's approach starts with a very concrete question: "how can we distinguish between real remembering and fabrication?" He was forced to address this question when asked by the police to analyze the credibility of a defendant's testimony of committing murder. He and his colleagues were able to identify different narrative forms in the defendant's remembering 'real experiences' and his murder narrative (Hara, Takagi, and Matsushima 1997; Ohashi, Mori, Takagi, and Matsushima 2002). Narratives of 'real experiences' took the form of what they called *agent-alteration*, that is, referring to agents of action (self and others) alternatively, such as "**I** did ... then **he** did ... so **I** did ..." This narrative form parallels Gibson's (1979) 'perception–action cycles,' the circular interaction between agent and environment in activity. In contrast, the murder narrative was characterized by *agent-succession*, that is, referring to agents successively, such as "**I** did ... there, then **I** did ..." – thus suggesting that it was confabulated.

Mori (2008) wondered if these same narrative forms – for real and confabulated experience – could be demonstrated in a controlled experiment. He constructed an experiment that models the real-life social context of an 'interrogation.' Participants *navigated* one of two university campuses and a month later *exchanged* information about the navigation with a participant who navigated the other university campus. Each participant thus had first-hand knowledge of one university campus and second-hand knowledge of another. Two weeks later, participants were individually *interrogated* about what happened during the two navigations by a third participant (who was told the participants had navigated both universities). Following Bartlett's (1932/1995) method of repeated reproduction, an additional two *interrogation* sessions took place at 2-week intervals. Four participants took part in the study but only one particularly illustrative case was analyzed, following an idiographic approach to theory building (Salvatore and Valsiner, 2010).

Mori (2008) found a number of differences between narratives for the two campuses. First, the *agent-alteration/agent-succession* contrast that Hara, Takagi, and Matsushima (1997) had found in the murder defendant's testimony appears again here. For the directly experienced university, agent-alteration made up 69.2 percent of the narrative, whereas the percentage is reversed for the indirect experience, in which alteration counts for 41.7 percent. Second, objects tended to be variously described (e.g., the stairs were 'pretty large,' 'curved,' and 'grey') in remembering the direct experience, whereas descriptions were poorer for the indirect experience. Third, in the narrative of the direct experience objects tended to be unstably named, while for the indirect experience naming was more stable. For example, a room was called 'a something room,' 'a classroom,' and 'a room related to information' in remembering the direct experience, whereas for indirect experience a room would be given a single name (Mori, 2008, pp. 300–1). Fourth, the motivation for certain behavior tended to be explained as being environmentally induced for the direct experience and internally induced (e.g., "I thought" or "I guessed") for the indirect experience. Fifth, the participant expressed hesitation in drawing a map for the direct experience (signaling a struggle to come into experiential contact with the past) and none for the indirect experience. For Mori, these all indicate the operation of different 'organization of schemata' in the two conditions. However, all these differences become less apparent with repeated remembering, as a result of inter- and intrapersonal conventionalization – the former describes what happens when a participant appropriates ways of talking about his or her experience from the interrogator.

Mori's original contribution is to develop an experimental methodology – 'the schema approach' (Mori, 2009) – that is true to Bartlett's insight that remembering is both personal and social.

He encompasses the social nature of remembering by devising an experimental situation that models the social context of an interrogation, in either a courtroom or police station. A participant, who was involved in the navigation, engages in the free flow of conversation with a participant 'interrogator,' who does not know that one of the participant's narratives is a confabulation. The fact that Mori (2008) found differences in narrative form in this experiment similar to the real murder testimony (i.e., agent-alteration/agent-succession) suggests that he has successfully modeled some features of the real situation. Personal experience is brought into his experiment by introducing the body. In most memory experiments, the participant is confined to a chair and guided to attend only to the memory stimulus; other features of the experimental situation are simply considered noise to be carefully controlled (Mori, 2010). In contrast, in Mori's experiment it is precisely the experience of bodily movement and perception that the participant remembers (in the direct experience) which the experimenter tries to discover. We see the personal experiential qualities of coming into bodily 'contact' with an environment expressing themselves subtly in a narrative's form. He shows that the 'organization of schemata' in each remembering is different – due to the qualitative dissimilarities in the experiences themselves – and that this difference can be uncovered by analyzing a narrative form.

Conclusion: Past, Present, and Future of Schema

The history of schema demonstrates how the concept was flexibly adapted to meet the needs of different social contexts, analogous to the process schema itself was meant to describe at an individual level. As the concept of schema has been continuously reconstructed, it has changed from an *embodied, dynamic, temporal, holistic,* and *social* concept into its opposite in cognitive psychology. To summarize the story told, Head developed the early concept to describe how we coordinate serial movements through time. Bartlett saw in Head's schema the foundation for a theory of remembering that did not rely on memory storage as its root metaphor. He elaborated it in order to describe higher mental functions, such as remembering, but did so only in a hesitant and sketchy way. Bartlett's student Northway further adapted the concept to investigate qualitative differences for the organization of schema as a function of age, social background, difficulty of material, and methods used to learn it. Cognitive psychology then radically changed the concept by using the computer metaphor to articulate it. Schema was transformed into a static knowledge structure composed of different slots or nodes that either accept incoming information or fill in default values where input is lacking. Schema is here severed from an organism's functioning in the world. Although there have been attempts by discursive and ecological psychologists to bring back the earlier notion of schema in a new form, these developments have not affected the way in which the concept is generally understood in psychology.

There are two major obstacles in bringing the Bartlettian concept of schema back into psychology: one meta-theoretical and one methodological. Meta-theoretically, the storage metaphor is both the common-sense and scientific taken-for-granted way of conceptualizing memory. As was seen with cognitive theories, theorists easily slip back into the language and assumptions of the storage metaphor. What is needed are powerful new metaphors to guide theory and research. One example is schema as 'stage setting,' advanced by Bransford, McCarrell, Franks, and Nitsch (1977) as an explicit development of Bartlett and Gibson's ideas. According to them, "a major role of past experience is to provide 'boundary constraints' that *set the stage* for articulating the uniqueness as well as sameness of information" (p. 434, emphasis in original). This is very different from the notion that past experience is stored as traces and compared to present inputs. Instead, it highlights organismic *attunement* to the environment based on past experience, operating as a background condition rather than as isolated and fixed traces or a static framework composed of isolated nodes that receive information. For example, if one is used to driving a pickup truck this will set the stage for articulating the smoothness of a car's ride. Likewise, remembering involves attunement (an attitude) and contextual information to set the stage on which previous experience is reconstructed within these given constraints.

Methodologically, psychology needs to invent new methods of bringing time, as an indivisible movement, back into its studies. Time is typically *spatialized* in psychological research by only considering clock time and by simply counting and averaging items between subjects at one point in time. This fails to address the two questions that Bartlett (1935) set as a research agenda, namely how schemas develop and what are the processes of memory reconstruction. Above I called these a long and short temporality, respectively, because they necessitate situating psychological processes in the 'irreversibility of time,' to borrow a phrase from Bergson. Time in this conception involves qualitative and accumulative change.

Bartlett (1928a) gives an example of the long temporality in relation to Watson and Rayner's (1920) famous experiment on 'little Albert,' who they taught to fear white rats (among other white fluffy things) by presenting a loud noise when the rat was present. From an ecological perspective, these psychologists were shaping a certain attunement or orientation to the environment. It is not possible to erase this earlier experience (i.e., reverse time) with white rats but the schema can nonetheless be further developed through new encounters. Bartlett (1928a) suggests introducing another boy into the setting to play with the white rat and for Albert to observe, which will stimulate curiosity to counterbalance the fear. Bartlett's (1932/1995) repeated reproduction method, which analyzes qualitative changes in single cases, is itself a powerful means of exploring the long temporality, as is its extension in Northway's (1940b) and Mori's (2008) studies focusing on the 'organization of schema.' These latter studies are interesting in that they explicitly look at how the dynamic social and cultural relations of a context of reproduction feed-forward into the next reproduction, setting the stage for reconstruction there. In other words, rather than seeing schema as simply in the head, they highlight how social and cultural aspects of the setting are continuously interwoven into the person's evolving schema. Others have also begun to develop schema in a more inclusive social and cultural direction to answer the questions about its long temporality: for example, McVee, Dunsmore, and Gavelek (2005) combine it with neo-Vygotskyian concepts of mediation within the field of education, and Beals (1998) extends it with Bakhtin's concepts of speech genres and heteroglossia.

Exploring the short temporality was more of a problem for Bartlett in that he had to rely on notes he took while carefully observing his subjects during the experimental task and their comments on their experience. Today, psychologists can use video recorders and other technologies, which were unavailable to Bartlett, to scrutinize the moment-to-moment processes of remembering in their details, as Middleton and Edwards (1990b) and Mori (2008) have done. These experiments set up a conversational task to create conditions in which subjects externalize and objectify their thinking, so as to record remembering as it occurs and then analyze it in its temporal dimensions. More recently, I have suggested conceptualizing the process of 'turning around upon schema' with theories of self-reflection from Vygotsky and G.H. Mead (see Wagoner, 2011a, 2012). As already noted, Bartlett could not *explain* the process of 'turning around upon schema' and at the end of his life he said it simply *described* what was happening. Vygotsky's 'sign' and Mead's 'significant symbol' can provide the missing mechanism that *explains* how we can experientially move outside ourselves and thereby reflect on our own activity. In Vygotsky's (1987) account this is possible because the sign is by definition a social relation, having been internalized through interaction with others in social practices (Veresov, 2010). Similarly, Mead

(1934) describes how I can take the perspective of the other toward myself through the vocal gesture, because I have heard it from both sides of a social act (Gillespie, 2007).

Applying this framework, the researcher can analyze 'turning around upon schema' as a process of sign mediation in which the person both stimulates and evaluates his memory with signs. A conversational replication of Bartlett's method of repeated reproduction (Wagoner and Gillespie, 2014) showed that people make suggestions to themselves and then either accept or reject them, ask themselves questions, and then answer them. In other words, people were continually turning around on their own efforts, reflecting managing their remembering as it unfolds. In this way, people are not simply the dupes of their own false suggestions, but often take active control of their remembering. This involves dancing around a memory, cajoling themselves to remember something in a gap of memory through self-suggestion and evaluation. It is here that we see the active interplay of different schema. From this, it follows that people do not simply output memories; instead, memories are produced through a constructive process that unfolds in time (Chapter 2). A method capable of analyzing the emergence of something qualitatively new (e.g., an adapted memory) in single cases through time is an invaluable resource (see 'microgenetic method' – Wagoner, 2009). In addition to providing an analytic strategy for investigating the short temporality, this experimental extension also bring back the social and cultural focus into the act of remembering by exploring the means and strategies people use to remember. From a cultural psychology approach, these are social in origin. Chapter 5 will elaborate the distinctly social dimensions of Bartlett's reconstructive theory of remembering and how this aspect was developed by others in a number of psycho-anthropological field studies from the 1930s until today.

Notes

1. Piaget is another source from which psychology takes the notion of 'schema,' but will not be considered here. Like Bartlett's friend and associate Henry Head, Piaget takes the term from philosopher Immanuel Kant who saw it as an imaginative link bridging sensation and understanding. Piaget's (1952) definition of schema as "a cohesive, repeatable action sequence possessing component actions that are tightly interconnected and governed by a core meaning" (p. 7) is not so far from Head and Bartlett.
2. Bartlett (1932/1995) was only against a version of the trace theory that excluded the active, holistic, flexible character of our memories: "Though we may still talk of traces, there is no reason in the world for regarding these as made complete at one moment, stored up somewhere, and then

re-excited at some much later moment. The traces that our evidence allows us to speak of are interest-determined, interest-carried traces. They live with our interests and with them they change" (pp. 211–12).

3. Contemporary neuroscience is increasingly moving toward a conceptualization of the brain as a contextual, holistic, and dynamic system that never returns to the same state twice, and as such the notion of memory as a static register of an experience looks more and more implausible even from a neurological perspective (see Singer, 2007). From this new neurological perspective, Nobel Prize winning scientist Gerard Edelman (2005) has developed alternative active and dynamic metaphors of memory using immunology and Darwinian natural selection as models.

4. The contemporary equivalent of this position is ecological psychology, which follows the work of J.J. Gibson.

5. Bartlett read Bergson with enthusiasm at the beginning of his career. The influence of Bergson is likely significant, though Bartlett does not cite him. A thorough study of this link still needs to be made.

6. Northway (1940a, p. 320) also pointed out the important influence of Bartlett's mentor James Ward, who built on philosopher Lotze's notion of the 'activity of memory,' in which memory is understood as a scheme or plan of action rather than a picture in the mind.

7. This notion of schema comes close to the way it is used by Johnson (1987).

8. Studies in memory expertise have made similar points. Chess masters, for instance, have excellent memory for chess positions in an actual game, but remember no better than novices for randomly placed pieces (Chase and Simon, 1973).

9. However, meta-cognition is a much more de-contextualized process of observation and control. Turning around on schema, in contrast, is a situated act of agency under definite constraints.

10. Halbwachs (1992) similarly argued that it was the unique interplay between different social frameworks in an individual that made memory feel personal (see Chapter 5).

11. In *Psychology and Primitive Culture*, Bartlett (1923) referred a group's activity of building together material from diverse sources as 'social constructiveness' (Chapter 3). Here we see the same idea applied at the individual level (see Wagoner, 2013).

12. Bartlett's thinking on this point in many ways resembles the pragmatist's theory of action and self-reflection (see Gillespie, 2007). Wagoner (2012) has argued that G.H. Mead's (1934) theory of self-reflection is superior to Bartlett's in that it provides a social mechanism for the process, whereas Bartlett (1968b) is content to remain at the level of description. However, the two approaches can also be fruitfully combined (Wagoner and Gillespie, 2014).

13. This image function, where information can be lifted from one setting and brought into another, parallels Bartlett's (1923) theorizing of 'diffusion by borrowing,' whereby an individual travels abroad and in returning home introduces a foreign element of culture into their group. For Bartlett cultural contact also freed the individual by providing multiple possible trains of thought (see Chapter 3; Wagoner, 2013).

14. Neisser (1976) later criticized his own earlier position, after having been persuaded by J.J. Gibson that an ecological approach was necessary.
15. Brewer (2000) and Brewer and Nakamura (1984) have also written a number of important meta-reflections on the concept of schema. His position is very much within the cognitive line of thinking and Minsky's theory in particular.
16. McVee, Dunsmore, and Gavelek (2005) have earlier criticized the cognitive concept of schema for failing to explore its origins and development.

Social Organization gives a persistent framework into which all detailed recall must fit, and it powerfully influences both the manner and the matter of recall. Moreover, this persistent framework helps to provide those 'schemata' which are a basis for the imaginative reconstruction called memory. It is equally probable that the social creation and clash of interests aid in the development of the specific images which ... may be present in individual recall.

(Bartlett, 1932/1995, p. 296)

In the previous chapters, we explored the core concepts and their relations in Bartlett's general theory of remembering. We saw how these concepts were later adopted by psychologists but in a transformed form. While concepts like 'schema' and 'construction' have become common parlance when discussing memory, their link to Bartlett's social psychology has been generally neglected. This was made possible by the structure of *Remembering* itself – Bartlett's 'theory of remembering' was highly phenomenological and placed at the end of Part I, while his explicit theorizing about the embeddedness of mind in social processes is relegated to Part II of the book, to which psychologists have paid much less attention. In Part II, Bartlett is very clear that most human schemata are social in origin and that remembering needs to be conceptualized first and foremost as part of an everyday social practice. It is here that he returns to some of the key ideas developed in his earlier book *Psychology and Primitive Culture* on the dangers of assuming various psychological processes as being 'pre-social,' that is, operating in independence of history.

In this chapter, I discuss Bartlett's distinctive social psychological approach to remembering and in so doing I make links between his experiments (Chapter 2), his anthropological ideas (Chapter 3), and his theoretical description of remembering (Chapter 4). First, I outline the theories of two of Bartlett's contemporaries (i.e., Jung and Halbwachs), who took up the question of the collective aspects of memory and thus set the stage for Bartlett's approach. These theories develop opposing perspectives on the subject: Jung did not escape the biologizing tendencies of the nineteenth century, while Halbwachs stressed the inescapable social character of memory. Second, I sketch out precisely what Bartlett understood by 'social psychology' and third, I proceed to show how he applies this understanding to the topic of remembering; the two sides of his social psychology are shown to correspond to his distinction between the 'matter and manner of recall.' Fourth, I will consider three generations of psycho-anthropological field studies, which have borrowed, criticized, and extended Bartlett's social psychological approach to remembering. Finally, this chapter concludes with a reflection on the meaning and place of the social in studies of remembering.

Collective Memory: Jung and Halbwachs

The notion of collective memory was being discussed in two contrasting ways when Bartlett was developing his own social psychological approach to remembering.[1] On the one side, collective memory was conceived in terms of biological inheritance and thus the product of phylogeny. This idea is the collective equivalent of the trace theory of memory, in which material is individually stored in the organism for later use (Chapter 4). G.G. Jung's theory of collective unconscious and archetypes exemplified this approach. On the other side were theories that aimed to shift the focus from the biological to the distinctly social aspects of the collective memory. From this perspective, the generational persistence of collective knowledge is not a result of phylogeny but rather socialization into the 'cultural patterns' or 'social frameworks' of a particular group. This approach is no better illustrated than in the classic work of Maurice Halbwachs (1925/1992). In this section, I sketch out these two approaches as well as Bartlett's (1932/1995) criticisms of them.[2]

The biological approach to collective memory is a form of Lamarckian evolution, whereby an individual has access to the past experiences of his or her ancestors. Sigmund Freud had argued that an act of patricide occurring in the primordial past continued to effect father–son relationships. Following this lead, Jung said that the unconscious contains both a personal and collective layer. The personal layer ends at the earliest memories of infancy, while the collective layer reaches back into the ancestral past. The collective unconscious contains images, ideas, formulas, and laws that express our ancestors' views about the world, which are biologically transmitted from one generation to the next. Jung located these in the brain, arguing that because all human brains are equally differentiated this meant that mental functions must also contain collective and universal elements. Bartlett counters this argument by pointing out that brains are the basis for the subsequent development of functions and not the storehouse of functions or images, especially not those from an ancestral past. Analogously, the human baby's possession of legs is neither sufficient for walking – that requires a process of learning – nor does the simple fact of having hands give the baby images of the tools he will later use.

A second piece of evidence Jung provides for his theory is the "extraordinary agreement of indigenous myths both as to theme and form" (quoted from Bartlett, 1932/1995, p. 285). Bartlett argues that psychoanalysts and symbolists have far too easily and uncritically identified the *same* symbols in different cultures around the world. Furthermore, even if a symbol was found to be universal it would not solve the problem of how it came to be so. Here we see Bartlett's preference for diffusionist explanation over 'psychic unity' (Chapter 3). Bartlett substantiates his position with River's (1922) article on 'the symbolism of rebirth,' in which he demonstrates that what was taken by psychoanalysts to be an exemplary case of a universal symbol, in fact, is not universal and the overlap found could be explained by population movements and the transmission of culture. Finally, Bartlett suggests that there could also be a 'fit' between psychological function and material that can be found in practically any environment. For instance, Jung's 'sun archetype' could be easily explained by similar environmental conditions rather than a biologically inherited memory trace.

The theory of the collective unconscious thus confused phylogeny and sociogenesis. Ideas, symbols, and the like are not passed on biologically from one generation to the next, but socially through the age overlap in members of a group. In contrast to the biological conceptualization, Halbwachs (1925/1992) powerfully developed a truly social psychological theory of collective memory. Using the same line of argument made by Durkheim with regard to the social nature of thought categories (Chapter 3), he argued that remembering is conditioned by social life. "It is in society that people normally acquire their memories. It is also in society that they recall, recognize, and localize their memories" (Halbwachs, 1925/1992, p. 38). From this perspective, psychologists' attempts to locate memories in the individual, or worse still the brain, entirely miss the point. What is most important about human memory is that it takes place through 'social frameworks.' These are first the other people one interacts with and secondly they can be taken at a more symbolic level to include condensed images of the past and a structure to give them order and meaning.[3] When we remember, we place ourselves within the perspective of a group and elaborate along its lines.

Halbwachs develops his argument by considering the collective memory of the family, the religious group, and social classes. Every group develops a mental life of its own, with its own memories, formulas, and images of the past, which it passes to its members. These in turn function as models, examples, a basis for education, and in doing so the group's identity is solidified around them. Consider Halbwachs's description of family memory:

> When we say "In our family we are long lived," or "we are proud," or "we do not get rich," we speak of some physical or moral property which we treat as inherent in the group and passing from it to its members. Sometimes it is the place or country of origin of the family, or again it may be some outstanding characteristic of one of its members, which becomes the more or less mysterious symbol of the common stock from which all the constituent individuals draw their peculiar qualities.
>
> (Halbwachs, 1925/1992; quoted from Bartlett, 1932/1995, p. 295)

For Bartlett (1932/1995), Halbwachs's book was 'a careful and attractive study' (p. 294), full of ideas that 'seem to be both true and important' (p. 296). Moreover, he saw it to be much in line with his own work, in that it highlighted how "social organization gives a persistent framework into which all detailed recall must fit, and it powerfully influences both the manner and the matter of recall" (p. 296). However, Bartlett was critical of the idea that the social group itself remembers. He is clear that we can only discuss with confidence "memory *in* the group, and not memory *of* the group" (p. 296). Whether Halbwachs actually held this view of the group's capacity to retain and recall its past can be disputed.[4] Nonetheless, Bartlett's discussion does provide some conceptual clarity. In everyday conversation we ask a person "do you remember X?" and genuinely believe their affirmation, even if they give little detail. It is difficult to see how this question could be posed to a social group and also have it answered in a unitary fashion. As such, the 'collective memory' remains an ambiguous metaphor.

This is not to say that group properties can be analyzed purely through the individuals in them. Interestingly, Bartlett feels perfectly comfortable applying the concept of temperament to the collective – that is, the 'group temperament.' Like Halbwachs, he is clear that "Social grouping produces new properties both of behavior and of experience" (Bartlett, 1932/1995, p. 298) and stresses that "we may ... legitimately speak of customs, traditions, institutions, technical secrets, formulated and unformulated ideals and numerous other facts are literally properties of groups, as the direct determinates of social action" (p. 254). Social groups develop institutions that are specific to them and which guide the thinking and action of their members (see Chapter 3). These 'preferred persistent group tendencies' must be taken into account in explaining psychological processes. In *Psychology and Primitive Culture*, Bartlett (1923) referred to them as 'group difference tendencies,' to emphasize that they differentiate one social group from another. Methodologically, this means that to adequately explain individual experience and action, psychologists need to attend to the customs and traditions *specific* to the social group of which the individual in question is a member. This insight is essential to understand his notion of social psychology, which we now turn to.

Bartlett on Social Psychology

The idea that one cannot understand individual experience and behavior in separation from group processes is key to Bartlett's delineation of social psychology as a discipline. Bartlett (1932/1995, p. 239) defined social psychology "as the systematic study of the modifications of individual experience and response due directly to membership in a group." Precisely what is meant here is best approached through examples. Bartlett tells two stories that he gathered during his 1929 visit to Swaziland in South East Africa to outline the discipline of social psychology. It was at this time that he was able to finally partially realize his earlier anthropological aspirations by doing some fieldwork among the Swazi. These stories began his Cambridge undergraduate lectures on social psychology as well as Part II of *Remembering* (pp. 239ff). We must, however, remember that Bartlett was never rigorously trained in ethnography, which often leads him to read too much into limited data. The stories are reports from others and as such we should be somewhat skeptical about their credibility, due to the very processes of change illustrated in his serial reproduction experiments (see Chapter 2). Our major interest here though is not in the stories' accuracy, but rather how Bartlett uses them to delineate social psychology's object of inquiry.

The first story is of a Swazi ceremony whereby those guilty of causing some calamity – e.g., loss of cattle, sudden death, illness, crop failure, etc. – through wizardry are identified and killed. It is called 'smelling out' by the Swazi because guilt is said to smell bad. The group sits in a circle each holding a spear, while a witch doctor dances around the inside of the ring, stopping in front of one man and jumping away. This is continued several times until finally other men sitting in the circle spear the man to death on the spot. Five or six men are said to be killed in wild excitement on the same night. Bartlett points out that the Swazi are generally law-abiding and not terribly excitable; they are no more likely to kill in the case of an ordinary neighborly meeting than a typical

European would. But under these specific social conditions, Swazis' emotions can be excited in such a way that they kill their comrades. This is a case of direct social guidance of individual conduct in the physical presence of a group, or what would today be called 'social influence.' According to Bartlett, these individuals are being regulated by the norms of the specific social setting.

In the second story, a Swazi native on a journey spends a night in a *kraal* (cattle enclosure). While he was sitting talking to the chief, a black mamba – the most deadly snake in the region and also highly aggressive – slithers toward him from a hole in the ground. The traveler immediately throws his spear at the snake and kills it, but just as quickly the chief picks up a heavy chunk of wood and knocks him to the ground with it. The traveler narrowly escapes but dies later as a result of poor medical treatment. Why would the chief all of a sudden attack the visitor? The answer: The snake was the chief's grandfather. In this region there is a close relationship between the spirit of dead ancestors and snakes, and in this village the black mamba was particularly important. What we see in this example is how individuals internalize their group's traditions, such that they guide individual conduct outside of the direct physical presence of the group.

Thus, social psychology is the study of how action is facilitated by a group's customs, conventions, and beliefs either through the direct influence of others or through the internalization of group norms. The first story might seem to describe what social psychology has indeed studied for the last 50 years: numerous studies have shown how social influences can lead 'normal' individuals to act against their character, even violently toward others (e.g., Milgram, 1974; Haney, Banks, and Zimbardo, 1973). Along these lines, Bartlett (1932/1995) himself said, "I may seem to know a man through and through, and still would not dare to say the first thing about what he will do in a group" (p. 24). However, his practice of social psychology differs from these in that he focuses on *specific* already existing social groups, and how their particular histories and conventions shape the behavior of their members. The basic unit of analysis is 'the-individual-in-a-given-social-group' (Bartlett, 1923, p. 11; see Chapter 3). In contrast, contemporary social psychology has typically dealt with artificial small group interactions and their short-term effects (Danziger, 1992), rather than historically existing social groups and the norms and traditions particular to them.[5]

This is related to the widespread tendency in psychology today to think of the individual as rational and free outside of the group, which social influence corrupts (Greenwood, 2003). Research on memory distortion tends to take a similar stance. For example, eyewitness testimony research since Loftus's (1975) classic study has tended to focus on how social influence leads to distorted or inaccurate memory. In contrast, for Bartlett and many others at this time, social life provided the framework for agency and constructive memory to develop in the first place – an assumption still held in much of cultural psychology today (for a review, see Wagoner, forthcoming). In short, according to Bartlett, social psychology must deal with how specific groups' persistent social frameworks shape their members' psychological processes and actions, through either direct social interaction or the internalization of social norms. The argument that psychological processes are always historically embedded was already put forward in *Psychology and Primitive Culture* (see Chapter 3, especially the section 'Bartlett's social psychological approach'). It is here used to understand the social processes involved in any act of remembering, which will be described in what follows.

Matter and Manner of Recall

Bartlett's description of two stories delineating social psychology directly parallels his distinction between the matter and manner of recall. The 'matter of recall' is about how internalized norms and traditions shape *what* we remember, while the 'manner of recall' concerns how the presence of other group members shapes *how* we remember. The latter thus involves attending to concrete social processes occurring *between* people. Bartlett's (1932/1995) experimental studies provided abundant evidence of the matter of recall (see Chapter 2), but only secondarily focused on the manner of recall.[6] In his experiments, he describes a participant, who when briefly presented with a hand pointing upward to some ambiguous object (see Figure 5.1) said he had seen an aircraft gun firing at an airplane. This experiment was conducted during the First World War, when people were constantly expecting and talking about air raids. Similarly, in his *serial reproduction* experiment, subjects changed a phrase in the Native American story *War of the Ghosts* to read "elderly relatives 'would grieve terribly' if he did not return" (p. 129). The social framework surrounding the First World War was clearly shaping his participants' perceiving and remembering – that is, the matter of recall. With regards to the manner of recall, Bartlett only mentions a comparison between oral and written recall he made using the method of serial reproduction; the story is never quite the same in the two cases, even if the matter is identical. Later in the book, he says that, "To write out a story which has been read is a very different matter from retelling to auditors a story which has

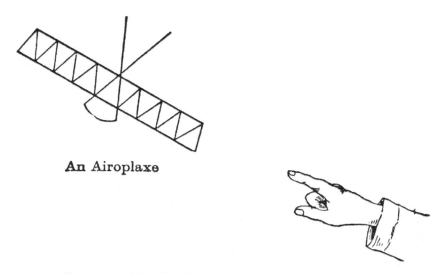

An Airoplaxe

Figure 5.1.   Stimuli in Bartlett's perceiving experiment

been heard. The social stimulus, which is the main determinant of form in the latter case, is almost absent from the former" (Bartlett, 1932/1995, p. 174).[7]

Although he makes a few connections to his experiments, Bartlett's principle source for elaborating his distinction between the matter and manner of recall came from observations he made on his 1928 trip to Swaziland in Southeast Africa. In relation to the matter of recall, Bartlett describes how a group of Swazis who had visited England remembered the police officers as being particularly friendly. This was because the hand gesture they made to stop traffic was similar to the Swazi gesture for greeting their fellows, demonstrating again how a social framework determines what is selectively attended to and remembered. In discussing Swazi memory, Bartlett also takes up the question of 'primitive' mentality, already discussed at length in his 1923 book *Psychology and Primitive Culture* (Chapter 3). European travelers to 'primitive cultures' had reported that the natives had exceptional memory capacities. Bartlett was perhaps the first to test this assumption in a number of field experiments, as his Cambridge mentors had done with regard to the special senses on the Cambridge Expedition to the Torres Strait (see Haddon, 1901). In one experiment, Bartlett instructed a random boy of 11 or 12 years of age to take a brief message of about 25 words from one end of a village to the other.[8] The result was that the boy did no better or worse than an English boy of the same age.

Bartlett also tried out experimental tests similar to those written up in *Remembering*, but with material understandable to the locals, and found similar levels of recall when compared to Europeans.

There was at least one context, however, in which the Swazi remembered with much greater detail and accuracy than Europeans: information concerning cattle.[9] Swazi society revolves around the care and possession of cattle. If an animal goes astray and gets mixed up with other herds, the owner can come with a description of the missing beast. No matter how long the interval of time passed, the owner's word is almost never questioned, because it is expected that the herdsman remembers the individual characteristics of his cattle. Bartlett decided to test this by having a herdsman recall a list of cattle bought by his employer the previous year, together with any additional information he would like to give. The native rapidly recited a list of nine transactions, for example: "From Mampini Mavalane, one black polly cow, with grey on the throat, for £3." Bartlett was able to compare this description against a record of transactions the owner had kept, and found that the herdsman had made only two 'trifling errors,' despite the fact that he had only overheard the transactions that were made by his employer. It is noteworthy that Bartlett's example here is of incredibly accurate memory, whereas his theory is now typically characterized as showing that memory is unreliable (Ost and Costall, 2002). According to Bartlett (1968b), accurate memory is possible, but it is domain-specific and socialized by the group. This being the case, memory cannot adequately be studied as a content- and context-free capacity (see Chapter 2).

In discussing the manner of recall, Bartlett again takes up the question of the memory of 'primitive' people. However, his characterization here is much more problematic than with the matter of recall. He suggests that primitive social organization has parallels with low-level remembering in individuals, in having few interests, all of which are concrete and of equal dominance. These factors are thought to favor remembering by rote recapitulation over constructiveness. Swazis' particular social interest in cattle leads them to swiftly recall the price, color, and origin of their beasts and to disregard all irrelevant detail. But in other contexts, where no such dominant interest lies, they tend toward rote recall. Bartlett (1932/1995) paints the following picture of Swazi customs to illustrate his point about social organization's facilitation of rote recall:

Two wanderers on a pathway meet, they make a clean breast one to another of all that they have lately done, seen and learned. Rote recital is easily the best method. The same style is exploited in the leisurely and wordy native councils. There is behind it the drive of a group with plenty of time, in a sphere of relatively uncoordinated interest, where everything that happens is about as interesting as everything else, and where, consequently, a full recital is socially approved.

(Bartlett, 1932/1995, pp. 265–6)

Clearly, Bartlett does not fully escape the condescending colonial perspective of his compatriots. According to him, this same manner of rote recall is present when Europeans examine 'relatively primitive people' in a court of law. The witness tends to recall chronologically everything that happened in detail without focusing on those details that are relevant to the case at hand. This was characteristic of 'unsophisticated' recall for Bartlett. It is a kind of all or nothing response, which is also how Bartlett's mentors characterized primitive sensitivity in their famous experiment on nerve regeneration (see Rivers and Head, 1908; and also Chapter 3). Bartlett gives the following abbreviated example of an actual court case involving attempted murder. In it, the woman seems unable to break the chronological sequence of events and focus on the detail relevant to the case at hand, much to the annoyance of the Magistrate:

The Magistrate: Now tell me how you got that knock on the head.
    The Woman: Well, I got up that morning at daybreak and I did ... (here followed a long list of things done, and of people met, and things said). Then we went to so and so's kraal and we ... (further lists here) and had some beer, and so and so said ...
    The Magistrate: Never mind about that. I don't want to know anything except how you got the knock on the head.
    The Woman: All right, all right. I'm coming to that. I have not got there yet. And so I said so and so ... (there followed again a great deal of conversation and other detail). And then after that we went on to so and so's kraal.
    The Magistrate: You look here: if we go on like this we shall take all day. What about that knock on the head?
    The Woman: Yes; all right, all right. But I have not got there yet. So we ... (on and on for a very long time relating all the initial details of the day). And then we went on to so and so's kraal ... and there was a dispute ... and he knocked me on the head, and I died, and that is all I know.

(Bartlett, 1932/1995, p. 265)

A second, more plausible account of the manner of recall was also given by Bartlett. He notes that whenever an event is recalled in the presence of others certain characteristics will spring forth, such as the comic, the pathetic, or the dramatic. The narrator will exaggerate certain features for the sake of the audience's interest. The two are attuned to one another and form a feedback loop: "There is social control from the auditors to the narrator" (p. 266).[10] This is one reason why one's style of speech and writing will be different. The focus on social relationships and their influence on psychological processes had earlier been elaborated by Bartlett in relation to the diffusion of culture, in particular folk stories (Bartlett, 1920a, 1923). He noted how stories tended to change as they entered new social groups, because the narrator adapts them to conform to the social interests of his or her audience. As a result of this, different characters, events, and morals will take prominence as a function of the group in which the story enters and its social framework. A similar effect also occurs with rumors or whenever information spreads within or between groups.[11]

In addition to the narrator's orientation to the social framework of his auditors, Bartlett also suggests that the form of relationship between them plays an important role. Here he draws on the distinction between *dominance* and *submissiveness* earlier discussed in *Psychology and Primitive Culture* (Chapter 3). This brings in the interesting topic of *power asymmetries* in remembering, especially those occurring between members of different social groups.

Change the audience to an alien group, and the manner of recall again alters. Here the most important things to consider are the social position of the narrator in his own group, and his relation to the group from which his audience is drawn. If the latter group are submissive, inferior, he is confident, and his exaggerations are markedly along the lines of the preferred tendencies of his own group. If the alien audience is superior, masterly, dominating, they may force the narrator into the irrelevant, recapitulatory method until, or unless he, wittingly or unwittingly, appreciates their own preferred bias. (p. 266)

This analytic focus provides an equal, if not more, convincing explanation of the woman's manner of recall in the above court case example. The Magistrate is certainly a member of a dominant group, whose social framework may not be immediately understandable to the woman. This leads her to recount much more information than he deems relevant. In this way, rote recall is not a matter of primitiveness of the people involved but the social relationship between narrator and audience. The social relationship unavoidably shapes both how and what is remembered. For this reason, Bartlett says that anthropologists need to be cognizant of their own position vis-à-vis their informants, a principle widely discussed in the field today (e.g., Bourdieu, 1999).

Although matter and manner of recall are analytically separate, Bartlett argues that they mutually influence one another. This point is, however, left largely unelaborated. Like his concept of schema (Chapter 4), his characterization of each and their coordination in remembering remained more suggestions to explore in future studies than fully worked-out analyses. What is clear is that Bartlett aimed to develop a thoroughly social approach to remembering, which highlighted individuals' remembering in relation to others (whether of their own or another group) and to the norms, customs, and traditions specific to the group(s) concerned. This involved attending to the audience of the person remembering, their form of social relationship, and the social frameworks that come into play in this dynamic. In what follows we will see how others developed Bartlett's social psychology of remembering in three generations of psycho-anthropological field studies.

Nadel and Bateson's Anthropological Reconstructions

Not long after the publication of *Remembering* in 1932, Bartlett's social psychological theory of remembering was tested by two anthropologists: Siegfried Frederick Nadel and Gregory Bateson. Both of them incorporated psychological concepts into their anthropological work, had direct contact with Bartlett, and published seminal studies in 1937. Nadel finished his thesis at the London School of Economics in 1935 on 'Political and Religious structure of Nupe Society' under the supervision of Malinowski and Seligman (who was on the Cambridge Expedition to the Torres Strait). That same year he was invited to join a group of social scientists assembled together by Bartlett, whose discussions resulted in *The Study of Society* (1939) (Chapter 1). Nadel remained in close contact with Bartlett from 1935 on, and decided to use Bartlett's *method of repeated reproduction* during his continued fieldwork among the Nupe. The results were published in the journal *Africa*, alongside an article by Bartlett (1937a) arguing that psychological methods could fruitfully be used by anthropologists, as Nadel had done.

Nadel's study focuses principally on the matter of recall by comparing the neighboring Nupe and Yoruba tribes, living in Northern Nigeria. In spite of the fact that they share the same material environment and similar levels of technology, the two tribes had developed 'entirely different, almost antagonistic, cultures' (p. 424). For example, the religion of the Yoruba was characterized by "an elaborate and rationalized hierarchical system of deities each of which has its specific, specialized duties and functions," whereas the Nupe believed in an 'abstract and impersonal power' (p. 424). In art, the Yoruba had the human figure as a principal motif, while the Nupe developed an ornamental, decorative form (cf. Haddon's description of figurative and abstract decorative patterns – Chapter 3). The Yoruba had a tradition of drama and the Nupe had none. Nadel claims that the general tendency toward integrated and concrete meanings among the Yoruba and abstract details among the Nupe was manifested in a diversity of other cultural forms in both tribes – their folklore, music, dance, habitual everyday behavior, etc.[12]

To test how the two groups' 'preferred persistent tendencies' guide the remembering of their members, Nadel constructed the following story to use in a repeated reproduction experiment on children in local schools of both communities:

Long, long ago there were a man and his wife. They had two children, sons. When these sons had grown up, they saw a beautiful girl, they both made friends with her and loved her very much. They loved her with one heart. But the girl did not love the elder brother, she only loved the younger. Thereupon the elder brother went to the younger and told him to give up the girl. He said: "I am the one to marry the girl for I am your elder brother." Thus he spoke. But the younger refused. They quarreled a great deal till the elder brother became furious. When night fell he went to the hut where the younger brother was sleeping and killed him with his sword, he killed him with one stroke. When the people heard the news they said, "He did an evil deed, God will revenge it." But the girl cried, she cried for twenty days and her heart was full of pain. When she had finished crying she left and went to another place. Nobody saw her again.

(Nadel, 1937, p. 427)

Bartlett's theory would predict that the Yoruba and Nupe would transform the story in the direction of their own cultural patterns: the Yoruba toward *logical coherence of narrative structure* and the Nupe toward *an enumeration of descriptive details*. This is in fact what he finds. Nadel notes that the Yoruba invent new links between parts of the story and faithfully reproduce existing links. The Nupe, on the other hand, retell the story in a much looser way, filling in details that are inessential to the narrative's progression. For example, the sentence "when these sons had grown up" is a logical link in the story – the brothers must grow up before having a love affair. The 18 out of 20 Yoruba children (90 percent) reproduced the sentence in the second reproduction, compared with only 4 out of 60 Nupe children (6.7 percent) doing so. Additionally, Nadel reports most Nupe reproduced the sentence "The elder brother did an evil deed, God will revenge him" simply as "God will revenge him," while the majority of Yoruba children strengthened the rational link with an elaboration, for example, "The elder brother has done very wrong. No man can judge him, but God will revenge it" (p. 428). It is worth noting here that Nadel is uninterested in the question of which tribe remembered more in his analysis; rather, like Bartlett, he is concerned with the *direction* of transformation in the two groups as a function of their preferred persistent group tendencies (see also Chapter 2).

Like Nadel, Bateson was concerned with understanding how a group's general cultural patterns (found across different social contexts) shape the remembering of their members. They differ in that Bateson employs an ethnographic rather than experimental method, and focuses mainly on the manner rather than on the matter of recall. Bateson did his M.A. in anthropology at Cambridge University in 1930 and became a research fellow at St. John's College from 1931 to 1937 (where both his grandfather and Bartlett were college notables). From 1932 to 1933, Bateson was engaged in fieldwork among the Iatmul of New Guinea, which he wrote up over the following two years for his celebrated book *Naven* (1937). At this time, he was also working under Bartlett in experimental psychology. In *Naven*, Bateson argued that every culture has its own general cognitive style or 'eidos,' which he analyzed in relation to the Iatmul's remembering. On this topic, Bateson is explicit about taking up Bartlett's (1932/1995) theory, in particular the issue of rote remembering and its relation to social customs.

Learned Iatmul men display a vast memory for totems and names, which they use in debates with one another. From a rough estimate of the number of songs possessed by each clan, each containing a number of names, Bateson estimated that these men have committed 10–20,000 names to memory. The names are compounds of four to six syllables that refer to details of an esoteric mythology. They are arranged in pairs which resemble each other (like Tweedledum and Tweedledee) and are connected by some association (e.g., in contrast or synonymous meaning). Thus, the names have tags that allow them to be memorized by word association as well as imagery, which I will focus on later. Bateson stresses that they are *not* recalled through a process of rote recapitulation where, according to Bartlett, accuracy in chronological sequence is strictly kept. When name pairs were given, their order was subject to 'slight but continual variation.' Moreover, the Iatmul never repeated already remembered names in an effort to produce more names. Instead, when the Iatmul are asked about some event in the past, they were able to give the relevant information without serially passing through other names.

Bateson connected the Iatmul skillful manner of remembering to their custom of debating. In these debates, competing clans can claim the right to a name by demonstrating their knowledge of the esoteric mythology to which it refers. Each clan needs to be careful not to give away too much knowledge or the other clan will have an improved means of claiming the name. Thus, the conflicting clans assert that they have superior knowledge of the mythology, while simultaneously sussing out how much the other actually knows.

In this context, the myth is handled by the speakers not as a continuous narrative, but as a series of small details. A speaker will hint at one detail at a time – to prove his own knowledge of the myth – or he will challenge the opposition to produce some detail. In this way there is, I think, induced a tendency to think of a story, not as a chronological sequence of events, but as a set of details with varying degrees of secrecy surrounding each – an analytic attitude which is almost certainly directly opposed to rote remembering.

(Bateson, 1936, p. 223)

In these debates, objects are also continuously offered for exhibition – for example, a shell necklace to represent a river or leaves used as emblems of a variety of objects and names are strategically placed within the debating grounds. Thus, visual and kinesthetic imagery as well as word and meaning association played an important role in the Iatmul's memory for names. In contrast, rote recall seemed to be rather unimportant in this context. Bateson does not argue that his findings contradict Bartlett's theory but rather that they show how particular social organization can facilitate a movement away from remembering by rote. Three decades later, cultural psychologist Michael Cole would be much more direct in his criticism of Bartlett's claim that primitive social organization leads to rote recall.

Cole's Cross-Cultural Investigations

Little was done with this seminal tradition of Bartlett, Nadel, and Bateson's psycho-anthropological studies for almost three decades. It was not until the 1960s that Michael Cole[13] and his colleagues revived it in their 'unorthodox ethnography' of Kpelle rice farmers in north central Liberia.[14] Their work is a notable exception to psychologists' typical neglect of the social and cultural side of Bartlett's theory of remembering (since the 1940s – see Chapter 2). The study's primary interest was in shedding further light on the perennial question of whether members of different cultures think and remember differently. To do this, they employed an experimental methodology, as Nadel had done, but focused on the manner of recall as with Bateson, especially the issue of rote remembering as an indicator of primitive social organization. They also had Americans of the same age do the experimental task, so as to have a group to compare with the Kpelle.

Cole and Gray (1972) used a 'free recall' experimental task, in which participants were presented with a list of words or objects and later allowed to recall them in whatever order they wished. This enabled the researchers to explore not only how much was remembered, but also more importantly *how* it was remembered. Earlier research had observed that when Western adults were given a free recall task they tended to 'cluster' their remembering of items around categories (e.g., clothing and food), rather than remembering them in the same order they were presented, indicating rote recall. In contrast to adults, young children tend not to cluster items when recalling them, nor do they improve much with practice. In applying the method in Liberia, Cole and Gray were careful to generate a list of items that were culturally familiar to the Kpelle and also that would be clusterable within their local social framework.

Given that the items to be remembered did not elicit social interest by the Kpelle nor was the task particularly familiar to them, Bartlett's theory would predict they would fall into a rote manner of recall. In fact, Cole and Gray found little pattern in their remembering in an initial free recall experiment; Kpelle adults neither recalled by rote nor by clustering. Moreover, there was little improvement across learning trials. In contrast, American College students remembered much more, improved with practice and readily clustered the items during recall. The authors, however, were careful not to read too much into this initial experiment: "We have only demonstrated differences in the way that adult representatives of two cultures recall a set of common nouns" (p. 1071). They went on to devise a number of other experimental manipulations to explore what factors condition these differences.

They next compared Kpelle children's performance on clusterable and non-clusterable lists, against American children. The clusterable list was much easier to remember than the non-clusterable list for both Kpelle and Americans, even though neither group showed much clustering. While the scores of Kpelle and Americans were similar, their pattern of recall varied considerably: American children showed considerable increases in recall and clustering scores from first to last trial, while Kpelle improvements were gradual and changed little in how much they clustered across the trials. However, the authors pointed out that the Kpelle are not learning by rote, as the order of input and output showed little correlation. In contrast, American children tended to rote recall on the first trial but not thereafter. The American children also had a much more pronounced *serial position effect* (where the first and last items in a list are recalled at a higher frequency than those in the middle – Ebbinghaus, 1885/1913). These differences in patterns of recall suggested that the Kpelle and Americans were approaching the task differently, but the nature of this difference remained unclear.

Earlier anthropologists, including Lévy-Bruhl (Chapter 3), had argued that 'primitive' or traditional people's thinking was concrete rather than abstract. Cole and Gray (1972) tested this with the free recall task by using physical objects rather than spoken word lists. They found recall improved slightly but did so for both Kpelle and Americans. They also compared educated and illiterate Kpelle to understand the role of schooling. There was in fact much higher recall among the educated who also showed marked improvement across the trials. To perform well on the free recall task requires the extraction of a rule (in this case semantic categories) to organize their memory for the list (Mandler, 1966). Improvement across trials can be understood as a result of learning to organize the material according to a rule, a familiar practice in formal schooling.

This led to the question: would making category membership more salient improve recall? One test of this compared random ordering versus 'blocked' ordering (where all items of a given category were presented together) of items in a list. Interestingly, in this experiment educated Kpelle did no better than the uneducated Kpelle, except when concrete objects were used, in which case education improved performance. As might be expected, 'blocked' ordering significantly increased clustering as well. Other means of making categories salient included a 'chair cueing method,' whereby concrete objects were presented over chairs representing one of four categories (i.e., clothing, tools, food, utensils). Under these conditions, recall dramatically improved and learning happened continuously across the trials, much like the American pattern. When objects were randomly presented above the four chairs, participants still recalled the items by the chair; however, here they did not improve significantly across the trials. In another experiment, they also found that they could greatly enhance Kpelle recall by having them recall items of a list one category at a time (e.g., "Tell me all the tools I named?"). In short, creating conditions for the Kpelle to organize their memory around categories greatly enhanced their performance in the free recall task.

In a final experiment, Cole and Gray tried embedding items-to-be-remembered within two narratives. Both narratives were constructed on the basis of familiar Kpelle folklore and were about a topic of social interest: marriage. The narratives differed in that in the first the items were serially presented and in the second they were clustered according to category. The first story described the marriage of the chief's daughter to a young man arriving in the village. The daughter soon learns that he is a witch and leaves objects along the path they travel to let her parents know where he has taken her. For example, at the edge of the town she leaves a handkerchief and crossing the bridge a spoon. The Kpelle are asked what objects she left behind? In the second narrative, four men come to ask for the chief's daughter. They all bring five different items, each man of a particular category (i.e., clothing, food, utensils, tools). Subjects were asked who ought to get the girl and which things each man brought. They found that presentation of items in a narrative correlated to a high degree with the order in which those items were later remembered (i.e., either serially or clustered). In other words, recall matched how the items were presented in the story.

Cole and Gray's (1972) study is powerful in that it provided a rigorous methodology for comparing the manner of recall in different social groups that went well beyond the typical two-group comparison to explore various situational factors. They also adapted their tests to the local customs and meanings of the Kpelle community, thereby avoiding the tendency of much cross-cultural research to quickly affirm the superior performance of Western groups, as indicated by a test that fit a Western social framework. However, while the sensitivity to local culture helps to set the groundwork for their study, the role of social institutions and local practices in remembering is not directly an object of analysis beyond the clustering of semantically related objects. Furthermore, the operationalization of 'constructiveness' as clustering in recall excluded the broader focus on the elaboration and simplification of culture in remembering (Chapter 2). Put differently, their methodology did not directly capture the qualitative meanings that connect an individual's recall to the cultural patterns of the group to which he or she is a member. Only the last experiment tapped into a central social practice within the Kpelle community, viz. story telling. It is clearly the closest link to Bartlett's (1932/1995) more naturalistic experimental methodology of remembering stories containing social content of interest that engages a person's 'effort after meaning.'

Since Cole and Gray's (1972) study, social scientists have increasingly identified narrative as a core mediator of remembering and other psychological processes. For example, Jerome Bruner (1990, 1991, 2002), himself building on Bartlett, has argued that narrative is at the foundation of our common sense or 'folk psychology,' which allows experience to be shared outside of a narrow interpersonal or ecological niche. In his words,

[Narrative] is a precondition for our collective life in culture. I doubt such collective life would be possible if it was not for our human capacity to organize and communicate experience in narrative form. For it is the conventionalization of narrative that converts individual experience into collective coin which can be circulated, as it were, on a base wider than a merely interpersonal one.

(Bruner, 2002, p. 16)

Many of Bartlett's own methods have focused on narrative as a window into a group's patterns of thought and directions of change, a point he argued in many places (e.g., Bartlett, 1920a, 1923, 1946b). Cultural psychologists in particular have highlighted the construction, use, and conflict of narratives in social interaction. In the next section, we will consider one powerful example of how narrative has been studied as a cultural tool used to mediate memory, and in doing so how it transforms both the matter and manner of recall.

Wertsch's Schematic Narrative Templates

Central to Cole, Bruner and other cultural psychologists' approach is the idea that symbolic forms of a social group mediate higher psychological processes, such as remembering. This idea is usually credited to Vygotsky but it has a much longer history in, for example, Cassirer, Durkheim, Wundt, and Hegel – Bartlett was most directly in contact with the idea through his association with Henry Head. Perhaps, the most powerful recent development of the notion of mediation in relation to remembering as a social process can be found in the work of James Wertsch (2002), who specifically focuses on 'collective remembering' through the mediation of narratives. It should be noted that 'collective' in his phrase refers to membership in a social group, not a transcendent property of the group. Wertsch avoids the 'strong version' of collective memory – that Bartlett (1932/1995) criticized in Halbwachs (1925/1992) – by arguing that collective remembering is a 'distributed' process in two senses of the term: first, it is distributed between individuals in a group and second, it is distributed between individuals and the cultural resources they use to remember, in particular narrative texts. In his own words,

Rather than being a thing, or possession, [collective memory] is best understood as a form of action. Specifically, it is a form of mediated action, meaning that it is fundamentally distributed between active agents, on the one hand, and the cultural tools – especially narrative texts – that they employ, on the other.

(Wertsch, 2002, p. 172)

In focusing on the issue of narratives, he makes an important distinction between 'specific narratives' and 'schematic narrative templates' (Wertsch, 2002, p. 60ff). Specific narratives include information about particular dates, settings, cast of characters, actions, motives, etc. (such as an invasion by x on date y for reason z), whereas schematic narrative templates are abstract and generalized plot structures that provide the background from which specific stories are constructed. In developing the latter concept, Wertsch very explicitly draws upon Bartlett's concept of schema (Chapter 4), highlighting his claim that schemata operate in an 'unreflective, unanalytic and unwitting manner' (quoted in Wertsch, 2002, p. 62).[15] Often we do not even realize how much we are committed to a particular version of the past until we start arguing with someone over it. Also following Bartlett, Wertsch stresses that narrative templates are not universal archetypes (as in Jung's theory), but rather belong to a particular group's narrative traditions, which may thus differ significantly from other groups. In fact, differences in narrative templates can be a major source of conflict among different groups. In short, narrative templates are implicit tools that are socially distributed among a group and used for grasping together a set of events into a coherent whole.

Wertsch powerfully illustrated his approach in a case study of the transformation of collective memory in the transition from Soviet to Post-Soviet Russia. Within this dramatic social transformation, narrative templates act as underlying conservative forces that resist change and thus provide the group continuity through time. The main source of evidence comes from Russian history textbooks and people's use of them. Wertsch found that a schematic narrative template, which he called *triumph-over-alien-forces*, was used in both Soviet and post-Soviet times to construct specific narratives of widely different events. This narrative template had the following structure:

1. An 'initial situation' (Propp, 1968, p. 26) in which the Russian people are living in a peaceful setting where they are no threat to others is disrupted by:
2. The initiation of trouble or aggression by an alien force, or agent, which leads to:
3. A time of crisis and great suffering, which is:
4. Overcome by the triumph over the alien force by the Russian people, acting heroically and alone.

(Wertsch, 2002, p. 93)

Consider how a 35-year-old man from Siberia in 1999 uses this narrative template to construct a specific narrative. His story is triggered by the instruction "write a short essay on the theme: 'What was the course of the Second World War from its beginning to end?'"

On September 1, 1939 German forces invaded the territory of Poland.

By the second month, they had seized all of Poland. The result of the occupation of Poland was that all of 6 million Poles (30 percent of the whole population) perished.

In 1940, the seizure of France and the Benelux countries took place.

In 1941 the USSR was attacked. By the end of October 1941 the Germans approached Moscow along a 100-kilometer front. At the price of incredible suffering the Soviet forces were able to throw the Germans back from Moscow at the end of 1941. 1942 was the year of massive resistance. It was the year in which our forces were surrounded at Kharkov and the year of the battle of Stalingrad. The turning point came in 1943. This was the year of the struggle at Kursk salient, the huge tank battle. In 1944 the second front was opened, and there was a rapid advance toward the west. 1945 saw the atomic bombing of Hiroshima and Nagasaki and the end of the Second World War.

(Wertsch, 2004, p. 53)

Although the text clearly starts in 1939 with the beginning of the Second World War, the focus is mainly on the Russia's 'Great Patriotic War' beginning in 1941. In nearly all Soviet and post-Soviet textbooks as well as subject's essays and interviews about the Second World War, four core events were included: "(1) the German invasion of USSR, 1941; (2) Battle of Moscow, winter of 1941–2; (3) the Battle of Stalingrad, winter of 1942–3; (4) Soviet victory over German army and the march to Berlin and victory, May 1945" (pp. 53–4). These elements occupy a mid-level between specific narrative and narrative template. In addition to them, the man in the above quote included a number of post-Soviet elements, such as mentioning the 'Poles' as a specific people rather than focusing on the 'Soviet People,' which was official discourse of the Soviet era. After the fall of the Soviet Union, the basic plot structure and mention of these four specific events changed little; however, the heroes of the story changed from Stalin and the Soviet Communist Party to the Russian masses. In short, although some of the details of the story changed there is much continuity from Soviet to post-Soviet society in the way the Second World War is narrated because of the persistent use of the *triumph-over-alien-forces* narrative template.

It should be noted that Wertsch is not claiming this is the only narrative template in the Russian tradition, but rather that it is the most ubiquitous tool used in Russian collective remembering. It provides the basic plot line for the most important events in Russian history, from the thirteenth-century Mongol invasion to Hitler's invasion in the twentieth century. In later writings, Wertsch has argued that this narrative template has also played a key role in Russia's recent conflicts with Georgia, which itself uses the narrative template 'foiled attempts to return to the golden age' to understand its past and present (Wertsch and Batiashvili, 2012, p. 39ff; see also Wertsch, 2017).[16] The *triumph-over-alien-forces* narrative template is even used to narrate the Russian revolution where the actors who were originally one of 'us' become the 'alien' actors who through their aggression spoil the peace. In all cases, the narrative template casts characters into the strictly separated dichotomies of us and them, good and evil, light and dark. Although one might find a similar narrative template being used in another country, its centrality and particular features give it a particular Russian character. For example, contrast it with the US key national narrative template 'a quest for freedom,' through which Americans tends to construct their history (Wertsch and O'Connor, 1994).

Wertsch's approach represents a substantial development of Bartlett's social psychology of remembering and his notion of schemata in particular. He has been one of the few recent thinkers to analyze schemata in their embeddedness within the cultural traditions of different communities. With regards to the matter of recall, he shows how particular historical events are selected and emplotted based on the cultural traditions of a community and the textual resources they make available to their members. Even as the specifics of historical narratives change, much continuity can be found on deeper levels. Moreover, as with Nadel (1937), the analytic focus is on *direction* in which a narrative is shaped based on the textual resources used and the function memory serves, rather than overemphasizing the narrative's accuracy. This is not to say accuracy is unimportant, but that the function of creating a usable past and accuracy work in tandem. In relation to the manner of recall, Wertsch (2002) describes how remembering varies between social contexts. He makes a distinction between the 'mastery' and 'appropriation' of textual resources: mastery concerns being able to effectively use them, while appropriation is about becoming emotionally committed to them (p. 119ff). In other words, the former involves having the necessary cognitive skills and the latter involves making the resources one's own. Drawing on Goffman's (1959) distinction between front and backstage, Wertsch describes how in the Soviet Union people were forced to master official narratives for public performance, while at the same time holding different ideas in private or backstage (cf. Bartlett's analysis of cultural contact and propaganda, where forcing cultural change results in ideas going underground – Chapter 3). There was even a joke told in private that "nothing is so unpredictable as the Russian past" (Wertsch, 2002, p. 77).

Conclusion: Rethinking the 'Social' in Remembering

The 'social' and 'collective' have meant very different things through the history of psychology. In the nineteenth century, there were intellectual tendencies to, on the one hand, turn psychological processes into biological ones, and on the other to analyze the emergent properties of social organization, such as language, myth, and ritual, as genuinely collective products. Carl Jung's notion of the 'collective unconscious' was an extreme version of the first tendency, turning even collective symbols into biological entities, while Halbwachs followed the latter tendency to develop the argument that even personal memory was fundamentally social. By social he meant that group interaction created emergent properties that condition the experience and action of its members. Although Bartlett rejected the suggestion that groups themselves have memories, his approach closely paralleled Halbwachs. Bartlett (1932/1995) thought social groups shape individual recall "by providing that setting of interest, excitement and emotion which follows the development of specific images and socially by providing a persistent framework of restrictions and customs which acts as the schematic basis for constructive memory" (p. 255). Methodologically, this meant looking at both how internalized group conventions shape *what* the individual recalls (powerfully illustrated by his own and later others' experimental studies) and how the concrete social process between people affects *how* remembering is done. Although the latter issue was much sketchier it sets interesting questions for us today, such as how power asymmetries affect the style and content of remembering, especially in relation to different groups' conventions. In short, Bartlett's social psychology of remembering focuses on the individual's particular position in and between groups and the group conventions that come into play in any act of remembering.

In the twentieth-century psychology, shifted as a discipline from a focus on the social as the specific values, norms, and traditions of different social groups, to a study of the short-term effects of social interaction on an individual's behavior (Danziger, 1992). This has mostly been the study of how social influence or suggestion leads to inaccuracy, distortion, and other forms of irrationality. In this approach, an individual's action is severed from the wider social-cultural context in which they are embedded. As such the focus on how group conventions are internalized and transformed by individuals to be used as a schematic basis for remembering is lost. As we saw, however, Bartlett's social psychological theory of remembering had a marked influence on a select but significant line of psycho-anthropologists. Both Nadel (1937) and Bateson (1936) demonstrated that a group's social customs powerfully shaped the content (matter) and the cognitive style (manner) of recall. Cole and Gray (1972) used a 'free recall' experimental task to explore Bartlett's primitive social organization lead to rote recall, where there is a slavish obedience to chronological order. They found no evidence for this; instead, the strongest determinant of order in recall was placement of items in a narrative. The topic of how narrative resources guide remembering in groups became central to cultural psychology and Wertsch's approach in particular. Wertsch (2002) reinvigorates Bartlett's concept of schema (Chapter 4) by analyzing how 'schematic narrative templates' are developed and used in a cultural tradition to construct a wide range of specific narratives about different historical events. Moreover, he shows that there is a difference between the 'mastery' and 'appropriation' of those narratives.

Central to a Bartlettian social psychology of remembering is the idea that we are not atoms of memory, sufficient unto ourselves. Instead, we stand in relationship to many others, including both collectives and individuals, when we remember. Remembering is a situated social act that adapts to the particular constraints and possibilities of the present context, while simultaneously retaining a sense of continuity through time. We loop back to some of the same information or episodes in our memory, reinterpreting and adapting them to fit our present concerns and circumstances. As such, remembering must be considered as being *both* personal and social at the same time. A number of recent memory theorists have likewise commented on the difficulty in strictly separating our individual and collective remembering (e.g., Brown and Reavey, 2015; Brockmeier, 2015). They argue that there are so many lines of intersection between the two that it is impossible to fully disentangle them without losing the phenomenon of interest. This idea runs counter to the notion that memories are first purely individual entities in the person which are then modified as a result of social processes, such as obedience and conformity. Instead, memories are from the start deeply embedded within a person's transaction with the social and material world. From this perspective, accuracy is just one of many criteria for exploring remembering, and in many contexts not the most important.[17] More often, one's sense of self and social bonds are at stake. These observations are fully compatible with emerging trends in psychology, such as extended or distributed cognition (Sutton, Harris, Keil, and Barnier, 2010). Bartlett's approach to remembering can serve as a useful guide in this effort to reconnect the social and cognitive in a unified whole. As Northway (1936) put it, "the problem of remembering is one of 'construction,' belonging both to individual and social psychology, it lies on the border line where the two meet" (p. 29).

Notes

1. Recently, the sociologist Jeffrey Olick (1999) has made a similar distinction between 'collected' and 'collective' memory, which maps on to Jung and Halbwachs, respectively. The first refers to the aggregated memories of members of a group, while the latter concerns genuinely collective phenomena that stands above individual minds.
2. Bartlett (1932/1995) also mentions Janet's (1928) theory in this context, as a distinctly social perspective on memory, which he sees as being complementary to his own. However, he gives it less attention than Jung's and Halbwachs's theories, saying that he only came to know it after his own ideas had already been developed.
3. This characterization of 'social frameworks' comes very close to Moscovici's Theory of Social Representations (see Chapter 3; Wagoner, 2015), which is somewhat unsurprising given their shared Durkheimian heritage.
4. In Halbwachs's (1950/1980) later book *The Collective Memory*, he responds to criticisms and clarifies his position. For example, "While collective memory endures and draws strength from its base in a coherent body of people, it is individuals as group members who remember" (p. 48). Bartlett would have fully agreed with such statements.

5. Much of what is considered a 'social' psychology today would not have been in the earlier twentieth century because it did not consider psychological processes in light of norms and values specific to real social groups. For example, Triplett's (1898) study of 'social facilitation' was first published in a physiology journal. Floyd Allport was responsible for labeling it the first experiment in social psychology, in his intentional effort to make the sub-discipline about individuals rather than groups (see Danziger, 1992, 2000; Farr, 1996).

6. Bartlett to some extent addressed this question in other places (viz. Bartlett, 1920a, 1923).

7. Similarly, Bartlett (1923, p. 63) had earlier remarked that story telling in 'primitive' cultures requires an audience and a social setting. Attempting to render the story in independence from these, as the ethnographer may try to do, kills the spirit of the story.

8. This experimental task is very similar to Istomina's (1975) classic experiment, in which she created a context for children to perform a memory task that was meaningful to them. She found children's memory was greatly improved compared to a more standard sterile experimental condition.

9. Cf. Mary Douglas (1980, p. 76ff) discussion of Azande memory also focused on cattle and contrasts Evans-Pritchard's cultural account of memory with Bartlett's.

10. On this point, Bartlett is clearly influenced by the emerging field of cybernetics (see Chapter 1).

11. The classic study of rumor was made by Allport and Postman (1947) using Bartlett's method of serial reproduction (see Chapter 2).

12. These two tendencies of culture were earlier discussed by Haddon (1894, 1895) in relation to the development of decorative art.

13. Michael Cole has since become a leading figure in the sub-discipline of cultural psychology. In his *Cultural Psychology: A Once and Future Discipline*, he demonstrates his engagement with Bartlett's social psychology of remembering as well as Nadel's and Bateson's extensions of it (see Cole, 1996, p. 57ff).

14. More details on the background and methods of the study can be found in Cole, Gay, Glick, and Sharp's (1971) *The Cultural Context of Learning and Thinking: An Exploration in Experimental Anthropology*.

15. Wertsch's study was included here, rather than the last chapter, because of his anthropological focus and concern with collective (as opposed to individual) remembering.

16. Narrative templates may also shape how a group remembers the history of another nation. Brescó and Rosa (in press) show how subjects with different national feelings of belonging (either Spanish or Basque) remembered texts about Irish history according to their position in the Spanish–Basque conflict, using Bartlett's method of repeated reproduction.

17. Accuracy in memory is itself not a transparent notion if one does not take literal recall as the ultimate standard. From a Bartlettian perspective, how accuracy is assessed could be conceptualized as varying with the conventions of different social contexts.

6   Thinking about Thinking

> The essence of thinking as a mental process ... may be found in two characteristics; it uses evidence which has already accumulated through perception or recall, and it moves beyond that evidence to something which so far claims no already attained sensorial or perceptual foundation.
>
> (Bartlett, 1950b, pp. 145–6)

> The thinker is more than a thinking machine.
>
> (Bartlett, 1958, p. 96)

Bartlett's interest in the topic of thinking extends back to his earliest publications. At the end of his 1916 *St. John's Dissertation*, Bartlett sketched out a number of experiments to explore thinking similar in form to those conducted in the dissertation. These experiments, however, would not be done until much later (Bartlett, 1938a) and would further come to fruition as the study of what Bartlett called 'everyday thinking,' though he published a number of theoretical reflections on thinking prior to this (Bartlett, 1925c, 1927d; Bartlett and Smith, 1920). However, it was not until the late 1940s and 1950s that thinking took a central position in Bartlett's research, at which time his own thinking had shifted as a result of the applied work on high-level skill in human–machine interactions that his laboratory did during the Second World War (Chapter 1). In his programmatic book *Thinking: An Experimental and Social Study* (1958), one finds both continuities and discontinuities with his earlier work. The continuities are in his analytic focus on a situated ongoing activity, and an experimental setup that aims to capture complexity by introducing ruptures such that the subject must constructively 'fill in the gaps.' The major discontinuity is the lesser emphasis of social and cultural processes. The word 'social' does appear in the subtitle (as in the subtitle of *Remembering*) but here it is given less attention than before and 'culture' is almost entirely absent.

This chapter contextualizes, outlines, and elaborates Bartlett's distinctive approach to the topic of thinking. First, it describes the Würzburg and Gestalt approach to thinking as a form of experience, which Bartlett builds upon in developing his own approach. This tradition of studying thinking was displaced in the 1960s by the emergence of cognitive psychology with its focus on correct thinking and how mental shortcuts lead to various kinds of errors. Second, the applied research done in Bartlett's laboratory during the Second World War on high-level skill in human operators is explained. This provides a starting point to approach thinking processes in Bartlett's research program, while at the same time remaining open to differences between bodily skill and thinking. Third, Bartlett's framework is applied to 'closed system thinking,' as one finds in numerical and logical puzzles. This kind of thinking is particularly amiable to experimental study but is by no means the most typical form of thinking, nor should it be taken as the standard upon which all thinking is assessed. Fourth, closed system thinking is contrasted with 'open' or 'adventurous thinking,' where new information must be sought. This is described in relation to thinking in experimental, everyday, and artistic contexts. In these contexts, constructive and social processes take the lead. This chapter concludes with an argument for a comparative study of thinking that looks for common principles between different types but avoids reducing one kind to another.

Thinking before Cognition

Bartlett's book on thinking was published at a time when psychology was making a radical shift in its approach to the subject. Whereas the earlier Würzburg and Gestalt approaches to thinking saw it in terms of the experience of solving a problem, it later came to be defined in terms of factors leading to mental errors. Bartlett's book belongs to the earlier era of research, which was clearly outlined in George Humphrey's monumental book *Thinking: An Introduction to Its Experimental Psychology* (1951). As a friend and colleague at Cambridge, Bartlett encouraged Humphrey to begin the book back in 1934. Bartlett (1958) even says that he would have included "some detailed and critical account of earlier psychological work" (p. 7) if Humphrey had not already published his 'splendid study' on it. Thus, Humphrey's book offers an excellent example of how thinking was approached before the cognitive revolution, and of Bartlett's particular understanding of it.

Humphrey begins his book by setting up the pre-experimental background against which the early twentieth psychology of thinking developed. Since Aristotle and through the nineteenth century, the question of thought processes had generally been answered philosophically by positing mechanical laws of association. In the theory of association, ideas are turned into objects that naturally follow one another because they have been linked together by contiguity, similarity, or contrast: contiguity implies co-occurrence in time, such that later when one idea appears the other follows; similarity means one idea will instate another when it is *like* it; and finally contrast highlights the link between opposite ideas. In this approach, thinking is the clash of different associations in relation to discrete objects. At the end of *Remembering*, Bartlett (1932/1995, p. 304ff) himself explicitly positioned his own approach against the theory of association, arguing that: "It tells us something about the characteristics of associated details, when they are associated, but it explains nothing of the activity of the conditions by which they are brought together" (p. 308).

Bartlett's own thinking on this point was influenced by the Würzburg School, which had its heyday in the first decade of the twentieth century under the leadership of Oswald Külpe (1862–1915) (see also Chapters 1 and 2). When Würzburgers initiated the earliest experimental studies of thinking, they found the theory of association to be inadequate and argued for the need to introduce task directedness. For example, Ach (1905) made a distinction between 'reproductive tendencies' (governed by associative laws) and 'determining tendencies,' which gave direction to thought. As we saw in Chapter 2, Bartlett adopted the term 'attitude' to theorize mental directedness from the Würzburg School. Bühler (1907) explicitly turned the Würzburg method to the topic of thought by having participants think through complex problems and then retrospectively describe the mental process through which they reached the solution. In his studies, the determining tendencies become 'thought' (*Gedanke*) itself. As this new mental content was not an image or sensation, he claimed to have demonstrated the existence of 'imageless thought,' countering the Aristotelian idea that there is no thought without images (see Humphrey, 1951, p. 55ff).

Gestalt psychology (*Gestalttheorie*)[1] of the Berlin School of experimental psychology took the Würzburg theory a step further by altogether doing away with the notion of 'reproductive tendencies' – that is, experiences reproduced from the past without change. One of the group's founders Max Wertheimer (1880–1943) argued that all true thinking is 'productive' (as opposed to 'reproductive') in that it involves the formation of a new gestalt (configuration or form) (see Wertheimer, 1945). In the process of thinking, a person arrives at an insight (an 'aha' moment) that brings together earlier disconnected experiences into a new configuration and thereby modifies them. The mechanism that brings about thinking and a new gestalt is a system in tension. Zeigarnik (1927, 1967) famously demonstrated the role played by tension in an experiment showing that unfinished tasks, where tension remains, are remembered more frequently than finished tasks. The study was inspired by Kurt Lewin's observation that waiters tend to remember open orders much better than closed orders. In continuity with the Gestalt tradition, Bartlett himself employed the notion of 'field' or 'pattern' into which the material of a situation becomes arranged and gaps stand out to be filled (see later).

One of the most illuminating examples of the Gestalt approach to thinking is Wolfgang Köhler's (1925) classic *The Mentality of Apes* (see also Humphrey, 1951, p. 161ff). This book was discussed widely in Cambridge in the 1920s. The Gestalt Psychologists Köhler and Koffka had actually visited Bartlett there in 1922.[2] Köhler's research involved creating a number of situations of varying difficulty in which chimpanzees had to solve the problem of using tools to access some food. In one case, the chimpanzees had to move a crate and then stand on it in order to reach food hanging from the ceiling. In another case, the chimpanzees had to put two sticks together to create an instrument that could be used to reach food outside of their cage. Köhler also noted a number of contextual factors, such as the physical arrangement, that increased the likelihood of reaching the solution – in other words, the whole field setup conditions for a successful reconfiguration. He stressed that chimpanzees' problem solving had nothing of the character of 'trial-and-error' learning emphasized by other psychologists such as Thorndike. Instead, the different elements of the situation are brought together in relation to the problem at hand in a moment of 'insight.' Bartlett (1958) himself makes insight, or what he called a 'leap' or 'flash', an important component of human thinking. Dogs and other animals, on the other hand, were unable to solve these problems.

In the conclusion of his massive study, Humphrey (1951) said "50 years' experiment on the psychology of thinking or reasoning have not brought us very far, but they have at least shown the kind of road which must be traversed" (p. 308). He argued that this earlier work identified a set of persistent problems, which future studies of thinking must take on. For example, what is the motor or motivation of its flow (e.g., association or system in tension)? How do conscious and unconscious processes interact (e.g., attitudes, determining tendencies)? What is the relation between motor and inner processes (e.g., acting out thought)? Ironically, shortly afterward, psychology would take a radically different road than the one suggested by Humphrey (1951). In Germany, most of those who had worked in the Würzburg School and the Gestalt psychologists were exiled or killed[3] by the Nazi regime for being Jewish or for political reasons (Ash, 1998). In America, behaviorism became dominant, which called for an abandonment of the mentalistic language of terms like thinking – for example, Watson (1913) reduced thought to subvocal speech (for a critique of this move based on Würzburg ideas, see Bartlett and Smith, 1920). Humphrey's definition of thought as "what occurs in experience when an organism, human or animal, meets, recognizes, and solves a problem" (quoted from Bartlett, 1952, pp. 88–9), based on the early twentieth-century European tradition, was largely abandoned and then later assimilated into a very different approach.

When the topic of thinking re-emerged in the 1960s with the rise of cognitive psychology, it took on a rather different form. In the typical experimental setup, subjects are given a problem with a single solution arrived at by a statistical or logical procedure, such as which of two possibilities is more probable. For example, Tversky and Kahneman's classic experiments in this line aimed to identify the 'mental shortcuts' or 'heuristics' people use to solve the problems, which in turn lead them into error (see e.g., Tversky and Kahneman, 1974). In memory research, the concept of schema fulfilled the same function of providing a mental entity to explain distortion that occurred between input and output (see Chapter 4). Gigerenzer et al. (1989) argued that the new thinking tasks sidelined the earlier focus on the experience of the organism and replaced it with the question of whether a person performs 'correct' calculations. The laws of thinking in this new approach were to be derived from the violations of the right outcomes and procedures. In contrast, Würzburg and Gestalt approaches had used problems with typically more than one solution and were more concerned with how contextual details changed the elements of the situation and likelihood of reaching a solution.

This difference in approach can partly be explained with the new metaphors of mind as a calculating machine or computer. Around the same time, the psychology of memory also shifted toward a study of inaccuracy and distortion based on the standard provided by a computer, against which people appeared cognitively lazy, lacking alertness, and largely irrational – in short, cognitive misers (Chapter 2). Bartlett's own laboratory in Cambridge in fact helped set the ground for this conceptual shift through the focus on human–machine interactions, such as flying an airplane or performing some industrial task (Chapter 1). While Bartlett's students began to subscribe to the metaphor of humans as machines, Bartlett himself remained committed to a bio-functional perspective. He is clear that "the thinker is more than a thinking machine" (1958, p. 96) and as such aimed to explore the diversity of thinking, not just logical puzzles. In the next section, we will discuss the Cambridge research on bodily skill that served as inspiration for these two very different approaches to thinking.

From Bodily Skills to Thinking

Bartlett had long been interested in the topic of skill as part of his enthusiasm for various sports. This topic, however, took on new urgency with the need to better understand human–machine interactions to aid the British effort in the Second World War (Chapter 1). As with his earlier critique of the psychophysical model of experimentation (Chapter 2) and his concept of schema (Chapter 4), Bartlett's approach to skill emphasized how it is organized in terms of a structured 'pattern' or 'field' within an ongoing activity, rather than a fixed succession of isolated stimulus-response reactions. Bartlett (1955a, p. 208) is clear that "nothing fundamental can be discovered or understood about skill by a study of the direct results of environmental stimulation in the production of what can be treated as single response items." Instead, every movement must be seen as possessing properties not only in relation to the immediate external stimulation but also to the preceding and succeeding movements in a series – in other words, the whole activity (or temporal gestalt) defines the nature of the parts.

Skilled activity fluidly progresses through a series of interconnected steps, in which there is a continuous regulation of flow between different signals given by the environment and the actions that must be carried out in proper timing so as to achieve the desired end:

> The player in a quick ball game; the operator, engaged at his work bench, directing his machine, and using his tools; the surgeon conducting an operation; the physician arriving at a clinical decision – in all these instances and in innumerable other ones ... there is the continuing flow from signals occurring outside the performer and interpreted by him to actions carried out; then on to further signals and more action, up to the culminating point of the achievement of the task, or of whatever part of the task is the immediate objective.
>
> (Bartlett, 1958, pp. 21–2).

Bartlett (1958) is at pains to point out the need to attend to bodily skills' 'temporal structure' (p. 15), how each movement builds on the previous ones and anticipates what is coming next in order to reach a goal. He outlines four main features of skilled performance (i.e., timing, stationary phases, point of no return, and direction), which all directly relate to a series of temporally organized steps or phases. Let us consider each one of these features in turn.

One defining feature of skilled versus unskilled action is the smoothness of performance in the former case. This is achieved by efficiently managing the interval between movements, what Bartlett calls *timing*. Learning a new skill involves shortening initially long intervals between components and lengthening initially short components. This is rather different from measuring the absolute speed (or reaction time) of any single movement, which was the standard method up until that time. Instead, the focus is on the proper timing of movements in a chain and the particular environmental demands of the moment. This approach is obviously far from the behaviorists' focus on stimulus-response reactions; in contrast, these are circular streams of action regulated by the changing environment, similar to Dewey's (1896) argument to replace the 'reflex arc' with a circle or spiral. Moreover, Bartlett points out that a focus on overall 'achievement' in some skilled action very rarely sheds light on the 'processes' involved, which he sees as key to his approach.[4]

The second important aspect of skill is the *stationary phases* or *halts*. For example, in the simple case of picking up an object and transporting it to another location the hand stretches out, hovers, picks up, transports, hovers again, and finally sets the object down. This kind of movement was typical of people working in industry during the Second World War. The hovering or halting occurs when the person has to pay special attention to the environmental conditions of the moment, such as the position, size, shape, and probable weight of the object. It is during these moments that the person picks out novelty from the environment in order to efficiently continue the performance. As a methodological principle, it is thus important to explore when, how, and with what effects these halts occur between steps in an activity.

Third, at a certain point in a skilled performance, actions reach *a region of no return*. At a certain point after an action has been launched, "any additional signals will either be ignored or will lead to an attempt to modify projected movements under conditions in which accurate timing is impossible" (p. 18). Bartlett describes how this plays out between a bowler and batsman in a game of cricket: the bowler tries to get the ball to do something unexpected at the last moment so that the batsman cannot correct his stroke in time to meet it. Meanwhile, the batsman tries to either meet the ball before this happens or delay making the stroke beyond the region of no return so as not to be caught by unexpected changes. The expression 'point of no return' is itself taken from pilots' description of actions that have reached the point to which they cannot be altered without serious consequences to performance.

Finally, skilled activities have a *direction*, meaning that the movements that make them up are being guided toward a goal. Rather than mechanically reacting to a stimulus or being determined by previous movements, skilled actions are oriented and organized to progress toward some future state, whether that be the batsman hitting the ball in cricket, the pilot landing the airplane, or a surgeon completing the operation. The direction, however, need not be clearly defined or consciously present to the person. In fact, the Würzburg School had found that task orientation (*Aufgabe*) was typically not conscious to the person and only became so under special conditions. Bartlett even argued that being overly conscious of direction could get in the way of skilled performance (see also 'turning around upon schema' in Chapter 4; cf. Sutton, 2007).

Bartlett used what had been learned about bodily skills to orient his inquiry into thinking. Thinking is approached as a 'high-level skill' that has as its material symbols and signs rather than bodily movements. With this analogy, Bartlett aimed to place thinking within its 'natural development' from earlier forms of behavior, while being well aware that it had new characteristics not found at this lower level. He says that the analogy "is essentially methodological and pragmatic" (p. 12), providing a novel way into the subject. Like bodily skill, "thinking also claims that it is based upon information or evidence which, again, must be picked up directly or indirectly from the environment and which is used in an attempt to satisfy some requirement of the occasion upon which the thinking takes place" (p. 12). For example, you meet someone after a long absence and try to account for how his appearance has changed in the time since he was last seen; or a man is tracking an airplane, which disappears and reappears, so that the man must figure out what happened in between.

The analogy between thinking and bodily skills suggested a methodology in which the researcher explores how the person, through a series of interconnected steps, selects and extends evidence or information so as to 'fill up gaps' in the evidence. In other words, the researcher attends to how the person must at each step 'move forward into a gap.' Consider the following example of finding one's way in a new city:

A man may find himself ... in a city with which he is not very familiar, whose inhabitants speak a language he does not know, and he may have to find his way from a given place to, say, a railway station. He could proceed at random, throwing dice or drawing lots at each road division. He would be much more likely, however, to 'think it out.' For this he would keep perception and recall both wide awake, but he would also build upon whatever he knew and could find out about the construction and plan of this and other cities in the same area or country. As he went along, if he was right, his journey would become more obviously directional, his decisions at the turning-points of the road would become easier and more decisive. Somewhere he would get to a stage at which he could say definitely that he was on the route desired and would finish up where he wanted to go.

(Bartlett, 1961a, p. 151)

We see here how thinking involves both perceiving and remembering but differs from them in its focus on combining multiple sources of information to achieve a specific goal. Moreover, as the activity proceeds its 'directional' qualities become more apparent, such that decisions come easier and the halts shorter. This example has all the major features of thinking Bartlett analyzes in relation to skill, especially as a temporally organized series of steps toward a terminal point. However, how precisely the different steps in a thinking activity are organized differs considerably between various kinds of thinking. The broadest and most important distinction is between 'closed system thinking' and 'open' or 'adventurous thinking.' I will describe these successively in the next two sections, while also introducing some other important distinctions to classify thinking activities.

Thinking within Closed Systems

Much of the psychology of thinking has been focused on how people solve problems of a numerical or logical nature. Bartlett (1958) says that these are neither the most typical nor the simplest kind of thinking. However, they are the most amiable to experimental demonstration – as such it is little wonder that psychology has concentrated on them.[5] For this reason, 'closed system thinking' or 'formal thinking' makes up the first part of his book. By closed system, he means "one possessing a limited number of units, or items, or members, and those properties of members which are to be used are known to begin with and do not change as the thinking proceeds" (p. 23). In other words, "all the properties are theoretically definable before they come to be used in any particular instance" (p. 23), but they may be rearranged in the process. As mentioned earlier, Bartlett understood all thinking as a form of gap filling. His experiments were designed to present participants with material containing gaps for which they are to be filled in through a series of articulated steps that the researcher can follow. He distinguishes between three processes of filling gaps: 'interpolation,' 'extrapolation,' and looking at evidence from a special point of view to see 'evidence in disguise.' I will discuss each of these in turn in this section. It should be noted here though that these three can also applied to 'adventurous thinking,' as one finds in science, art, and everyday life – more on that to come.

Interpolation occurs when there is information up to a point, and then there is a gap, followed by more information that progresses from where the gap ended to a terminal point. For example, you are reading a book and find a missing page which you must fill in on the basis of what came before and after it. Bartlett (1958) begins his discussion with a simple experiment with numbers in which the following information is given:

1   17

The experimenter instructed the participant: "take 1 as the first and 17 as the last number, and fill up the gap between them in any way that seems to be indicated" (p. 24). Bartlett notes that a few people treated the problem as an opportunity to engage in 'flights of fancy,' where the gap is filled with imaginative drawings, words, or symbols preferred by the particular individual. These participants effectively treat a closed system as a completely free and open one. Cases such as these are particularly important in relation to 'artistic thinking' (see later), but do not directly contribute to contexts of thinking where there is a demand that evidence be extended in an 'objective' fashion within a community of thinkers. Putting these cases aside for now, a random sample of educated people from Britain or America will fill in the series in one of the following ways:

(a) 1, 3, 5, 7, ..., 17;
(b) 1, 2, 3, 4, ..., 17;
(c) 1, 9, ..., 17;
(d) A number of other ways, each of which occurs rarely, so that it is possible to treat them as all falling into a single group of 'individual responses.'

(Bartlett, 1958, p. 25)

In terms of frequency of occurrence within the population, Bartlett notes, "for every instance of (d) there will be approximately two of (c), five of (b) and six of (a)" (p. 25). Thus, (a) and (b) are by far the most common responses. In this and many other cases of closed system thinking, there are many more logical possibilities for filling the gap than are actually taken by people. In other words, there is a significant uniformity in the ways members of a cultural group fill an empty interval. This social character to thinking is the key ingredient to 'everyday thinking,' which will be discussed later. Bartlett also noted that if you add one step between 1 and 17, such as 3, 2, or 9, the rest of the steps were pretty well-determined. People tend to quickly extract a 'rule' (e.g., odd numbers) that guides their gap filling. This applies equally to graphic material, such as in Figure 6.1 below.

The figure on the right in Figure 6.1 was also used in Bartlett's (1932/1995, p. 22) experiments on perceiving. In connection with thinking, Bartlett (1950b, p. 151) points out that there are at least 20 different

Figure 6.1.   Stimuli used in perceiving and interpolation experiments

possibilities that can be taken at the first step to fill in the gap between the two figures (i.e., transform the left figure into the right figure) in accord with the evidence. However, after the second step the rest are determined in terms of their character, number, and order. One could say objectivity and generality emerges at a stage in the sequence. As we will see in what follows, this 'point of no return' will vary with the kind of material at hand.

In contrast to interpolation, extrapolation concerns cases in which there is evidence up to a point and then no more, but the thinker demands to take it further. It is generally more difficult than interpolation because with the latter the thinker is provided with the goal, whereas with extrapolation it needs to be discovered. Consider the verbal puzzle Bartlett uses to introduce extrapolation:

A, GATE, NO, I, DUTY, IN, CAT, BO, EAR,
O, TRAVEL, ERASE, BOTH, GET, HO, FATE.

ERASE
FATE

The participant was instructed to use "the group of words at the top to complete the verbal arrangement indicated by the two words 'erase' and 'fate' taking 'erase' as the middle word in the column. Not all words given need to be used" (p. 35). In order to complete the puzzle, the participant must extract and apply two rules: (1) focusing on the fact that the letter E comes before the letter F often led to the rule of 'alphabetical sequence' and (2) attending to the point that Erase had one letter more than Fate could lead to the rule of 'length of word sequence.' Only two out of a hundred taken at random applied both rules and produced the following:

A
BO
CAT
DUTY
ERASE
FATE
GET
HO
I

Unlike the two interpolation series discussed earlier, adding another step (DUTY) to this arrangement made little difference for participants. But when CAT and GET were included, nearly all completed the puzzle. Here we see different 'regions of no return' between this thinking series and the previously discussed ones. Bartlett also highlighted that there is a clear difference between extracting a rule and applying it. For example, alphabetical sequence might be adopted and then abandoned, or replaced by the rule of word-length. Others followed a more random placement of words or attempted to arrange them in a semantically meaningful way. The same participants who did this puzzle were used in another similar puzzle. Bartlett found much 'transfer of training' from the first puzzle to the second. Participants who managed to extract a rule or rules from the first puzzle attempted to do so in the second through perhaps different rules; while those who adopted a random selection of words continued to do so. In some cases, an approximation of the terminal point presented itself in 'leap' of intuition as being a diamond shape in the first extrapolation puzzle and as two triangles touching each other at a point in the second. This image sets a frame into which the missing steps must fit and thereby turns extrapolation into an interpolation situation. In this way, the leap and the extraction of a rule are similar; both set a definite direction and give meaning to the steps taken toward it.

The last process of gap filling Bartlett discussed within closed system thinking is what he calls 'evidence in disguise.' This concerns cases in which all items are already present but need to be seen from a new perspective in order to use them. In this context, Bartlett investigated the process by which people solve crossword puzzles. For example, one clue read, "ARE WE, LAD, IN THE RIGHT STATE." Over half of the university participants correctly wrote down DELAWARE without requiring any steps. Some typical comments were: "The answer suddenly 'clicked,'" "DELAWARE occurred 'in a flash,'" "The word 'lad' seemed unnecessary: try anagram: fits DELAWARE" (p. 65). Although the answer appeared in a leap, one can still identify how evidence is used in a sequential manner. The first thing that the problem solver must determine is what sort of situation he or she is dealing. In this case, participants must recognize that 'this is an anagram,' which requires a rearrangement of letters for its solution. This brings the problem into a regular interpolation or extrapolation situation. Bartlett also points out that solving the puzzle involves using information from memory but emphasizes that it takes a highly flexible form; it becomes active in relation to the immediate evidence and the circumstances of the moment, such as the task of solving an anagram (see also Chapter 4).

Adventurous Thinking: Science, Everyday Life, and Art

Whereas 'closed system thinking' deals with situations in which all the required information for solving the problem is already present, 'adventurous thinking' necessitates that new information be sought and put in relation to what is already given. The latter points to the fact that human beings not only try to avoid uncertainty by reducing knowledge to the closed system (and ultimately interpolation), but also have a zest for chase, risk, adventure, and sport which leads them to struggle to break out of the closed system. If this is the case, the human thinker cannot be adequately understood through the metaphor of a machine that mechanically responds to information; at best this only fits closed systems thinking. Thus, the implicit approach of early work in the cognitive psychology of thinking (see earlier) describes only a subset of thinking. Bartlett (1958) explicitly argued against the view that "thinking, when it is effective, is bound to be narrowly directed, to favour short cuts, and to adopt the style and method most suited to certain 'closed situations'" (p. 145). Far from the notion of human thinker as a calculating machine, the investigation of adventurous thinking brings us closest to Bartlett's earlier focus on constructive (or in Gestalt terms 'productive' – see earlier) processes and how they are conditioned by social factors. Bartlett saw adventurous thinking as characteristic of science, everyday life, and art, each of which will be described in what follows.

To discuss experimental thinking Bartlett provides three case studies, two historical and one personal.[6] The first historical case deals with medicine's experimental investigation of infective agents (viz., bacteria and viruses) and the second with research on reaction times. The personal case is a description of his own extended process of investigation that culminated in the publication of *Remembering*. Thus, he has in mind both the long development of a particular research area as well as extended pursuit of gentlemen scientist. Like his study of bodily skills as an organized series of movements, his focus here is not on thinking with regards to particular experiments but their place within a prolonged development of research. Bartlett highlighted that experimentation comes at a rather late stage in the search for knowledge and is preceded by much accumulation and classification of information through other sources. Nonetheless, once experimental thinking gets under way it tends to follow a wandering, uneconomical path in its search – Bartlett himself accumulated much more material than he used in the write up of his experiments. There will always be more potential paths at each step than the experimentalist can take. Thus, he or she needs to have the 'sensitivity' to be able to exclude many dead-end paths before having gone down them, and more importantly, be able to 'predict' or 'prophesize' the direction of lines of research that are most likely to be fruitful.[7] Prediction in this sense is the long-term equivalent of 'anticipation' in relation to bodily skills. Like his study of bodily skills, the emphasis is again on the series of steps rather than on a single event as well as on the 'halts' between experiments where openings occur. This kind of prediction needs to be distinguished from that of correctly forecasting the outcome of a single experiment based on assumptions already assumed to be correct, which Bartlett thought added little to one's knowledge – in this case it would be more informative if the prediction was found to be incorrect.[8]

The experimentalist is thus constructive in his approach. He or she must look ahead and with foresight select or experimentally construct the appropriate and significant evidence from a range of possibilities. Original experimental thinking in this sense typically involves either inventing new methods or borrowing them from other fields. Methods can be an impediment to further progress when they become too standardized and thoughtless; part of Bartlett's own experimental originality came from breaking away from the dominant Ebbinghausian approach to memory (Chapter 2). But more than method, original research often has the characteristic of bringing together different streams of inquiry: "Perhaps all original ideas and developments come from the contact of subject–matter with different subject–matter, of people with different people" (Bartlett, 1958, p. 147). Bartlett himself developed his ideas through contact with people in anthropology, neurology, philosophy, mathematics, history, philology, and literature (p. 140) (see also

Chapter 1). Original and routine experimental thinking differ in that with the former we will find different interests at play, while the latter is more circumscribed in a particular field of study. Originality comes from seeing where different streams of evidence seem to be converging and working to constructively bring them together. In this we find a diffusionist explanation of scientific development, where the contact of different cultural groups leads to the constructive growth of new ideas and practices from within (Chapter 3). However, we cannot lose sight here of the characteristics of the scientist as a person. Bartlett emphasizes that the original experimentalist scientist is adaptive, has foresight, is willing to make and admit mistakes, pinpoints problems, takes risks, and is not only oriented to closing gaps but also to opening new possibilities. Traveling down the long, winding road to significant scientific discoveries is 'emotionally sustained' through the scientist's own love of chase, risk, and adventure. In this, experimental thinking differs considerably from the function and aim of everyday thinking.

By 'everyday thinking' Bartlett (1958) means, "those activities by which most people, when they are not making any particular attempt to be logical or scientific, try to fill up gaps in information available to them" (p. 164). It concerns public opinion, fashion, social policy, and more broadly, just about any topic of general social interest. Like experimental thinking, everyday thinking is a response to an indeterminate situation where several solutions are possible, rather than the single solution characteristic of closed systems. However, while the experimental scientist carefully proceeds through a series of detailed steps in order to bring together different strands of evidence, 'everyday thinking' is based largely on a single jump in which the thinker finds evidence to confirm what he or she believed from the start. This is usually done on the basis of some conventional idea, giving everyday thinking its strong 'social coloring.' Bartlett also refers to it as 'immediate communicative thinking' in that it is instantly expressed in a social setting with the hopes of gaining approval and acceptance from one's peers. Bartlett said, "It is directed towards convincing by strong assertion rather than towards compelling proof" (p. 187). In this process, individuals as group members tend to concentrate on a single detail or group of details, which in turn overdetermines their thinking and leads them to ignore or bend all other information toward it. This is similar to Moscovici's (1981, p. 190) description of everyday thinking, in which the conclusion justifies the steps to reach it, or put differently the verdict justifies the trial (Chapter 3).[9] To study this process, Bartlett "devised a number of concrete situations, all involving group relations not too far removed from the possible experience of the people who would deal with them.

They were left in an incomplete state, and the subjects in the experiments were to be asked to continue them to what they thought would be their most likely issue" (Bartlett, 1958, p. 168). This research strategy comes close to his earlier methods for the study of remembering narratives, such as *War of the Ghosts* (chapter 2).[10] However, in this case, the gaps are introduced from the start, rather than occurring as a result of the passing of time and with it the disintegration of memory.

The earliest study of thinking using incomplete narratives was a 1938 article titled 'the cooperation of social groups,' in which two prose passages were used which described a conflict and resolution between two groups. In the first story, this concerned the Union of Agricultural Engineers and the Association of Agricultural Labourers, while the second story depicted a small village in North England, in which Roman Catholics and Anglicans were forced to work together as a result of a drought in the community. The friendly and unfriendly contact of groups was earlier discussed through ethnographic cases in *Psychology and Primitive Culture* (chapter 3). Here Bartlett is concerned with probing the way in which the bulk of people think and talk about this pressing social issue. Bartlett (1938a) asked subjects "to try to express an opinion, based on psychological grounds only, as to whether the co-operation sought between the two groups is likely to be successfully maintained, or must inevitably break down" (p. 38). His 50 subjects were divided into two general classes: (1) persons associated with the university (i.e., students, researchers, and lecturers) and (2) "persons having practical, wage earning activities or the like, without a university training, but with a wider experience of everyday human affairs" (p. 38). Thus, Bartlett is able to compare the patterns of responses of these two already existing social groups. In doing so, he conceptualizes his subjects as socially embedded as he had in his earlier work. He finds in the first case that the 'university group' was equally divided between probable permanence and probable breakdown, whereas in the 'practical group' 20 percent were for permanence and 80 percent for breakdown; however, with regards to the second conflict, there was no difference between the groups. In the first case, there was also a difference between the university group and practical group in what 'evidence' was selected from the passages to justify their conclusions. For example, "To the practical group a difference in I.Q. appeared far more important and more antagonistic to co-operation than to the university group" (p. 39).[11]

Bartlett and his students collected a great quantity of data using this method with a wide range of stories involving the cooperation of social groups as well as personal matters. This program of research aimed to be widely comparative between different groups inside of England and around the world. For example, Bartlett's student Carmichael (1939a, b) compared the thinking of experts and nonexperts. He used an article from the newspaper about the increasing cooperation of an amateur and national rowing association, and had both rowers (the experts) and non-rowers (the nonexperts) as participants. Whereas 60 percent of the experts thought that the attempted cooperation was 'doubtful,' only 16 percent of the nonexperts arrived at that conclusion. Furthermore, the nonexperts, on the one hand, felt more certain of their views, which were constructed on the basis of a conventional generalization. The experts, on the other hand, brought forward many more points of evidence but mostly from their personal experience rather than what was presented in the article. With regards to comparison of different national groups, everyday thinking experiments were done in India, Africa, and the Middle East. Unfortunately, almost all of this data was lost in the war and thus never saw publication. The one exception to this was Carmichael's (1940) study of 'constructive thinking amongst Greenlanders,' which used some of the same stories in England and Greenland. It thereby provided experimental data to counter Lévy-Bruhl's notion of 'primitive mentality' as being wholly distinct from the European thinking (see Chapter 3). Following Bartlett (1923), Carmichael (1940) argued "the contention that civilized persons strive always to reach a well-balanced coherent conclusion, while the primitive is willing to tolerate incoherence and even 'considerable contradictions and contrasts' is, if not unfair to the primitive, at least highly flattering to ourselves" (p. 313). Bartlett (1958) concluded that in all the groups studied:

Everyday thinking ... consists in the main of some single generalization, advanced as if it were incontestable, with or without evidence; but if with evidence, usually with less than might be used. Generalization and selective evidence are alike strongly socially determined. The first can nearly always be found to be current in some group of which the thinker is a member, and the second, provided it is not just personal recall, is precisely the same evidence that many other members of the group also select. (p. 178)

As a final example of adventurous thinking, Bartlett (1958) explored the thinking of the artist. In this, he aimed to understand the process by which the artist creates a piece of literature, painting, or music through 'a consideration of the performance stages' (p. 190). His material for analysis was mainly biographies of great artists, especially novelists and painters.[12] According to him, the artistic process begins with a 'preparatory' stage in which the artist collects experiences that will later be used as the material for his or her work. These experiences, however, need to settle in such a way that the artist can transform what began as individual experiences into something with objective qualities, recognizable to members of the group. In connection with this, Bartlett recalled an episode walking through a Turkish city with an artist, who pointed to some working class men sitting in a row on a rough seat and told him "Some day I shall paint a picture of those men." Bartlett asked her, "Why not now?" to which she replied "No, it is not ready yet" (p. 189). From this initial preparation, the process of painting often proceeds as follows:

> There is the preparation, which may or may not be with quick sketches, quickly discarded, or in part only to be retained. Then the picture begins to grow, and as its maker moves along the succession of his adventure, the watcher will see how opportunity seems to be opening out all the time, and may from stage to stage continually ask himself 'What next?' The painter, like Velasquez, with much groping and trying, with many sketches, with rejections and partial acceptances, moving tentatively, and then at last with certainty towards the final picture. (pp. 192–3)[13]

Similarly, when the novelist first launches at his or her task, possibilities abound. Characters are developed and scenes play out in such a way that many lines of sequent development are possible. However, as the novel reaches its completion as a work of art the events depicted increasingly take the character of inevitability until the artist can say, "This is what must happen. This alone is satisfying" (p. 191).

The intermediate stages of the process may occur in 'a flash' of intuitive insight, "the product itself is brief and short – the small, brilliant drawing, the short story with but a single incident, the musical theme, the momentary poem" (p. 194). Of all the kinds of thinkers discussed, the artist uses the leap or flash most frequently. The intuitively produced fragments must then, however, be worked by further steps into a finished form. This comes close to Obeyesekere's (2012) description of 'visionary experience' as a process by which potent insights arrived at through an unreflective consciousness must be elaborated into a rationally ordered form at the next stage if they are to serve as knowledge.[14] In Bartlett's words, it "passes to an achievement lying beyond the 'flash' itself" (Bartlett, 1958, p. 194). All these efforts of the artist are driven by a service to a 'standard,' which he or she both seeks and expresses. This standard "remains in part within the thinker and in his affinity to other human beings" (p. 196). The artist does not provide proof through evidence like the scientist, nor does he or she simply make a point by assertion like the everyday thinker, but is persuasive to the extent he or she satisfies the standard. Like the flash, conventions are highly important to the artist's work (Chapter 3), but the artist must pass beyond them in his or her pursuit of a standard. For this reason, mere copying of a style is unfulfilling to the serious artist. Ultimately, the artist aims to arrive at a finished work that is "at once convincing and satisfying, and yet question-making and disturbing ... so that ... the spectator or the listener ... generally want to go back to it again and again ... not because they failed to understand it, but because by going back to it they can understand better and more, asking new questions and discovering the answers" (p. 196).[15]

Conclusion: The Comparative Study of Thinking Processes

Bartlett's approach to thinking is interesting to us today in that it is comparative along three dimensions: with bodily skills, between different kinds of thinking, and between different social groups. First, in order to show how thinking grows out of earlier forms of flexible adaptation to the environment, Bartlett explored formal parallels between bodily skills and thinking as a high-level skill. Both are directed at 'filling in gaps' through a series of steps in an ongoing activity. They differ in that those steps are expressed as bodily movements in the former case and as signs and symbols in various media in the latter. Moreover, bodily skills are tightly coupled to the immediate environment, whereas thinking provides a means through which the person can *distance* him- or herself from the here-and-now situation in various different directions, some of which may even appear to have no time and place. At the end of *Remembering*, Bartlett (1932/1995, p. 314) had argued that constructive imaging, remembering, and thinking all have this characteristic of distancing, and in this way overlap with each other (cf. Werner and Kaplan, 1963; Zittoun and Gillespie, 2016). They can, however, be distinguished in that remembering is more fixed on recalling a particular episode from the past, imaging is much more unconstrained in its movements, while thinking aims to reconfigure whatever information is available (from perceiving, imagining, and remembering) in order to solve a particular problem. In this way, Bartlett's approach is similar to the Gestalt and to some extent the Würzburg approach in its focus on the steps involved and information used in completing a given task.

Second, Bartlett compared different kinds of thinking processes – namely, closed system, experimental, everyday, and artistic thinking. This was by no means an exhaustive list: in the book's conclusion he suggests extending the comparison to other contexts, such as religious (especially mystical) thinking (see also Bartlett, 1950c) and legal thinking. He was careful to look for common principles between kinds of thinking while recognizing that each will have its own particular characteristics: "Each kind of thinking possesses its own balance of properties, its own characteristic variety of most of them, and some features that are all of its own" (Bartlett, 1958, p. 199). There is an important lesson to learn here about *not evaluating one form of thinking on the criteria appropriate for another*.[16] As we saw earlier, Gigerenzer et al. (1989) was critical of how the psychology of thinking became the study of errors, distortions, and biases in the 1960s and 1970s; the principles of thinking were here to be discovered by looking at deviations from the right procedures to arrive at the 'correct' calculations. In this way, all kinds of thinking are evaluated according to the principles of closed systems thinking, where "steps taken towards filling up a gap increases, the number of probable next steps decreases, until a stage is reached beyond which all thinking must proceed through the same number and order of steps to the same terminus" (Bartlett, 1958, p. 191). These steps are tightly connected to one another, and only rarely does a leap occur.

Experimental thinking is similar to closed system thinking with respect to carefully following a meticulous series of steps toward a terminus; however, Bartlett emphasized the constructive dimensions of combining different streams of investigation, inventing and borrowing methods, and having intuition with regards to which lines of research are likely to be successful and which are not. This is because, unlike closed system thinking, many possible pathways open up to the experimental scientist at each halting point. His or her orientation is simultaneously to close gaps in knowledge through compelling proof and to open new possibilities for further exploration. In contrast, the everyday thinker makes the evidence and steps fit a conclusion already reached at the start of the process. The gap is here typically filled by using a conventional principle which has been picked up from some earlier social environment, such as the home or school – for example, "Englishmen are always good sports," "All's fair in politics," or "The biggest step is from idea to action" (Bartlett, 1951, p. 135). The evidence is then selected and bent to fit the conventional generalization, which is asserted as if it were incontestable. In fewer cases, personal memories may be used in place of the convention. Finally, artistic thinking also uses memories and conventions but puts them in service of a standard, which is in the thinker and his or her sensitivity to the experience of other human beings. Like the experimenter, the artist often tests out different possibilities (e.g., in sketches) to find what best satisfies the standard. This form of thinking is most likely to employ the intuitive leap or flash, but must then take its products a step further by sequentially arranging them to achieve the artistic goal.

Third, there is a comparison of how members of different social groups fill up gaps. Even with closed system thinking, Bartlett found uniformity in gap filling among members of a group. But the conventions of different groups played a much more important role throughout the study of adventurous thinking. This comes across most strongly in his discussion of everyday thinking, where different social groups are directly compared in terms of how they interpret the outcome of a situation and what evidence they bring to bear to support their claim. Bartlett's incomplete story method provides a powerful methodology to the role of conventions in thinking and traces how thinking changes as a function of group membership. There are many possibilities for taking this methodology forward, such as by analyzing and comparing the group conversations through which consensus is reached. Another possibility would be to ask people both how they thought the situation depicted would be resolved and how they thought a member of another social group might fill in the missing information. In this way, the researcher could also explore what individuals think of other groups' ways of thinking (see Gillespie, 2008 on 'alternative representations').

What Bartlett (1958) did not explicitly say is that closed system, experimental, everyday, and artistic thinking are themselves each socially embedded in different groups within which a person may move. Taking this step, we arrive at the observation that "a plurality of modes of thought can coexist within the same individual" (Moscovici, 1976/2008, p. 185), each becoming dominant within its own social sphere (see also Chapter 3). Doctors, lawyers, scientists, and artists will approach a situation in different ways depending on whether they are doing so as a professional or merely giving an opinion as part of everyday communication. In his *Psychology and Primitive Culture*, Bartlett (1923) had himself argued that a conflict of tendencies was managed by relegating them to different spheres of expression in society. This is particularly the case in modern societies, where according to Moscovici (1976/2008) we find "the dynamic coexistence – interference or specialization – of the distinct modalities of knowledge, corresponding to definite relations between man and his environment" (p. 186). Moscovici called this state of affairs 'cognitive polyphasia' and argued that it was 'the rule rather than the exception' (p. 186). Bartlett's method for studying everyday thinking would be a powerful tool to better understand this socially situated character of thinking. However, in contrast to Bartlett's methods and concepts for studying remembering (Chapter 2), little has been done to develop his approach to thinking.[17] Bringing Bartlett (1958) into the contemporary psychology of thinking would help to outline the diversity of thinking processes, resist the tendency to reduce one to another (viz. logical or numerical thought), and stress thinking's social character as well as provide powerful methodological tools to further its study.

Notes

1. Although the English-speaking world tends to know only about the so-called Berlin School of Gestalt psychology, there were in fact several different schools of thought. For example, in contrast to the Berlin school of Wertheimer, Koffka, and Köhler, the Leipzig Institute put much more emphasis on feeling (see Diriwächter, 2008; Krueger, 1928; Wagoner, 2011b). Bartlett, however, was most influenced by the Berlin School.
2. Bartlett first met Köhler at the International Congress of Psychology, held in 1922 at the University of Oxford. Afterward both Köhler and Koffka were Bartlett's guests at St. John's College, where they had lively discussions with other Cambridge psychologists. Bartlett continued to meet Köhler intermittently over many years (see Bartlett, 1961b). The influence of the two approaches ran both ways. Koffka published a review of Bartlett's *Psychology and Primitive Culture* in 1926 and provided a detailed discussion of *Remembering* in his magnum opus *Principles of Gestalt Psychology* (1935). Moreover, researchers who followed in the 1940s and 1950s saw the affinity between the approaches and aimed to bring them together in their work – for example, Allport and Postman's (1947) classic study of rumor.
3. One of the last important Würzburg psychologists, Otto Selz, was killed in the concentration camps. Maurice Halbwachs, discussed in the last chapter, suffered the same fate.
4. Werner (1937) also outlines this key distinction between 'process' and 'achievement.' He adds that in the transition from one skill level to another there is often a temporary drop in achievement – for example, in making the transition between two finger touch typing and the use of all 10 fingers. It is possible that Bartlett borrowed the distinction from Werner, who attended a 1955 symposium on thinking with Bartlett in Cambridge.
5. Psychology as a whole (not just in relation to thinking) has tended to investigate what can be quantified and experimentally studied, while sidelining messier, more complex phenomena.
6. Bartlett also approached 'scientific thinking' in an article published a year later (see Bartlett, 1959). His focus was similar to the one in *Thinking*, attending to 'prediction,' 'the development of method,' 'detecting the direction of evidence,' and the scientist's 'sensitivity' to evidence.
7. This idea can be further elaborated with Polanyi (1982): "Scientific discovery reveals new knowledge, but the new vision which accompanies it is not knowledge. It is *less* than knowledge, for it is a guess; but is *more* than knowledge, for it is a foreknowledge of things yet unknown and at present perhaps inconceivable. Our vision of the general nature of things is our guide for the interpretation of all future experience. Such guidance is indispensable. Theories of the scientific method which try to explain the establishment of scientific truth by any purely objective formal procedure are

doomed to failure. Any process of enquiry unguided by intellectual passions would inevitably spread out into a desert of trivialities" (p. 135).

8. Gigerenzer (2004) has forcefully made this argument against the method of 'null hypothesis testing,' experimental psychology's dominant approach today (see Chapter 2).

9. Moscovici also uses this phrase to describe the research focus of social representations theory. For him, social representations "concern the contents of everyday thinking and the stock of ideas that gives coherence to our religious beliefs, political ideas and the connections we create as spontaneously as we breathe" (1988, p. 214). Although very close to Bartlett's notion of everyday thinking, Moscovici does not cite him on this point, though he undoubtedly knew of his work on thinking.

10. Bartlett also tried this task on both single persons and with people in groups, whereas his earlier studies were focused on individuals doing the memory task. This adds a potentially interesting comparative dimension which is unfortunately not explicitly developed as part of his analysis. He is also very explicit that "It would have been worth while to make tape recordings of some of (the group discussions); but I did not do that" (p. 173). This would be a fruitful extension of the everyday thinking method to analyze how decisions about some topic of social interest are arrived at in a group versus individually.

11. It is unfortunate that these results are presented mainly as aggregated outcomes of the social groups compared, rather than processes. The method could, however, be transformed to look more carefully at the steps involved in filling in the gap – e.g., by analyzing conversations between people (see footnote 10).

12. The focus on great artists is what Glăveanu (2010) has described as the 'he-paradigm' for researching creative thinking, as opposed to the 'I-paradigm' (exploring each individual's creativity whether a great inventor or not) and the 'we-paradigm' (looking at how people are creative in cooperation with each other). Interestingly, Bartlett (1958) consistently stressed the group (or 'we') character of both experimental and everyday thinking, but tended to underplay it when discussing the artist's thinking. However, in Bartlett's (1923) earlier book *Psychology and Primitive Culture*, he emphasized how the folk artist is strongly socially situated and guided in their actions.

13. This description has much in common with Bartlett's (1932/1995) characterization of constructive remembering, in which the rememberer encounters gaps and asks him- or herself "what must have been the case" (see Chapter 4).

14. Like Bartlett, Obeyesekere (2012) aimed to show that mystical or intuitive thinking was not simply a deficit form of knowing when compared to thinking in science and logic. In fact, he shows that in all these cases there is a dialectic between intuitive and rational forms of inquiry.

15. Philsopher of aesthetics Robert Innis (2007) has likewise characterized an encounter with a great work of art as one in which we are continuously drawn back to it to ask new questions and discover new 'vital messages.'

16. Lévy-Bruhl (1926/1985) also made this point in relation to 'primitive mentality' that we should not evaluate the thinking processes of other cultural

groups on the principle of noncontradiction, which he saw as characteristic of Western thinking.

17. *Thinking* (1958) did have an influence on early cognitive psychology (e.g., Neisser, 1967) but has since been largely forgotten. Although, rarely cited for his influence on this point (Jahoda, 1988), Bartlett's notion of 'everyday thinking' was also important for Moscovici's development of social representations theory (Chapter 3). It also helped cultural psychologists argue for the need to study thinking in real-life situations rather than in the laboratory (see e.g., Cole, McDermott, and Hood, 1978).

Conclusion: From Past to Future

> To understand and value current practice [in psychology] it is necessary to know something of the past, but never by it to be wholly ruled.
> (Bartlett, 1961b, p. 393)

This book has explored the human tension between conservation of the past and construction of the new in both individuals and social groups. In the process of living forward, human beings both modify old patterns and construct genuinely new forms to meet the challenges of a complex and changing environment. Major innovations typically arise from contacts with groups having different social organization and cultural forms. For example, original scientists like Bartlett have been influenced by several disciplines and have had the foresight to weld together distinct streams of ideas. Change in scientific disciplines is guided by contemporary conventions of practice and thinking, but also involves the selective borrowing from the more distant past in order to develop new ideas. This has helped psychologists to understand and value current practice as well as critique and move beyond it. The latter use of the past has more in common with cultural contact with foreign groups than with the flexible conservation of conventions from the immediate past. Like visiting a foreign country, this way of engaging the past can help us to take distance from our conventional ways of doing things. The exploration of Bartlett's work and legacy has here helped us to consider human beings as much more than simply reacting to or caused by various external influences. Instead, humans have been conceptualized as agents constrained by their past and present environment, but also capable of moving beyond them.

This concluding chapter aims to consolidate the ideas put forward in this book by outlining first the key features of Bartlett's constructive approach and second the historical reconstruction of his ideas over time. It begins by analyzing how the notion of 'construction' provides an integrative framework to investigate human action on and between individual and group levels. Although Bartlett argued that these levels should

not be confused (e.g., by applying the concept of memory to the group –
see Chapter 5), he often used models developed for one level as an analogy to understand the other. After having outlined Bartlett's integrative
constructive approach, this chapter applies his analysis of the reconstruction of cultural forms to the fate of his own ideas. This historical analysis
provides a case to illustrate how ideas and practices move, change, are
integrated, are forgotten, and are rediscovered. In this way, the study of
how culture is transmitted, maintained, and transformed can be applied
equally to scientific communities as well as to other groups in society.
The interdisciplinary contact and exchange Bartlett emphasized in relation to scientific development is needed to construct a psychology for the
third millennium. Bartlett's own synthesis of biological, anthropological,
sociological, and psychological ideas provides an instructive example of
an integrative approach to knowledge construction.

A General Theory of Constructiveness

Throughout this book, I have stressed how constructiveness involves a
flexible adaption to new circumstances rather than a response that exactly
reproduces what was done in the past. What is needed for human life is
a usable past. This is because "the external environment ... partially
changes and in part persists, so that it demands a variable adjustment,
yet never permits an entirely new start" (Bartlett, 1932, p. 224). Bartlett
applied this principle to different levels of organization from bodily
skills to group processes. Although he is clear that new properties emerge
at higher levels, he frequently used analogies from one level to understand another, such as the analogy he made between 'cultural patterns'
(Chapter 3) and 'schemata' (Chapter 4). This is apparent from Bartlett's
(1932) unstable terminology to refer to these concepts: his preferred
names for schema were 'active developing patterns' and 'organized settings,' while he also used 'group schemata' to discuss what he had earlier
called 'cultural patterns.' In what follows I will explore some of the parallels between his theorizing of individual and group processes in relation
to the notion of constructiveness. More elaborate distinctions between
levels of organization can easily be made,[1] but for our purposes the simple distinction is sufficient to explore the different sides of Bartlett's constructive approach. I will highlight five points of comparison between the
two levels that bring constructiveness to the fore: (1) readiness to receive,
(2) dominance of the past over the present, (3) stability through plasticity,
(4) radical reconstruction, and (5) de- and re-contextualization.

A person is not equally ready to receive all impressions. What is
experienced is a function of the person's attitude, interests, personal

history, and group membership. These factors constitute a person's active orientation to the world, aspects of which change from moment to moment, while others endure through one's lifetime. This is highly functional in that not all details of a situation are equally relevant to one's action. Bartlett was especially critical of Ebbinghaus's (1885/1913) method because it assumed a subject that passively received impressions. The Würzburg School did a variation of Ebbinghaus's study, where nonsense syllables of different colors, letters, and arrangements were presented to subjects who were instructed to observe a particular feature. Although there was a sensory experience of all stimulus aspects, subjects remained oblivious to those aspects that were unrelated to the task instructions (Ogden, 1951). Throughout his career Bartlett emphasized what a person brings to an action or experience in his studies, rather than assuming that the stimulus itself determines the response. Likewise, groups do not notice or adopt every new element of culture they encounter in other groups; this requires making the connection to an existing setting. Only those cultural elements for which there is some active interest or perceived utility for the group enter into it. As such, new technologies are frequently adopted while forms of social organization are particularly resistant to outside influence. History is replete with examples of cultural contact without transmission: groups without large administrative structures found little interest in adopting or recreating systems of writing (Diamond, 1997) nor did Japanese painters adopt the new perspective painting developed during the Renaissance though they knew about it. In short, groups like individuals need to be ready for some material if they are to attend to it.

This active orientation to the world is set up through the individual's or group's history. This is why the past tends to be dominant over the present. Bartlett (1932) famously argued that all psychological processes involve 'an effort after meaning,' whereby something given in the present is connected to a 'setting,' 'scheme,' 'schema,' which he understood as an organized mass of previous experience following Head's (1920) work in neurology (Chapter 4). Schemata thus provide the basis through which action and experience take form, like a figure emerging from a background; they are a person's accumulated history flexibly carried into new situations. In his experiments on perceiving, subjects saw a briefly displayed image in accordance with conventional expectations of what it should look like. When shown inkblots in his imagining experiment, subjects were reminded of entirely different things as a function of their previous experience (Chapter 2). And in his 'everyday thinking' experiments, subjects tended to ignore most of the evidence present and instead arrive at a solution based on some conventional generalization taken over from their social group or by personal recall (Chapter 6). The past's influence on the present was why Bartlett (1932) likened the experimentalist to a clinician. Similarly, in relation to the life of groups, Bartlett pointed out how a group's existing frame of reference provides a setting and explanation for new elements that enter into it. The group will not incorporate what cannot be given a place within its existing cultural patterns. The same principle holds true of propaganda produced by a ruling party for the public, although sometimes this can be prepared for by education (Chapter 3). In *Psychology and Primitive Culture*, Bartlett (1923) emphasized the conservative nature of 'primitive' groups; they tend to hold on to traditional ways of acting in and interpreting the world. This is mainly because of the minimal differentiation within the group and lack of contacts with other groups. And even when change is compulsory, as with forced conversions to Christianity, indigenous beliefs and traditions simply go underground and as such are retained at a deeper level.

Thus, both schemata and cultural patterns impose a stable but flexible framework on the novelty of the present. In this way, there is continuity in change, stability through plasticity. Schemata are described as active and developing, a constantly updated standard against which any new response is made. The fact that a continuous standard exists ensures continuity, while the fact it is developing in response to present conditions ensures change. Bartlett (1932) famously gave an example from tennis: "When I make the stroke I do not, as a matter of fact, produce something absolutely new, and I never merely repeat something old" (p. 202). The new response is channeled through the person's accumulated past experience and in meeting new conditions revises it. In his repeated reproduction experiments, Bartlett (1932) noted: "The most general characteristic of the whole of this group of experiments was the persistence, for any given subject, of the 'form' of his first reproduction" (p. 83). It is in the initial perception and reproduction that the material is put into relation with a person's schemata; this connection is difficult to break even when people are allowed to reread the original (Kay, 1955). The brilliance of Bartlett's repeated and serial reproduction methods is that they enable the researcher to explore continuity and change through a series of reproductions. Change and stability are here seen as interdependent opposites: it is precisely through the flexible application of a stable framework that continuity through time is ensured (see also Collins, 2006). In *Remembering*, Bartlett began to speak of this characteristic as 'constructive' in contrast to theories that saw memory as a static register of the past. However, in his earlier book *Psychology and Primitive Culture* Bartlett had used the term 'conservation' to describe how groups assimilate novelty to their existing cultural patterns, so that change is only slight. A group is able to preserve its traditions by flexibly adapting them to meet new needs. In short, both individuals and groups create continuity for themselves by adapting the old to new circumstances. There is change and reconstruction here but not of a radical nature- that requires an additional mechanism.

Bartlett implicitly discussed two forms of construction or reconstruction. In the first, changes are introduced through assimilation, simplification, and retention of apparently unimportant details (Bartlett, 1932, p. 268ff). This describes the conservation through plasticity discussed earlier. Bartlett illustrates this process both through his own experiments (Chapter 2) and with anthropological reports on the transformation of decorative art, cultural artifacts, and social practices as they move from one group to another (Chapter 3). However, a more radical reconstructive process can also occur, which he called 'turning around upon ones schemata' in relation to individual processes and 'social constructiveness' in relation to social groups. Bartlett is clear that imagining, remembering, and thinking in the full human sense is a conscious and self-reflective act, rather than the rudimentary work of schemata. This understanding of construction tends to be missed in contemporary discussions that see schemata as a distorting influence on memory and thereby ignore the reflective use of multiple schemata in remembering and also in thinking (Chapter 4; see later). In the process of remembering, a person constructively weaves together influences from a number of sources. It is in this process of 'turning around' that human agency emerges (see also Brown and Reavey, 2015). Similarly, Bartlett highlighted that groups not only assimilate cultural elements into a familiar social framework but also are capable of developing genuinely new forms by welding "together elements of culture coming from diverse sources and having historically, perhaps, very diverse significance" (Bartlett, 1932, p. 275). This occurs because groups have both a past and a future orientation or 'prospect.' The fact that a group has a 'prospect' creates conditions for 'social constructiveness' (Bartlett, 1928b). In *Psychology and Primitive Culture*, Bartlett gave the example of the emergence of a new religious cult through the weaving together of a number of distinct cultural groups' artifacts and ideas; in *Remembering*, he described sports teams as 'socially constructive' in their ability to creatively integrate new influences; and in *Thinking*, he discussed innovative scientific groups that borrow from numerous sources in order to better understand some phenomenon, as happened with the investigation of infective agents in medicine. More recently, Bloor (2000) has followed Bartlett in using the term 'social constructiveness' to analyze efforts during the First World War to develop radar detection systems, which also illustrates different national thinking styles.

In the more radical kind of reconstruction parts of one setting must be picked out and placed in another without losing their identity. This process involves de-contextualizing and re-contextualizing of material. At the individual level, Bartlett (1932) argued that this is done through the function of images. As his experiments aptly showed, images are not fixed entities but living and constantly changing with our interests. They arise when streams of interest conflict which introduces a rupture into our ongoing activities and triggers a process of self-reflection. The function of images is to allow us to 'pick out' bits from schemata and integrate it with other contexts, thereby increasing our variability of response:

> a man can take out of its setting something that happened a year ago, reinstate it with much if not all of its individuality unimpaired, combine it with something that happened yesterday, and use them to help him solve a problem which he is confronted to-day.
>
> (Bartlett, 1932, p. 219)

With regard to social groups, cultural elements are picked out of one group and brought into another stimulating social change from within. However, this happens under various conditions of cultural contact: one particularly important factor is whether there is a power asymmetry between the groups in question. When one group is dominant over another, this tends to foster an all-or-nothing adoption of the dominant group's culture and thus should not be considered as a form of radical reconstruction. Similarly, a submissive auditor in relation to a dominant audience when remembering tends to lead to literal recall (Chapter 5). Thus, whereas symmetrical relations between groups enables a free exchange of distinct cultural elements, asymmetrical relations creates conditions for whole bundles of cultural elements to be transmitted together.[2] In the former case, subgroups will typically develop around newly adopted distinct foreign cultural elements, re-contextualizing them in relation to other material and the group's ongoing project. In sum, at both individual and group levels the mixing and blending of material promote flexibility within a world filled with variability and constant change.

Although there are conceptual parallels between individual and group levels – schemata and cultural patterns – neither one is reducible to the other. On the one hand, properties of social groups (their norms, values, and traditions) cannot be reduced to the sum of individual members within them. Certain behaviors do not occur outside of a social group's framework. On the other hand, the individual is not an automaton within the group. One can say that a person's character is shaped by the social group but not determined by it (Nadel, 1937). As a result of their unique

history and combination of different schemata, an individual's experience
has a *personal* quality. To say that individual and group processes cannot
be reduced to the other, however, is not to say that they are independent
of each other. In many ways, they overlap and support one another.
Bartlett's notion that mind is a social formation and yet irreducible to
social processes comes close to other social-cultural theorists such as
Vygotsky, Mead, Baldwin, and Janet (Rosa, 1996; for a history of this
idea, see also Valsiner and van der Veer, 2000). Bartlett's work is particularly insightful in that he offers us both a socially situated psychological
theory as well as a psychologically informed theory of cultural dynamics.
These two inform each other in Bartlett's thinking to such a degree that
one cannot adequately interpret the one without the other. Thus
Bartlett's approach cannot be classified as *either* cognitive *or* sociocultural; it should by now be clear that it spans this divide.

Bartlett in Reconstruction

Having outlined some basic principles of Bartlett's constructivist theory,
our focus shifts to the different ways his ideas have been reconstructed
by others. In this effort, Bartlett's analytic framework provides us with
powerful tools to explore how ideas move and transform in science. As
he showed, cultural items are selectively borrowed and reconstructed
based on the conventions and the prospect of the receipt group. The
most successful and well-known channel through which his ideas have
been propagated has been cognitive psychology, but this is by no means
the only interpretation available. In this book, we have seen many different and often-conflicting representations of Bartlett developed based
on the diverse theoretical orientations (e.g., anthropological, cognitive,
social, ecological, discursive, and cultural). Different researchers have
selected particular dominant details from Bartlett's work, based on their
own background, and reconstructed the whole around those points
of interest, omitting what did not fit and rationalizing the rest, as
Bartlett's experiments also aptly showed (Chapter 2). This section briefly
describes 'three waves' of heightened interest in Bartlett's work (see also
Johnston, 2001), highlighting how constructiveness was understood in
each. The first wave is characterized by empirically testing different
aspects of Bartlett's approach to remembering. The second wave takes
place during the cognitive revolution, at which point much attention was
aimed at reinterpreting the concept of schema. And the third wave, of
which this book is a part, is focused on revitalizing the social and cultural aspects of Bartlett's work and integrating them with cognition.

The earliest elaborations of Bartlett's ideas explored constructive
remembering in relation to social and cultural factors (e.g., Bateson,

1936; Maxwell, 1936; Nadel, 1937; Northway, 1936). These studies illustrated how social groups and customs condition the recall of individuals in terms of both content and style, or 'the matter and manner of recall' in Bartlett's (1932) terms.[3] The direction to qualitative changes introduced into some material in remembering is largely a function of social interest and cultural patterns. In other words, the focus here is on how different groups give meaning to the material to be remembered. Constructiveness can be seen in how individuals as members of groups select, transform, and make use of some material. This called for a qualitative analysis revealing different 'preferred persistent group tendencies.' Many experiments in the 1940s to mid-1950s continued in this line of analysis in, for example, Allport and Postman's (1947) study of how rumors are transmitted and transformed to confirm conventional social prejudices, a line of investigation that has been more recently continued by Kashima (2000, 2008). Well into the 1950s, Talland (1956) was looking at 'cultural differences in serial reproduction,' the title of his article. Despite all the studies dealing with the issue of cultural dynamics, there are surprisingly few references to Bartlett's early book *Psychology and Primitive Culture*. After the 1930s, this work seems to have been largely forgotten, at least until the third wave of interest in Bartlett (see later). It is also noteworthy that Allport and Postman (1947), Talland (1956), and several others at this time incorporated Gestalt terms and ideas into their Bartlettian studies, especially from Wulf's (1922) classic work on the reproduction of simple visual forms (see Wagoner, 2017). In this period, there is a genuine integration of two streams of research, illustrating Bartlett's idea of 'social constructiveness.'

In the 1950s, the character of replication studies began to shift from the analysis of how social factors condition different directions of qualitative change in recall to a focus on individual recall as a primarily cognitive process. At this time, psychology experienced a shift in the meaning of an experiment from an open exploration of a qualitative phenomenon to a manipulation of an independent variable while holding all others constant (see also Winston and Blais, 1996). The latter notion of an experiment became popular partly because it allowed for a statistical analysis of scores that fit the administrative ethos of prediction and control of populations (Danziger, 1990). This approach was already on the rise when Bartlett published *Remembering*, in which it was criticized by him for not specifying the relationship between variables or how they operated within a single person. In contrast, the older, more open, and flexible style of experimentation he adopted made systematic interventions into a phenomenon in order to probe it through concrete and contextualized cases, thereby remaining experientially close to the phenomenon of interest. Bartlett used this approach to study remembering through his varied experimental setup (e.g., method of description, method of repeated reproduction, etc.), comparison with studies on other processes (e.g., perceiving and imaging), use of a wide range of material (e.g., different stories, images, argumentative texts), testing recall after different time intervals, and complementing subjects' reproductions with their verbal reports (Chapter 2).

With the restricted notion of an experiment, researchers sought to obtain definitive answers regarding the truth or falsity of a given aspect of Bartlett's theory of remembering, understood as a cognitive process. The terminology for describing qualitative changes in reproductions in these replications was at first quite varied, often incorporating key terms from Gestalt psychology. But over time these and other terms, indicating constructiveness, become subsumed under the umbrella 'distortion.' The most decisive turning point in this history was a study by Gauld and Stephenson (1967) who concluded that memory reconstruction was a result of Bartlett's task instructions rather than inherent in memory itself. Their assumptions about the phenomena could not be more different than Bartlett's. First, they assumed that memory to be a context-free faculty and second that 'construction' meant 'distortion' and 'error.' In the 1990s, many memory researchers continued with similar assumptions (viz. focusing on memory distortion) and remembered only Gauld and Stephenson's (1967) failed replication. In this history, we see how Bartlett's experiments were assimilated to a different framework and how additions such as the notion of 'distortion' transformed the meaning of the whole. Until this day, Bartlett is remembered within much of psychology for showing that 'distortions' and 'errors' increase in memory over time. Although this is not entirely wrong, it was not Bartlett's aim. Moreover, it ignores his own description of what makes remembering constructive, in which accurate memories were also understood as constructed (Ost and Costall, 2002).

In the same year that Gauld and Stephenson (1967) effectively put an end to replications until the 1990s, Neisser (1967) published *Cognitive Psychology*, which outlined a new field of study that focused on how the mind works with information. Bartlett was the chosen ancestor for this approach:

The present approach is more closely related to that of Bartlett (1932, 1958) than to any other contemporary psychologist, while its roots are at least as old as the 'act psychology' of the nineteenth century. The central assertion is that seeing, hearing, and remembering are all acts of *construction*, which may make more or less use of stimulus information depending on circumstances.

The constructive processes are assumed to have two stages, of which the first is fast, crude, wholistic, and parallel while the second is deliberate, attentive, detailed, and sequential.

(Neisser, 1967, p. 10, original emphasis)

It is noteworthy that Neisser mentions both *Remembering* and *Thinking*, but apparently did not take notice of *Psychology and Primitive Culture*. There is nonetheless much that is certainly correct in the quote – for example, the roots of Bartlett's approach in act of psychology (of Brentano and those who followed him), the centrality of 'construction,' and his description of its two stages, which parallel the two kinds of construction in Bartlett's work that were outlined earlier. What is more problematic is his use of the computer metaphor to describe mind and 'construction' processes. Although the metaphor first took hold in the Cambridge laboratory with its studies of human–machine interactions (Chapter 1), Bartlett (1958) himself argued that it was inappropriate and remained committed to a bio-functional perspective. When the machine or computer metaphor was applied back to Bartlett's approach, 'meaning' got replaced with 'information' (Bruner, 1990).[4] As such, Bartlett's key phrase 'effort after meaning' is never mentioned in Neisser's book. Instead, the book is explicitly about what happens to information as it travels from the senses through various mental systems. It is only in the last chapter that Neisser addresses the 'higher mental processes' (viz. Memory and Thinking), focusing his discussion on Bartlett's critique of the trace theory of memory or what Neisser called 'the reappearance hypothesis' (p. 280ff). Construction in his account becomes little more than a recombination of elements according to an already existing plan, thus leaving little room for human innovation.[5]

As cognitive psychology grew, Neisser's keyword 'construction,' as a general description of what the mind does, would itself be replaced with 'information processing.' A more limited notion of construction would continue in the study of memory research but mostly as a synonym of distortion (Chapter 2). The word 'processing' implies working with finite information found 'out there' rather than constructively going beyond it. In other words, construction becomes a de facto recombination of elements according to an existing plan. Within this expanding approach, it became popular to discuss theoretical mental entities that occurred between stimulus and response, and inputs and outputs. The concept of schema fit this part wonderfully by explaining all kinds of memory distortions. Although Oldfield (1954), a former student of Bartlett, was the first to translate schema into the language of information storage on a computer, he emphasized the constant recoding of elements (to economize storage) occurring to the plan provided by schema. In contrast, later schema theories (including frames, scripts, and story schema) saw schemata as generally static structures with nodes into which elements fit or were forgotten (Chapter 4). There is little room here for the notions of agency and radical reconstruction discussed earlier, as the question of how a person might reflect on and manipulate schema was largely ignored. Moreover, because the structure was presumed to be static no one felt the need to do *repeated* reproduction experiments until much later (see Bergman and Roediger, 1999). A more dynamic notion of schema has more recently been developed in cognitive psychology with the parallel processing approach (McClelland, 1995), but this still falls short of capturing radical reconstruction.

One of the first thinkers to re-energize the social and cultural dimensions of Bartlett's work was Serge Moscovici. His theory of social representations explicitly aimed to counterbalance the individualistic focus that had become characteristic of much social psychology. Like Bartlett (1923, 1932), Moscovici stressed that social representations are dynamic and plastic structures that thus need to be studied in their *transformation* as they move from one social group to another. Moreover, both thinkers situate human action and experience within complex systems of culture that are historically developed but treated as natural; in this way, human beings are constantly rehearsing or re-enacting their traditions while remaining largely oblivious that they are doing so. Moscovici's theory is also one of the few approaches to bring together ideas from throughout Bartlett's career (another is Michael Cole's cultural psychology, see later). From *Psychology and Primitive*, Moscovici borrowed Bartlett's insight that "Lévy-Bruhl compares primitive man to Kant" (Moscovici, 2000, p. 248) and thereby ignores the diversity of thinking found in contemporary society. *Remembering* and particularly the notion of 'conventionalization' helped Moscovici to articulate the key processes of 'objectification' (whereby abstract ideas are projected into the world and treated as if they were real) and 'anchoring' (which makes 'the unfamiliar familiar'). Finally, the notion of 'everyday thinking', borrowed from *Thinking* (1958), was key to formulating the idea of common sense or social thought, which needs to be assessed within its own logic and functions. Moscovici's (1984) statement, "Social thinking owes more to convention and memory than to reason" (p. 26) is exactly in line with Bartlett (1958). Social representations theory reconfigured the different aspects of Bartlett's work to answer the specific question of how science is transformed into common sense. This process of transformation can be dramatically illustrated using Bartlett's method of serial reproduction (see Bangerter, 1997).

It was only in the 1980s, however, that we find a wider rediscovery of the distinctly social aspects of Bartlett's work. Anthropologist Mary

Douglas (1980, 1986) drew attention to the important insight of *Psychology and Primitive Psychology* that humans are social beings and must be studied as such (e.g., Bartlett's unit of analysis was the 'individual-in-a-given-social-group'). In particular, she highlighted Bartlett's (1923) idea that the conflict of tendencies in a group is often resolved by relegating each to its own sphere of expression within a community (Chapter 3). Although Douglas drew on the concept of schema in her earlier work (Douglas, 1960/1984, p. 36), for her *Remembering* was a retrograde step in that it backed away from the stronger social position of the *Psychology and Primitive Culture*: "The author of the best book on remembering forgot his own first convictions" (Douglas, 1980, p. 19). This is not an entirely fair assessment, as the second half of *Remembering* explores social psychological issues, such as how social factors condition recall (Chapter 5). These social dimensions of remembering have been powerfully developed in discursive psychology and cultural psychology.

Discursive psychologists Edwards and Middleton (1987) highlighted the neglected aspects of Bartlett's famous book, such as 'feeling and attitude,' 'cross-modal remembering,' and most importantly for them 'conversation.' They pointed out the 'task-oriented dialogues' Bartlett (1932) carried out with his participants. However, they also argued that Bartlett experiments were 'not really social enough' (Middleton and Edwards, 1990a, p. 24). The circulation of story through a group, as studied by the method of serial reproduction, usually happens through medium of conversation; remembering is done by question and answer with others. The discursive approach thus shifted the analytic focus from internal cognitive processes to the contextual and pragmatic aspects of conversation. Rather than looking at input and outputs, their analysis compares "two outputs at different times, serving different communicative purposes, and requiring the same sort of analysis" (Middleton and Edwards, 1990b, p. 43). For example, they compared differences between remembering a film in an experimental context and conversation going on post-experiment (by leaving the tape recorder running after the experiment is over). They found in the experimental context that remembering is oriented to sequentially ordering and connecting events, whereas post-experiment the participants focus on remembering their evaluation of the film and emotional reaction to it. Schema or 'organized setting' in this account becomes a contextualized social practice (Middleton and Brown, 2005). In the same book, like Middleton and Edwards (1990a, b), Shotter (1990) furthered the discursive approach by comparing Bartlett's theory of remembering and Wittgenstein's notion of language as a form of life, and more recently Beals (1998) has done something similar in relation to Bakhtin's dialogical theory.

Cultural psychology's revival of Bartlett's work could be said to begin with Michael Cole and his colleagues' study of recall among Kpelle rice farms (Chapter 5). They found little evidence for the rote recall that Bartlett's theory might have predicted, nor for chunking of items to be remembered around categories (e.g., tools or clothing) – chunking can be seen as a sign of high-level schematic organization, characteristic of constructiveness, as opposed to low-level rote recall. These experiments in some ways followed the new conventions of an experiment described earlier, where one statistically compares different groups on a standard task, while keeping all other factors constant. However, they go well beyond the typical two-group comparisons of cross-cultural psychology to probe various contextual factors that might contribute to differences in recall. Cole, McDermott, and Hood (1978) later fortified this argument for the need to study psychological processes in real-life situations rather than in a neutral laboratory using Bartlett's (1958) notion of 'everyday thinking.' More recently, Cole (1996) further nuanced the notion of cultural context to mean 'that which weaves together' rather than 'that which surrounds.' In other words, instead of acting as an external factor that 'influences' psychological processes, social practices, cultural artifacts, and others are seen as directly participating in and constituting them. This comes close to Bartlett's notions of conventions and schema (which Cole acknowledges) as well as a number of other sociocultural interpretations of schema that followed (e.g., McVee, Dunsmore, and Gavelek, 2005). More recently, James Wertsch (2002) has extended the schema concept in a cultural direction with his notion of 'schematic narrative templates,' which are deep-seated cultural tools that mediate a person's memory of the past. Like Cole (1996) and social representations theory, his concept situates schema within a specific group's evolving traditions. The narrative and meaning-making dimensions of Bartlett's work have also been the focus of cultural psychologist Jerome Bruner (1990, 1991, 2002).

Although one could criticize cognitive psychology three decades ago for neglecting the social, cultural, and holistic, this is not the case today. A number of emerging trends have aimed to approach psychological processes as integrated and embedded systems providing flexible adaptation to the environment. Cognitive psychology and neuroscience are now arguing that imagination and memory are two sides of the same process by which an organism anticipates and plans for the future (e.g., see Schacter, Addis, and Buckley, 2007). This comes very close to Bartlett's description of 'remembering as an imaginative reconstruction' that increases variability of response. Schacter (2012) has also drawn attention to the neglected notion of 'turning around upon schema,' which for Bartlett occurs whenever the situation demands more than a fully learned response. While construction is understood as functional, there is still a tendency here to emphasize how it leads to 'distortion' and 'error.' Again, this is not in itself wrong but simply one-sided in that it limits the possibilities for exploring the reasons and nature of change in remembering. True and false memories are constructed on the basis of the same mechanisms and are experienced as being the same. If distortion and accuracy are going to continue to be key codes, they will have to be used in a much more nuanced, layered, and context-dependent way than has been typical.

Since the 1990s, new trends in the social sciences have shifted the focus from a look at remembering and thinking as individual cognitive processing to seeing them as integrated into networks of social practices, material artifacts, and other people (e.g., see Wagoner, forthcoming). Researchers are beginning to look beyond what is happening within the cranium, and are considering resources of remembering and thinking as *distributed* across brain, body, and world (see e.g., Sutton, Harris, Keil, and Barnier, 2010). This work connects up well with Bartlett's theorizing of material artifacts' role in sustaining conventions, which set the ground for psychological processes (see Cole and Cole, 2000), as well as how forms of social relationship shape remembering (Chapter 5). It also points to the fact that remembering serves many other functions than creating accurate representations of the past, such as motivating action, guiding innovation, and social bonding (see social representations and discursive psychology earlier). If this is indeed the case more emphasis needs to be put on affective processes over cognitive ones, a key argument that was in fact already made in *Remembering* but since has been largely ignored. However, there seems to be converging consensus that we need to consider culture, cognition, and affectivity together to develop adequate models of what it means to be human. It is at this intersection that we can begin to grapple with the processes at work in human being's creative adaptability. The recent explosion of research inspired by Bartlett's work attests to its potential in shedding new light on a range of issues surrounding constructiveness in psychological and social processes.

Reconstructions for the Future

Bartlett will inevitably continue to be reconstructed in the future, through different theoretical and methodological orientations of researchers. Exactly how and what directions this reconstruction will take is not a wholly predictable process. What is of importance is not simply that Bartlett continues to be used but that real scientific innovations grow out of his ideas. In the pages of this book, I have argued that this might occur in a number of places such as: reinventing the psychological experiment (Chapter 2); updating the idea of reconstruction in diffusion for a globalized and media-saturated world (Chapter 3); creating a concept of schema that is simultaneously temporal, dynamic, embodied, holistic, and social (Chapter 4); theorizing remembering as the coordination of individual and social processes within specified cultural contexts (Chapter 5); and exploring the diversity and social relationship among different forms of thinking, especially with Bartlett's method to study 'everyday thinking' (Chapter 6). Most of all, however, we need to consider human beings themselves as innovating agents. Construction is not a mechanical reassembly of elements but a living and forward-oriented response that takes the person beyond what is given. This was at the heart of Bartlett's key phrase 'an effort after meaning,' whereby we invest personal force with material in which we become entangled. We act on the meaning we give to the present, which is done on the basis of the past, in order to move toward the future. This process can be studied in individuals and social groups by adapting Bartlett's analysis of stability and change in cultural forms and experience, often leading to the emergence of something new and unpredictable. We must recognize that human beings are future-oriented meaning-makers and thus cannot be explained according to mechanical principles. The adventure of human life will remain open, ensuring that constructiveness will have its place whatever the future may bring.

Notes

1. The notion of levels of organization can be distinguished and elaborated in many different ways – for example, genetic, neural, behavioral, and environmental (Gottlieb, 1992); intrapersonal, interpersonal, positional, and ideological (Doise, 1986); and micro-, onto-, and socio-genesis (Duveen and Lloyd, 1990; Saito, 2000c; Valsiner, 2007).
2. Bartlett's mentor Rivers articulated this theory of cultural dynamics using a physiological model of two types of sensibility: a more primitive all-or-nothing sensitivity that only registered blunt pressure on the skin, and a localized sensitivity that repressed the former (see Rivers and Head, 1908).
3. For example, Nadel (1937) showed that a story was remembered in terms of *rationalized meaning* in the Yoruba tribe and *an enumeration of details* among the Nupe tribe (Chapter 5).
4. In *Thinking*, Bartlett (1958) even began to occasionally use the term 'information' as a synonym for 'evidence.'
5. Neisser (1976) himself later recanted his early cognitive position and went on to develop a more ecological approach. His later notion of 'repisode,' the representation of a series of events rather than a single event or 'episode,' is reminiscent of Bartlett's concept of schema (Neisser, 1982; see also Takagi and Mori, 2017).

References

Ach, N. (1905). *Über die Willenstätigkeit und das Denken*. Göttingen: Vandenhoeck & Ruprecht.

Ahlberg, S.W. and Sharps, M.J. (2002). Bartlett revisited: Reconfiguration of long-term memory in young and older adults. *The Journal of Genetic Psychology*, 163(2), 211–18.

Allport, G.W. and Postman, L. (1947). *The psychology of rumor*. New York: Henry Holt.

Ash, M.G. (1998). *Gestalt Psychology in German Culture 1890–1967: Holism and the quest for objectivity*. Cambridge: Cambridge University Press.

Baddeley, A. and Gregory, R. (2000). Remembering Bartlett. In A. Saito (Ed.), *Bartlett, culture and cognition* (pp. 36–45). UK: Psychology Press.

Bangerter, A. (1997). Serial reproduction as a method for studying social representations. *Papers on Social Representations*, 6(2), 141–54.

   (2000). Transformations between scientific and social representations: The method of serial reproduction. *British Journal of Social Psychology*, 39, 521–35.

Bartlett, F.C. (1913). *Exercises in logic*. London: W.B. Clive, University Tutorial Press.

   (1914). *Key to exercises in logic*. London: W.B. Clive, University Tutorial Press.

   (1916a). An experimental study of some problems of perceiving and imagining. *British Journal of Psychology*, 8, 222–66.

   (1916b). Transformations arising from repeated representation: A contribution towards an experimental study of the process of conventionalization. *Fellowship Dissertation, St. John's College*, Cambridge.

   (1918). The development of criticism. *Proceedings of the Aristotelian Society*, 18, 75–100.

   (1920a). Psychology in relation to the popular story. *Folk-Lore*, 31, 264–93.

   (1920b). The functions of images. *British Journal of Psychology*, 11, 320–37.

   (1923). *Psychology and primitive culture*. Cambridge, UK: Cambridge University Press.

   (1924). Symbolism in folk-lore. In *Proceedings of the VIIth international Congress of psychology* (pp. 278–89), Cambridge, UK: Cambridge University Press.

   (1925a). Group organisation and social behaviour. *International Journal of Ethics*, 35, 346–67.

(1925b). The social functions of symbols. *Australasian Journal of Psychology and Philosophy*, 3, 1–11.

(1925c). Feeling, imaging and thinking. *British Journal of Psychology*, 16, 16–28.

(1925d). James Ward 1843–1925. *American Journal of Psychology*, 36, 449–53.

(1926). Psychology of culture contact. In *Encyclopaedia Britannica*, Vol. 1 (13th edn., pp. 765–71). London and New York: Encyclopaedia Britannica Co. Ltd.

(1927a). Critical notice of Watson's behaviorism. *Mind*, 36, 77–83.

(1927b). *Psychology and the soldier*. Cambridge: Cambridge University Press.

(1927c). The psychology of the lower races. In *Proceedings of the VIIIth international Congress of psychology* (pp. 198–202). Gröningen: P. Noordhoff.

(1927d). The relevance of visual imagery to the process of thinking: Pt. III. *British Journal of Psychology*, 18, 23–9.

(1928a). The psychological process of sublimation. *Scientia*, 43, 89–98.

(1928b). Social constructiveness: Pt. 1. *British Journal of Psychology*, 18, 388–91.

(1930). Experimental method in psychology. *The Journal of General Psychology*, 4, 49–66.

(1932/1995). *Remembering: A study in experimental and social psychology*. Cambridge: Cambridge University Press.

(1935). Remembering. *Scientia*, 57, 221–6.

(1936). Frederic Charles Bartlett [autobiography]. In C. Murchison (Ed.), *A history of psychology in autobiography*, Vol. III (pp. 39–52). Worcester, MA: Clark University Press.

(1937a). Psychological methods and anthropological problems. *Africa*, 10, 401–20.

(1937b). Some problems in the psychology of temporal perception. *Philosophy*, 12, 457–65.

(1937c). Cambridge, England, 1887–1937. *American Journal of Psychology*, 50, 97–110.

(1938a). The co-operation of social groups. *Occupational Psychology*, 12, 30–42.

(1938b). Friendliness and unfriendliness between different social groups. (Sectional Trans.) *British Association for the Advancement of Science* (August 1938).

(1940). *Political propaganda*. Cambridge, UK: Cambridge University Press.

(1941). Fatigue following highly skilled work. *Nature*, 147, 717–18.

(1943). Anthropology in reconstruction. *Journal of the Royal Anthropological Institute*, 72, 9–16.

(1944). Psychology after the war. *Agenda*, 3, 1–11.

(1946a). Kenneth J.W. Craik, 1914–45 [obituary]. *The Eagle*, March, 454–65.

(1946b). Psychological methods for the study of "hard" and "soft" features of culture. *Africa*, 16, 145–55.

(1947a). Bartlett emphasizes value of words as determinant of social behavior. *Daily Princetonian*, 71(26th February), 36.

(1947b). The third Vanuxen lecture at Princeton [report]. *The Princeton Herald*, 23(March 7), 19.

(1947c). Some problems of "display" and "control". In *Universitas Catholica Lovaniensis, Miscellanea Psychologica Albert Michotte: etudes de psychologie offertes à MA. Michotte à l'occasion de son jubilé professoral* (pp. 440–52). Paris: Libraire Philosophique.

(1950a). Human tolerance limits. *Acta Psychologica*, 7, 133–41.

(1950b). Programme for experiments on thinking. *Quarterly Journal of Experimental Psychology*, 2, 145–52.

(1950c). *Religion as experience, belief, action*. London: Oxford University Press.

(1951). *The mind at work and play*. London: George Allen & Urwin.

(1952). Review of thinking: An introduction to its experimental psychology by George Humphrey (1951). *Quarterly Journal of Experimental Psychology*, 4(1), 87–90.

(1954). Intelligence tests: Assumptions, uses, and limitations. *Times Science Review*, 12, 9.

(1955a). Timing – A fundamental character in human skill. *Proceedings of the XII Congress of the international association of applied psychology*. London: IAAP.

(1955b). Contact of cultures in the present social world. *Twentieth Century*, 158(943), 269–78.

(1956). Changing scene. *British Journal of Psychology*, 47, 81–7.

(1957). *Some recent developments of psychology in Great Britain*. Istanbul: Baha Mathaasi.

(1958). *Thinking: An experimental and social study*. London: George Allen & Unwin Ltd.

(1959). Some problems of scientific thinking. *Ergonomics*, 2, 229–38.

(1960). La cinema et la transmission de la culture. *Revue Internationale de Filmologie*, 10(32/33), 3–12.

(1961a). On getting and using information. In N. Mitchison (Ed.), *What the human race is up to* (pp. 145–55). London: Victor Gollancz.

(1961b). The way we think now. *Psychologische Beitrage*, 6, 387–94.

(1962). The future of ergonomics. *Ergonomics*, 5, 505–11.

(1963). Propaganda and technique of mass persuasion. *Financial Times* (11 February, 75th Anniversary Issue), 69–70.

(1968a). W.H.R. Rivers. *The Eagle, St. John's College Cambridge*, 62(269), 156–60.

(1968b). Notes on remembering. Retrieved from http://www.bartlett.psychol. cam.ac.uk/

(2010[1959]). What makes a good experimental psychologist? *The Psychologist*, 23, 988–9.

Bartlett, F.C., Ginsberg, E.G., Lingren, E.J., and Thouless, R.H. (Eds.) (1939). Preface. In *The study of society: Methods and problems* (pp. 24–45). London: Routledge & Kegan Paul.

Bartlett, F.C. and Smith, E.M. (1920). Is thinking merely the action of language mechanisms? Part I. *British Journal of Psychology*, 11, 55–62.

Bauer, M.W. and Gaskell, G. (1999). Towards a paradigm for research on social representations. *Journal for the Theory of Social Behaviour*, 29(2), 163–86.

Bateson, G. (1936). *Naven*. Cambridge: Cambridge University Press.

Beals, D.E. (1998). Reappropriating schema: Conceptions of development from Bartlett and Bakhtin. *Mind, Culture, and Activity*, 5, 3–24.

Beckstead, Z., Cabell, K.R., and Valsiner, J. (2009). Generalizing through conditional analysis: Systemic causality in the world of eternal becoming. *Humana Mente*, 11, 65–80.

Bergman, E.T. and Roediger, H.L. (1999). Can Bartlett's repeated reproduction experiments be replicated? *Memory & Cognition*, 27, 937–47.

Bergson, H. (1907/1911). *Creative evolution*. New York: Henry Holt.

Betz, W. (1910). Vorstellung and Einstellung: I. Über Wierdererkennen. *Archiv für die gesamte Psychologie*, 17, 266–96.

Billig, M. (2013). *Learn to write badly: How to succeed in the social sciences*. Cambridge: Cambridge University Press.

Bloor, D. (1997). Remember the strong programme? *Science, Technology and Human Values*, 22, 373–85.

(2000). Whatever happened to 'social constructiveness'? In A. Saito (Ed.), *Bartlett, culture and cognition* (pp. 194–215). UK: Psychology Press.

Boas, F. (1901). *Kathlamet texts*. Washington: G.P.O.

Boivin, N. (2008). *Material cultures, material minds: The impact of things on human thought, society, and evolution*. Cambridge: Cambridge University Press.

Boring, E. (1950). *A history of experimental psychology* (2nd edn.). New York: Appleton-Century-Crofts.

Bourdieu, P. (Ed.) (1999). Understanding. In *The weight of the world* (pp. 607–26). Cambridge: Polity.

Branco, A. and Valsiner, J. (1997). Changing methodologies: A co-constructivist study of goal orientations in social interactions. *Psychology and Developing Societies*, 9(1), 35–64.

Bransford, J.D., McCarrell, N.S., Franks, J.J., and Nitsch, K.E. (1977). Toward unexplaining memory. In R.E. Shaw and J.D. Bransford (Eds.), *Perceiving, acting, and knowing: Toward an ecological psychology* (pp. 431–66). Hillsdale, NJ: Lawrence Erlbaum Associates.

Brentano, F. (1874/1973). *Psychology as an empirical science*. London: Routledge.

Brescó, I. and Rosa, A. (in press). Narrative form and identity in the conventionalization and remembering of national histories. *Studies in Psychology*, 38(1).

Brewer, W.F. (2000). Bartlett's concept of schema and its impact on theories of knowledge representation in contemporary cognitive psychology. In A. Saito (Ed.), *Bartlett, culture and cognition* (pp. 69–89). UK: Psychology Press.

Brewer, W.F. and Nakamura, G.V. (1984). The nature and functions of schemas. In R.S. Wyer and T.K. Srull (Eds.), *Handbook of social cognition*, Vol. 1 (pp. 119–60). Hillsdale, NJ: Erlbaum.

Brewer, W.F. and Treyens, J.C. (1981) Role of schemata in memory for places. *Cognitive Psychology*, 13, 207–30.

Brinkmann, S. (2010). *Psychology as a moral science*. New York: Springer.

Broadbent, D.E. (1970). Frederic Charles Bartlett. In *Biographical memoirs of fellows of the Royal Society*, Vol. 16 (pp. 1–13). London: Royal Society.

Brockmeier, J. (2015). *Beyond the archive: Memory, narrative and the autobiographical process*. Oxford: Oxford University Press.

Brown, S. and Reavey, P. (2015). *Vital memory and affect: Living with a difficult past*. London: Sage.

Bruner, J. (1990). *Acts of meaning*. Cambridge, MA: Harvard University Press.

(1991). The narrative construction of reality. *Critical Inquiry*, 18, 1–21.

(2002). *Making stories: Law, life, literature*. Cambridge, MA: Harvard University Press.

Bunn, G.C., Lovie, A.D., and Richards, G.D. (Eds.) (2001). *Psychology in Britain*. Leicester: BPS books.

Bühler, K. (1907). Tatsachen und Probleme zu einer Psychologie der Denkvorgänge: Über Gedanken. *Archiv für die gesamte Psychologie*, 9, 297–305.

(1908). Tatsachen und Probleme zu einer Psychologie der Denkvorgänge II: Über Gedankenzusammenhange. *Archiv für die gesamte Psychologie*, 12, 1–23.

Cabell, K. and Valsiner, J. (2014). *The catalyzing mind: Beyond theories of causality*. New York: Springer.

Carmichael, D.M. (1939a). The co-operation of social groups: Part I. *British Journal of Psychology*, 19, 206–31.

(1939b). The co-operation of social groups: Part II. *British Journal of Psychology*, 19, 329–44.

(1940). Some examples of constructive thinking amongst the Greenlanders. *British Journal of Psychology*, 30(4), 295–315.

Carmichael, L., Hogan, H.P., and Walter, A.A. (1932). An experimental study of the effect of language on the reproduction of visually perceived form. *Journal of Experimental Psychology*, 15, 73–86.

Chase, W.G. and Simon, H.A. (1973). The mind's eye in chess. In G.H. Chase (Ed.), *The psychology of learning and motivation*, Vol. 16 (pp. 1–58). New York: Academic Press.

Cole, J. and Cole, M. (2000). Re-fusing anthropology and psychology. In A. Saito (Ed.), *Bartlett, culture and cognition* (pp. 135–54). UK: Psychology Press.

Cole, M. (1996). *Cultural psychology: A once and future discipline*. Cambridge, MA: Harvard University Press.

Cole, M. and Gray, G. (1972). Culture and memory. *American Anthropologist*, 74(5), 1066–84.

Cole, M, Gray, G., Glick, J.A., and Sharp, D.W. (1971). *Cultural contexts of learning and thinking*. New York: Basic books.

Cole, M., McDermott, R.P., and Hood, L. (1978). *Ecological niche-picking: Ecological invalidity as an axiom of experimental cognitive psychology*. New York: Rockefeller University, Laboratory of Comparative Cognition.

Collins, A. (2001). The psychology of memory. In: G.C. Bunn, A.D. Lovie, and G.D. Richards (Eds.), *Psychology in Britain: Historical essays and personal recollections* (pp. 150–68). Leicester: BPS books.

(2006). The embodiment of reconciliation: Order and change in the work of Frederic Bartlett. *History of Psychology*, 9, 290–312.

Cornejo, C. (2016). From fantasy to imagination: A cultural history and moral for psychology. In B. Wagoner, I. Bresco, and S.H. Awad (Eds.), *The psychology of imagination: History, theory and new research horizons*. Charlotte, NC: Information Age.

Costall, A. (1992). Why British psychology is not social: Frederic Bartlett's promotion of the new academic discipline. *Canadian Psychology/Psychologie canadienne*, 33(3), 633–9.

(1996). Sir Frederic Bartlett. *The Psychologist, July*, 307–8.

(2001). Pear and his peers. In G.C. Bunn, A.D. Lovie, and G.D. Richards (Eds.), *Psychology in Britain: Historical essays and personal recollections* (pp. 188–204). Leicester: BPS books.

Craik, K. (1943). *The nature of explanation*. Cambridge: Cambridge University Press.

(1948). Theory of the human operator in control systems: 2. Man as an element in control systems. *British Journal of Psychology*, 38, 142–8.

Crampton, C.P. (1978). The Cambridge School: The life, works, and influence of James Ward, W.H.R. Rivers, C.S. Myers, and Sir Frederic Bartlett. Doctoral Dissertation, University of Edinburgh.

Danziger, K. (1990). *Constructing the subject*. Cambridge: Cambridge University Press.

(1992). The project of an experimental social psychology: Historical perspectives. *Science in Context*, 5(2), 309–28.

(1997). *Naming the mind: How psychology got its language*. London: Sage.

(2000). Making social psychology experimental: A conceptual history, 1920–1970. *Journal of the History of the Behavioral Sciences*, 36(4), 329–47.

(2002). How old is psychology, particularly concepts of memory? *History and Philosophy of Psychology*, 4, 1–12.

(2008). *Marking the mind: A history of memory*. Cambridge: Cambridge University Press.

Daston, L. (1992). Objectivity and the escape from perspective. *Social Studies of Science*, 22, 597–618.

Dewey, J. (1896). The reflex arc concept in psychology. *Psychological Review*, 3, 357–70.

Diamond, J. (1997). *Guns, germs, and steel: The fates of human societies*. New York and London: W.W. Norton & Company.

Diriwächter, R. (2008). Genetic Ganzheitspsychologie. In R. Diriwächter and J. Valsiner (Eds.), *Striving for the whole: Creating theoretical syntheses* (pp. 21–45). Somerset, NJ: Transaction Publishers.

Doise, W. (1986). *Levels of explanation in social psychology*. Cambridge: Cambridge University Press.

Douglas, M. (1960/1984). *Purity and danger: An analysis of the concepts of pollution and taboo*. London: Ark paperbacks.

(1980). *Evans-Pritchard*. London: Fontana.

(1986). *How institutions think*. London: Routledge.

(2000). Memory and selective attention. In A. Saito (Ed.), *Bartlett, culture and cognition* (pp. 179–93). UK: Psychology Press.

Durkheim, E. (1912). *The elementary form of the religious life*. Oxford: Oxford University Press.

Duveen, G. (2008). Social actors and social groups: A return to the heterogeneity in social psychology. *Journal for the Theory of Social Behaviour*, 38, 369–74.

Duveen, G. and Lloyd, B. (Eds.) (1990). Introduction. In *Social representations and the development of knowledge* (pp. 1–10). Cambridge: Cambridge University Press.

Ebbinghaus, H. (1885/1913). *Memory: A contribution to experimental psychology.* New York: Teachers College, Columbia University.

Edelman, G. (2005). *Wider than the sky: The phenomenal gift of consciousness.* New Haven, CT: Yale.

Edwards, D. and Middleton, D. (1987). Conversation and remembering: Bartlett revised. *Applied Cognitive Psychology*, 1, 77–92.

Everett, M.R. (2003). *Diffusion of innovations.* New York: Free Press.

Farr, R. (1996). *Roots of modern social psychology.* Oxford: Blackwell.

Fechner, G. (1860/1912). Elements of psychophysics. In B. Rand (Ed.), *The classical psychologists* (pp. 562–72). Boston, MA: Houghton Mifflin.

Forrester, J. (2008). 1919: Psychology and psychoanalysis, Cambridge and London – Myers, Jones and Maccurdy. *Psychoanalysis and History*, 10, 37–94.

Frazer, J. (1890). *The golden bough.* New York: Macmillian.

Gadamer, H. (1989). *Truth and method.* New York: Crossroad.

Gardner, H. (1985). *The mind's new science: A history of the cognitive revolution.* New York: Basic Books.

Gaskell, G. and Bauer, M. (Eds.) (2000). Towards public accountability: Beyond sampling, reliability and validity. In *Qualitative research with text, image and sound* (pp. 336–50). London: Sage.

Gauld, A. and Stephenson, G.M. (1967). Some experiments related to Bartlett's theory of remembering. *British Journal of Psychology*, 58, 39–49.

Gibson, J.J. (1979). *An ecological approach to visual perception.* Boston, MA: Houghton Mifflin.

Gigerenzer, G. (2004). Mindless statistics. *Journal of Socio-Economics*, 33, 587–606.

Gigerenzer, G., Swijtink, Z., Porter, T. et al. (1989). *The empire of chance: How probability changed science.* Cambridge: Cambridge University Press.

Gillespie, A. (2007). The social basis of self-reflection. In J. Valsiner and A. Rosa (Eds.), *The Cambridge handbook of socio-cultural psychology* (pp. 678–91). Cambridge: Cambridge University Press.

  (2008). Social representations, alternative representations and semantic barriers. *Journal for the Theory of Social Behaviour* 38(4), 376–91.

Glăveanu, V.P. (2010). Paradigms in the study of creativity: Introducing the perspective of cultural psychology. *New Ideas in Psychology*, 28(1), 79–93.

Goffman, E. (1959). *Presentation of self in everyday life.* Garden City, NY: Doubleday.

Gomulicki, B.R. (1956). Recall as an abstractive process. *Acta Psychologia*, 12, 77–94.

Gonzalez-Ruibal, A. (2012). Archeology and the study of material culture: Synergies with cultural psychology. In J. Valsiner (Ed.), *The Oxford handbook of culture and psychology* (pp. 132–62). New York, NY: Oxford University Press.

Gottlieb, G. (1992). *Individual development and evolution: The genesis of novel behavior.* New York: Oxford University Press.

Gould, S.J. (1981). *The mismeasure of man.* New York: Norton & Company.

Greenwood, J.D. (2003). *The disappearance of the social in American social psychology.* Cambridge: Cambridge University Press.

Haddon, A.C. (1894). *The decorative art of British New Guinea: A study of Papuan ethnography.* Dublin: The Academy House.

(1895). *Evolution in art: As illustrated by the life histories of designs.* London: Walter Scott Publishing.

Haddon, A.C. (Ed.) (1901). *Report of the Cambridge anthropological expedition to the Torres Straits,* Vol. 2. Cambridge: Cambridge University Press.

Halbwachs, M. (1925/1992). *On collective memory.* Chicago: University of Chicago Press.

(1950/1980). *The collective memory.* New York: Harper.

Hall, K.R.L. (1950). The effect of names and titles upon the serial reproduction of pictorial and verbal material. *British Journal of Psychology,* 41, 109–21.

Haney, C., Banks, C., and Zimbardo, P. (1973). Interpersonal dynamics in a simulated prison. *International Journal of Criminology and Penology,* 1, 69–97.

Haque, A. and Sabir, M. (1975). The image of the Indian army and its effects on social remembering. *Pakistan Journal of Psychology,* 8, 55–61.

Hara, S., Takagi, K., and Matsushima, K. (1997). Psychological analysis of the communication style of the accused in trial (II) – A murder case at Ashikaga. *Surugadai University Studies,* 14, 109–76.

Harré, R. (2002). *Cognitive science: A philosophical introduction.* London: Sage.

Head, H. (1920). *Studies in neurology.* London: Hodder & Stoughton.

(1926). *Aphasia and kindred disorders of speech (2 vols.).* Cambridge: Cambridge University Press.

Hearnshaw, L.S. (1964). *A short history of British psychology.* London: Methuen.

Herle, A. and Rouse, S. (1998). *Cambridge and the Torres Strait: Centenary essays on the 1898 anthropological expedition.* Cambridge: Cambridge University Press.

Humphrey, G. (1951). *Thinking: An introduction to its experimental psychology.* London: Wiley.

Innis, R.E. (2007). Dimensions of an aesthetic encounter. In S.K. Gertz, J. Valsiner, and J.-P. Breaux (Eds.), *Semiotic rotations: Modes of meaning in cultural worlds.* Charlotte, NC: Information Age Publishers.

Iran-Nejad, A. and Winsler, A. (2000). Bartlett's schema theory and modern accounts of learning and remembering. *Journal of Mind and Behavior,* 23, 5–36.

Istomina, Z.M. (1975). The development of voluntary memory in preschool-age children. *Soviet Psychology,* 13, 5–64.

Jahoda, G. (1988). Critical notes and reflections on 'social representations'. *European Journal of Social Psychology,* 18, 195–209.

James, W. (1890). *Principles of psychology.* New York: Dover.

Janet, P. (1928). *L'évolution de la mémoire et de la notion du temps.* Paris: Éditions Chahine.

Johnson, M. (1987). *The body in the mind: The bodily basis of meaning, imagination and reason.* Chicago: Chicago University Press.

Johnson, R.E. (1962). The retention of qualitative changes in learning. *Journal of Verbal Learning and Verbal Behavior*, 1, 218–23.

Johnston, E.B. (2001). The repeated reproduction of Bartlett's remembering. *History of Psychology*, 4, 341–66.

Kashima, Y. (2000). Maintaining cultural stereotypes in the serial reproduction of narratives. *Personality and Social Psychology Bulletin*, 26, 594–604.

(2008). A social psychology of cultural dynamics: Examining how cultures are formed, maintained and transformed. *Social and Personality Psychology Compass*, 2, 107–20.

Kay, H. (1955). Learning and retaining verbal material. *British Journal of Psychology*, 46, 81–100.

Kintsch, W. (1995). Introduction. In F.C. Bartlett (Ed.), *Remembering: A study in experimental and social psychology*. Cambridge: Cambridge University Press.

Kleining, G. (1986). Das qualitative experiment. *Kölner Zeitschrift für Soziologie und Sozialpsychologie*, 38, 724–50.

Klugman, S.F. (1944). Memory for position, among children, as measured by serial reproduction. *British Journal of Psychology*, 35, 17–24.

Koffka, K. (1926). Review of Bartlett's psychology and primitive culture. *Psychologische Forshung*, 7, 285–6.

(1935). *Principles of Gestalt psychology*. London: Routledge.

Köhler, W. (1925). *The mentality of apes*. London: Kegan Paul.

Krueger, F. (1928). The essence of feeling: Outline of a systematic theory. In M.L. Reymert (Ed.), *Feelings and emotions*. Worcester, MA: Clark University.

Külpe, O. and Bryan, W.L. (1904). Versuche über Abstraktion. In F. Schumann (Ed.), *Kongress für experimentelle Psychologie* (pp. 58–68). Leipzig: Barth.

Kusch, M. (1999). *Psychological knowledge: A social history and philosophy*. London: Routledge.

Lakoff, G. and Johnson, M. (1980). *Metaphors we live by*. Chicago: University of Chicago Press.

Larsen, S.F. and Berntsen, D. (2000). Bartlett's trilogy of memory: Reconstructing the concept of attitude. In A. Saito (Ed.), *Bartlett, culture and cognition* (pp. 90–113). UK: Psychology Press.

Latour, B. (2008). *Reassembling the social: An introduction to actor-network theory*. New York: Oxford University Press.

Le Bon, G. (1895/1966). *The crowd*. London: Fisher Unwin.

Lévy-Bruhl, L. (1926/1985). *How natives think*. Princeton, NJ: Princeton University Press.

Loftus, E.F. (1975). Leading questions and eyewitness reports. *Cognitive Psychology*, 7, 560–72.

Mallery, G. (1894). *Picture-writing of the American Indians*. Washington: Government Printing Office.

Mandler, G. (1966). Organization and memory. In K.W. Spence and J.T. Spence (Eds.), *The psychology of learning and motivation*. New York: Academic Press.

Mandler, J.M. and Johnson, N.S. (1977). Remembrance of things parsed: Story structure and recall. *Cognitive Psychology*, 9, 111–51.

Martin, J. (2013). Life positioning analysis: An analytic framework for the study of lives and life narratives. *Journal of Theoretical and Philosophical Psychology*, 33, 1–17.

Mayer, A. and Orth, J. (1901). Zur qualitativen Untersuchung der Association. *Zeitschrift für Psychologie*, 26, 1–13.

Maxwell, R.S. (1936). Remembering in different social groups. *British Journal of Psychology*, 27, 30–40.

McClelland, J.L. (1995). Constructive memory and memory distortions: A parallel distributed processing approach. In D.L. Schacter, J.T. Coyle, G.D. Fischbach, M.-M. Mesulam, and L.E. Sullivan (Eds.), *Memory distortion: How minds, brains, and societies reconstruct the past* (pp. 69–90). Cambridge, MA: Harvard University Press.

McDougall, W. (1908). *An introduction to social psychology*. London: Methuen.

McVee, M.B., Dunsmore, K., and Gavelek, J.R. (2005). Schema theory revised. *Review of Educational Research*, 75, 531–66.

Mead, G.H. (1934). *Mind, self and society: From the standpoint of a social behaviorist*. Chicago: University of Chicago.

Mesoudi, A. and Whiten, A. (2004). The hierarchical transformation of event knowledge in human cultural transmission. *Journal of Cognition and Culture*, 4, 1–24.

Mesoudi, A., Whiten, A., and Dunbar, R. (2006). A bias for social information in human cultural transmission. *British Journal of Psychology*, 97, 405–23.

Middleton, D. and Brown, S.D. (2005). *The social psychology of experience: Studies in remembering and forgetting*. London: Sage.

(2008). Issues in the socio-cultural study of memory: Making memory matter. In J. Valsiner and A. Rosa (Eds.), *Cambridge handbook of socio-cultural psychology* (pp. 205–37). New York: Cambridge University Press.

Middleton, D. and Edwards, D. (Eds.) (1990a). Introduction. In *Collective remembering* (pp. 1–22). London: Sage.

Middleton, D. and Edwards, D. (1990b). Conversational remembering: A social psychological approach. In *Collective remembering* (pp. 23–46). London: Sage.

Milgram, S. (1974). *Obedience to authority*. New York: Harper & Row.

Minsky, M. (1975). A framework for representing knowledge. In P.H. Winston (Ed.), *The psychology of computer vision* (pp. 99–128). New York: McGraw-Hill.

Moghaddam, F.M. (2013). *The psychology of dictatorship*. Washington, DC: American Psychological Association.

(2016). *The psychology of democracy*. Washington, DC: American Psychological Association.

Molenaar, P. (2004). A manifesto on psychology as idiographic science: Bringing the person back into scientific psychology, this time forever. *Measurement*, 2(4), 201–18.

Mori, N. (2008). Styles of remembering and types of experience: An experimental investigation of reconstructive memory. *Integrative Psychological and Behavioral Science*, 42, 291–314.

(2009). The schema approach. In J. Valsiner, P. Molenaar, N. Chaudhary, and M. Lyra (Eds.), *Handbook of dynamic process methodology in the social and developmental sciences* (pp. 123–40). New York: Springer.

(2010). Remembering with others: The veracity of an experience in the symbol formation process. In B. Wagoner (Ed.), *Symbolic transformation: The mind in movement through culture and society* (pp. 142–58). London: Routledge.

Moscovici, S. (1973). Foreword. In C. Herzlich (Ed.), *Health and illness: A social psychological analysis*. London: Academic Press.

(1976/2008). *Psychoanalysis: Its image and its public*. Cambridge: Polity.

(1981). On social representations. In J. Forgas (Ed.), *Social cognition: Perspectives on everyday understanding* (pp. 181–210). New York: Academic Press.

(1984). The phenomenon of social representations. In R. Farr and S. Moscovici (Eds.), *Social representations* (pp. 3–68). Cambridge: Cambridge University Press.

(1988). Notes towards a description of social representations. *European Journal of Social Psychology*, 18, 211–50.

(1990). Social psychology and developmental psychology: Extending the conversation. In G. Duveen and B. Lloyd (Eds.), *Social representations and the development of knowledge*. Cambridge: Cambridge University Press.

(2000). *Social representations: Explorations in social psychology*. Cambridge, UK: Polity.

Moscovici, S. and Marková, I. (1998). Presenting social representations: A conversation. *Culture & Psychology*, 4(3), 371–410.

Munk, H. (1890). *Über die Functionen der Grosshirnrinde, 2. Aufl.* Berlin: Hirschwald.

Myers, C.S. (1915). A contribution to the study of shell shock. *Lancet*, 1, 316–20.

Myers, C.S. and Bartlett, F.C. (1925). *A text-book of experimental psychology with laboratory exercises*. Cambridge: Cambridge University Press.

Nadel, S.F. (1937). Experiments on culture psychology. *Africa*, 10, 421–35.

Nahari, G., Sheinfeld, V., Glicksohn, J., and Nachson, I. (2015). Serial reproduction of traumatic events: Does the chain unravel? *Cognitive Processes*, 16, 111–20.

Neisser, U. (1967). *Cognitive psychology*. New York: Appleton-Century-Crofts.

(1976). *Cognition and reality*. New York: W.H. Freeman.

(1982). John Dean's memory: A case study. In U. Neisser (Ed.), *Memory observed: Remembering in natural contexts* (pp. 139–59). New York: Freeman.

Nelson, T.O. (1996). Consciousness and metacognition. *American Psychologist*, 51, 102–16.

Nisbett, R.E. (2005). *The geography of thought: How Asians and Westerners think differently ... and why*. London: Nicholas Brealey Publishing.

Northway, M.L. (1936). The influence of age and social group on children's remembering. *British Journal of Psychology*, 27, 11–29.

(1940a). The concept of "schema": Part I. *British Journal of Psychology*, 30, 316–25.

(1940b). The concept of "schema": Part II. *British Journal of Psychology*, 31, 22–36.

Obeyesekere, G. (2012). *The awakened ones: Phenomenology of visionary experience*. New York: Colombia University Press.

Ohashi, Y., Mori, N., Takagi, K., and Matsushima, K. (2002). *Psychologists meet trials*. Kyoto: Kitaooji Shobo (In Japanese).

Ogden, R.M. (1951). Oswald Külpe and the Würzburg school. *American Journal of Psychology*, 64, 4–19.

Oldfield, R.C. (1954). Memory mechanisms and the theory of schemata. *British Journal of Psychology*, 45, 14–23.

(1972). Frederic Charles Bartlett: 1886–1969. *The American Journal of Psychology*, 85, 133–40.

Oldfield, R.C. and Zangwill, O.L. (1942a). Head's concept of the schema and its application in contemporary British psychology I: Head's concept of the schema. *British Journal of Psychology*, 32, 267–86.

(1942b). Head's concept of the schema and its application in contemporary British psychology II: Critical analysis of Head's theory. *British Journal of Psychology*, 33, 58–64.

(1943). Head's concept of the schema and its application in contemporary British psychology III: Bartlett's theory of memory. *British Journal of Psychology*, 33, 113–29.

Olick, J.K. (1999). Collective memory: The two cultures. *Sociological Theory*, 17(3), 333–48.

Ost, J. and Costall, A. (2002). Misremembering Bartlett: A study in serial reproduction. *British Journal of Psychology*, 93, 243–55.

Paul, I.H. (1959). Studies in remembering. *Psychological Issues*, 1(2), 1–152.

Pear, T.H. (1922). *Remembering and forgetting*. London: Methuen.

Philippe, J. (1897). Sur les transformations de nos images mentales. *Revue Philosophique*, 43, 54–68.

Piaget, J. (1930). *The child's conception of physical causality*. NJ: Transaction Publishers.

(1952). *The origins of intelligence in children*. New York, NY: International Universities Press.

Polanyi, K. (1982). *Personal knowledge: Towards a post-critical philosophy*. London: Routledge.

Propp, V. (1968). *The morphology of the folktale*. Austin: University of Texas Press (translated by Laurence Scott),

Rapaport, D. (1942). *Emotions and memory*. New York: Science Editions.

Richards, G. (1998). Getting a result: The expedition's psychological research 1898–1913. In A. Herle and S. Rouse (Eds.), *Cambridge and the Torres Strait: Centenary essays on the 1898 anthropological expedition* (pp. 136–57). Cambridge: Cambridge University Press.

Rivers, W.H.R. (1911). The ethnological analysis of culture, presidential address to Section H of *The British Association for the Advancement of Science*. *Science*, 34, 385–97.

(1912a). Conventionalism in primitive art. *Reports of British Association for the Advancement of Science (Sección H)*, 599.

(1912b). The disappearance of useful arts. *Report of the British Association*, 598–9.

(1914). *The history of Melanesian society*. Cambridge: Cambridge University Press.

(1916). Sociology and psychology. *Sociological Review*, 9, 1–13.

(1922). The symbolism of rebirth. *Folklore*, 33, 14–33.

Rivers, W.H.R. and Head, H. (1908). A human experiment in nerve division. *Brain*, 31, 323–450.

Robertson, R. (1992). *Globalization: Social theory and global culture*. London: Sage.

Roediger, H.L. (1997). Remembering: Review of Bartlett, F.C. Remembering: A study in experimental and social psychology. *Contemporary Psychology*, 42, 488–92.

Roediger, H.L., Bergman, E.T., and Meade, M.L. (2000). Repeated reproduction from memory. In A. Saito (Ed.), *Bartlett, culture and cognition* (pp. 115–33). UK: Psychology Press.

Roediger, H.L., Meade, M.L., Gallo, D.A., and Olson, K.R. (2014). Bartlett revisited: Direct comparison of repeated reproduction and serial reproduction techniques. *Journal of Applied Research in Memory and Cognition*, 3, 266–71.

Roiser, M. (2001). Social psychology and social concern in 1930s Britain. In G.C. Bunn, A.D. Lovie, and G.D. Richards (Eds.), *Psychology in Britain: Historical essays and personal recollections* (pp. 169–87). Leicester: BPS books.

Roldán, A.A. (1992). Looking at anthropology from a biological point of view: A.C. Haddon's metaphors on anthropology. *History of the Human Sciences*, 5(4), 22–32.

Rosa, A. (1996). Bartlett's psycho-anthropological project. *Culture & Psychology*, 2(4), 355–78.

(2000). Bartlett's psycho-anthropological project. In A. Saito (Ed.), *Bartlett, culture and cognition* (pp. 46–66). UK: Psychology Press.

Rumelhart, D.E. (1980). Schemata: The building blocks of cognition. In: R.J. Spiro, B.C. Bruce, and W.F. Brewer (Eds.), *Theoretical issues in reading comprehension* (pp. 33–58). Hillsdale, NJ: Lawrence Erlbaum.

Saito, A. (Ed.) (2000a). *Bartlett, culture & cognition*. UK: Psychology Press.

Saito, A. (2000b). Psychology as a biological and social science. In *Bartlett, culture and cognition* (pp. 3–12). UK: Psychology Press.

Saito, A. (Ed.) (2000c). Multilevel analyses of social bases of cognition. In *Bartlett, culture and cognition* (pp. 155–77). UK: Psychology Press.

Salvatore, S. and Valsiner, J. (2010). Between the general and the unique: Overcoming the nomothetic versus idiographic opposition. *Theory & Psychology*, 20, 817–33.

Schacter, D. (1996). *Searching for memory: The brain, the mind and the past*. New York: Basic books.

(2012). Adaptive constructive processes and the future of memory. *American Psychologist*, 67(8), 603–13.

Schacter, D.L., Addis, D.R., and Buckley, R.L. (2007). Remembering the past to imagine the future: The prospective brain. *Nature Reviews Neuroscience*, 8, 657–61.

Segall, M.H., Campbell, D.T., and Herskovitz, M.J. (1966). *The influence of culture on visual perception*. Indianapolis, IN: Bobbs-Merill.

Shank, R. and Abelson, R. (1977). *Scripts, plans, goals and understanding*. Hillsdale, NJ: Erlbaum.

Shephard, B. (2003). *A war of nerves: Soldiers and psychiatrists in the twentieth century*. Cambridge, MA: Harvard.

Shotter, J. (1990). The social construction of remembering and forgetting. In D. Middleton and D. Edwards (Eds.), *Collective remembering* (pp. 120–38). London: Sage.

Shweder, R. (1991). *Thinking through culture: Expeditions in cultural psychology*. Cambridge, MA: Harvard.

Singer, W. (2007). Understanding the brain. *European Molecular Biology Organization Reports*, 8, 16–19.

Slobodin, R. (1997). *W.H.R. Rivers: Pioneer anthropologist, psychiatrist of The Ghost Road*. Thrupp-Stroud-Gloucestershire: Sutton Publishing.

Smith, E.M. (1915). *The investigation of mind in animals*. Cambridge: Cambridge University Press.

Smith, E.M. and Bartlett, F.C. (1920a). On listening to sounds of weak intensity, Part I. *British Journal of Psychology*, 10, 101–29.

    (1920b). On listening to sounds of weak intensity, Part II. *British Journal of Psychology*, 10, 133–65.

Sutton, J. (2007). Batting, habit and memory: The embodied mind and the nature of skill. *Sport in Society*, 10, 763–86.

Sutton, J., Harris, C.B., Keil, P.G., and Barnier, A.J. (2010). The psychology of memory, extended cognition and socially distributed remembering. *Phenomenology and Cognitive Science*, 9(4), 521–60.

Tajfel, H. (1972). Experiments in a vacuum. In J. Israel and H. Tajfel (Eds.), *The context of social psychology: A critical assessment* (pp. 69–121). London: Academic Press.

Takagi, K. and Mori, N. (2017). Approaches to testimony: Two current views and beyond. In B. Wagoner (Ed.), *Oxford handbook of culture and memory*. Oxford: Oxford University Press.

Talland, G.A. (1956). Cultural differences in serial reproduction. *The Journal of Social Psychology*, 43, 75–81.

Taylor, C. (1989). *Sources of self: The making of the modern identity*. Cambridge, MA: Harvard.

Taylor, I. (1883). *The alphabet: An account of the origins and development of letters*. London: Kegan Paul.

Taylor, W. (1947). Remembering: Some effects of language and other factors. *British Journal of Psychology*, 38, 7–19.

Titchner, E.B. (1909). *Lectures on the experimental psychology of thought-processes*. New York: Macmillan.

Toomela, A. (2007). Culture of science: Strange history of methodological thinking in psychology. *Integrative Psychological and Behavioral Science*, 41, 6–20.

Tresselt, M.E. and Spragg, D.S. (1941). Changes occurring in the serial reproduction of verbally perceived materials. *The Journal of Genetic Psychology*, 58, 255–64.

Triplett, N. (1898). The dynamogenic factors in pacemaking and competition. *American Journal of Psychology*, 9, 507–33.

Tversky, A. and Kahneman, D. (1974). Judgment under uncertainty: Heuristics and biases. *Science*, 185, 1124–31.

Valsiner, J. (2000). *Culture and human development*. London: Sage.

(2007). *Culture in minds and societies*. New Delhi: Sage.

(2012). *A guided science: Psychology in the mirror of its making*. Charlotte, NC: Transaction.

(2014). *An invitation to cultural psychology*. London: Sage.

Valsiner, J. and van der Veer, R. (2000). *The social mind: Construction of the idea*. Cambridge: Cambridge University Press.

Veresov, N. (2010). Forgotten methodology: Vygotsky's case. In A. Toomela and J. Valsiner (Eds.), *Methodological thinking in psychology* (pp. 267–96). Charlotte, NC: Info Age.

Vygotsky, L. (1987). *The collected works of L.S. Vygotsky. Volume 4: The history of the development of higher mental functions*. New York: Plenum Press.

Wagoner, B. (2009). The experimental methodology of constructive microgenesis. In J. Valsiner, P. Molenaar, N. Chaudhary, and M. Lyra (Eds.), *Handbook of dynamic process methodology in the social and developmental sciences* (pp. 99–212). New York: Springer.

(2011a). Meaning construction in remembering: A synthesis of Bartlett and Vygotsky. In P. Stenner, J. Cromby, J. Motzkau, and J. Yen (Eds.), *Theoretical psychology: Global transformations and challenges* (pp. 105–14). Toronto: Captus Press.

(2011b). What happened to holism? *Psychological Studies*, 56(3), 318–24.

(2012). Culture in constructive remembering. In J. Valsiner (Ed.), *Oxford handbook of culture and psychology* (pp. 1034–55). Oxford: Oxford University Press.

(2013). Culture and mind in reconstruction: Bartlett's analogy between individual and group processes. In A. Marvakis, J. Motzkau, D. Painter, R. Ruto-Korir, G. Sullivan, S. Triliva, and M. Wieser (Eds.), *Doing psychology under new conditions* (pp. 273–8). Concord, ON: Captus Press.

(2015). Collective remembering as a process of social representation. In G. Sammut, E. Andreouli, G. Gaskell, and J. Valsiner (Eds.), *Cambridge handbook of social representations* (pp. 143–62). Cambridge: Cambridge University Press.

(2017). What makes memory constructive? A study in the serial reproduction of Bartlett's experiments. *Culture & Psychology*, 23.

(forthcoming). *Oxford handbook of culture and memory*. Oxford: Oxford University Press.

Wagoner, B., Chaudhary, N., and Hviid, P. (2014). *Cultural psychology and its future: Complementarity in a new key*. Charlotte, NC: Information Age.

Wagoner, B. and Gillespie, A. (2014). Sociocultural mediators of remembering: An extension of Bartlett's method of repeated reproduction. *British Journal of Social Psychology*, 53, 622–39.

Ward, J. (1918). *Psychological principles*. Cambridge: Cambridge University Press.

Ward, T.H.G. (1949). An experiment on serial reproduction with special reference to the changes in the design of early coin types. *British Journal of Psychology*, 39, 142–7.

Watson, G. (1934). Psychology in Germany and Austria. *Psychological Bulletin*, 31(10), 755–76.

Watson, J.B. (1913). Psychology as the behaviorist views it. *Psychological Review*, 20, 158–77.

(1925). *Behaviorism.* London: Kegan Paul.

Watson, J.B. and Rayner, R. (1920). Conditioned emotional reactions. *Journal of Experimental Psychology*, 3, 1–14.

Watt, H.J. (1905). Experimentelle Beitrage zu einer Theorie des Denkens. *Archiv für die gesamte Psychologie*, 4, 289–436.

Werner, H. (1937). Process and achievement. *Harvard Educational Review*, 7, 353–68.

Werner, H. and Kaplan, B. (1963). *Symbol formation: An organismic-developmental approach to language and the expression of thought.* Hillsdale, NJ: Lawrence Erlbaum Associates.

Wertheimer, M. (1945). *Productive thinking.* New York: Harper.

Wertsch, J.V. (2002). *Voices of collective remembering.* Cambridge, UK: Cambridge University Press.

(2004). Specific narratives and schematic narrative templates. In P. Seixas (Ed.), *Theorizing historical consciousness* (pp. 49–62). Toronto: University of Toronto Press.

(2017). National memory and where to find it. In B. Wagoner (Ed.), *Oxford handbook of culture and memory.* Oxford: Oxford University Press.

Wertsch, J.V. and Batiashvili, N. (2012). Mnemonic communities and conflict: Georgia's national narrative template. In I. Markova and A. Gillespie (Eds.), *Trust and conflict: Representations, culture and dialogue* (pp. 37–49). London: Routledge.

Wertsch, J.V. and O'Connor, K. (1994). Multivoicedness in historical representation: American College students' account of the origins of the U.S. *Journal of Narrative and Life History*, 4(4), 295–310.

Wheeler, M.A. and Roediger, H.L. (1992). Disparate effects of repeated testing: Reconciling Ballard's (1913) and Bartlett's (1932) results. *Psychological Science*, 3, 240–45.

Wiener, N. (1948). *Cybernetics: Or control and communication in the animal and the machine.* Cambridge, MA: MIT Press.

Winston, A.S. and Blais, D.L. (1996). What counts as an experiment?: A transdisciplinary analysis of textbooks, 1930–1970. *American Journal of Psychology*, 109(4), 599–616.

Winter, A. (2012). *Memory: Fragments of a modern history.* Chicago: University of Chicago Press.

Wittgenstein, L. (1958). *Philosophical investigations.* Oxford: Blackwell.

Wulf, F. (1922). Beiträge zur Psychologie der Gestalt; VI Über die Veränderung von Vorstellungen. (Gedächtnis und Gestalt). *Psychologische Forschung*, 1, 333–73. Translated extract reprinted as "Tendencies in figural variation". In W.D. Ellis (Ed.) (1938). *A source book of Gestalt psychology* (pp. 136–48). London, UK: Routledge & Kegan Paul Ltd.

Wundt, W. (1907). Psychologie. In W. Windelband (Ed.), *Die Philosophie im Beginn des zwanzigsten Jahrhunderts: Festschrift für Kuno Fischer* (pp. 1–57). Heidelberg: Carl Winter's Universitätsbuchhandlung.

Wynn, V.E. and Logic, R.H. (1998). The veracity of long-term memories: Did Bartlett get it right? *Applied Cognitive Psychology*, 12, 1–20.

Zangwill, O.L. (1972). Remembering revisited. *The Quarterly Journal of Experimental Psychology*, 24, 123–38.

Zeigarnik, B.V. (1927). Das Behalten erledigter und unerledigter Handlungen. *Psychologische Forschung*, 9, 1–85.

(1967). On finished and unfinished tasks. In W.D. Ellis (Ed.), *A sourcebook of Gestalt psychology*. New York: Humanities Press.

Zittoun T. and Gillsepie, A. (2015). Integrating experiences: Mind and body moving between contexts. In B. Wagoner, N. Chaudhary, and P. Hviid (Eds.), *Integrating experiences: Mind and body moving between contexts*. Charlotte, NC: Information Age.

(2016). *Imagination in human and cultural development*. London: Routledge.

Zittoun, T., Valsiner, J., Vedeler, D. et al. (2013). *Human development in the life course: Melodies of living*. Cambridge: Cambridge University Press.

Index

Lightning Source UK Ltd.
Milton Keynes UK
UKOW05n0952100417
298764UK00004B/13/P